The Visual Turn
and the
Transformation of the Textbook

The Visual Turn
and the
Transformation of the Textbook

James Andrew LaSpina
University of California
Humanities Research Institute

 LAWRENCE ERLBAUM ASSOCIATES, PUBLISHER

1998   Mahwah, New Jersey   London

Lawrence Erlbaum Associates, Inc., Publishers
10 Industrial Avenue
Mahwah, New Jersey 07430

Library of Congress Cataloging-in-Publication Data

LaSpina, James Andrew.
   The visual turn and the transformation of the textbook / James
Andrew LaSpina.
      p. cm.
  Includes bibliographical references and index.
  ISBN 0-8058-2701-3 (cloth : alk. paper) , -- ISBN 0-8058-2702-1
(pbk. : alk. paper)
   1. Textbooks--Publishing--Data processing.   I. Title.
LB3045.5.L37 1998
371.3'2--DC21   97-44944
                                              CIP

Printed in the United States of America
10 9 8 7 6 5 4 3 2 1

Contents

Figures and Tables

I would like to thank Regina Clay and Lisa Jacobson of the Permissions Department, and Melody English of the School Design-Image Resource Group of the Houghton Mifflin Company for assistance in sorting out the artists, agencies, institutions and various sources credited for the illustrations, photographs, maps, graphs, and so forth, cited in this study. All page numbers listed below are from the Houghton Mifflin Social Studies Program, 1991 First Edition.

1.1: Copyright © 1989, Ligature, Inc.

2.1: Copyright © 1989, Ligature, Inc.

2.2a, b, c: ILLUSTRATION: P. 356. From A MESSAGE OF ANCIENT DAYS in HOUGHTON MIFFLIN SOCIAL STUDIES by Armento et al. Copyright © 1991 by Houghton Mifflin Company. Reprinted by permission of Houghton Mifflin Company. All rights reserved. PHOTOGRAPHS: p. 356-357, © P. Sclarandris, Black Star Publishing.

2.3: ILLUSTRATION: p. xi. From I KNOW A PLACE in HOUGHTON MIFFLIN SOCIAL STUDIES by Armento et al. Copyright © 1991 by Houghton Mifflin Company. Reprinted by permission of Houghton Mifflin Company. All rights reserved. PHOTOGRAPHS: p. xi-1. © Will and Deni McIntrye, Photo Researchers, Inc.

2.4: ILLUSTRATION: p. 91. From FROM SEA TO SHINING SEA in HOUGHTON MIFFLIN SOCIAL STUDIES by Armento et al. Copyright © 1991 by Houghton Mifflin Company. Reprinted by permission of Houghton Mifflin Company. All rights reserved. PHOTOGRAPH: Stephen Kennedy (r).

2.5: ILLUSTRATION: p. 187. From SOME PEOPLE I KNOW in HOUGHTON MIFFLIN SOCIAL STUDIES by Armento et al. Copyright © 1991 by Houghton Mifflin Company. Reprinted by permission of Houghton Mifflin Company. All rights reserved.

2.6: Copyright © 1989 Ligature, Inc.

2.7: ILLUSTRATION: p. 298. From ACROSS THE CENTURIES in HOUGHTON MIFFLIN SOCIAL STUDIES by Armento et al. Copyright © 1991 by Houghton Mifflin Company. Reprinted by permission of Houghton Mifflin Company. All rights reserved.

2.8: ILLUSTRATION: p. 233. From ACROSS THE CENTURIES in HOUGHTON MIFFLIN SOCIAL STUDIES by Armento et al. Copyright © 1991 by Houghton Mifflin Company. Reprinted by permission of Houghton Mifflin Company. All rights reserved.

2.9: Copyright © 1989 Ligature, Inc.

2.10: ILLUSTRATION: p. 226–227. From A MESSAGE OF ANCIENT DAYS in HOUGHTON MIFFLIN SOCIAL STUDIES by Armento et al. Copyright © 1991 by Houghton Mifflin Company. Reprinted by permission of Houghton Mifflin Company. All rights reserved. PHOTOGRAPHS: p. 226, © Paolo Koch, Photo Researchers, Inc.; p. 227, Karachi Museum, Pakistan, Art Resources, Inc., New York (t); © Dilip Mehta, Woodfin Camp & Associates (c); Ralph Brunke (bl); Government of India, Department of Archaeology (br).

3.1: Copyright © 1989 Ligature, Inc.

3.2: PHOTOGRAPH: p. 118. © Corbis-Bettman Newsphoto.

3.3: PHOTOGRAPHS: p. 8. © Mike Clemmer (tr, bl); Stephen Kennedy (cl, br). From SOME PEOPLE I KNOW in HOUGHTON MIFFLIN SOCIAL STUDIES Armento, et al. Copyright © 1991 by Houghton Mifflin Company. Reprinted by permission of Houghton Mifflin Company. All rights reserved.

3.4: GRAPH: p. 163. From SEA TO SHINING SEA in HOUGHTON MIFFLIN SOCIAL STUDIES Armento et al. Copyright © 1991 by Houghton Mifflin Company. Reprinted by permission of Houghton Mifflin Company. All rights reserved. PHOTOGRAPH: © Jack Parsons, the Stock Broker.

3.5: PHOTOGRAPH: p.202–203. © Jerry Jacka Photography.

3.6: PHOTOGRAPH: p. 78–79. The Shelburne Museum, Shelburne, Vermont. From A MORE PERFECT UNION in HOUGHTON MIFFLIN SOCIAL STUDIES Armento et al. Copyright © 1991 by Houghton Mifflin Company. Reprinted by permission of Houghton Mifflin Company. All rights reserved.

3.7: PHOTOGRAPHS: p. 206. I.N. Phelps Stokes Collection, Miriam and Ira D. Wallach Division of Art, Prints and Photographs, The New York Public Library, Astor, Lenox and Tilden Foundations (c); Peabody Museum of Archaelogy and Ethnology, Harvard University, photo by Hillel Burger (bl); p. 207. Oakland Museum History Department, Oakland, California, (b); ILLUSTRATION: © Gilcrease Museum, Tulsa, Oklahoma (t). From THIS IS MY COUNTRY in HOUGHTON MIFFLIN SOCIAL STUDIES by Armento et al. Copyright © 1991 by Houghton Mifflin Company. Reprinted by permission of Houghton Mifflin Company. All rights reserved.

3.8: PHOTOGRAPHS: P. 267. Wan-go H.C. Weng (tr); Ralph J. Brunke (cr, bl, bc, br); From A MESSAGE OF ANCIENT DAYS in HOUGHTON MIFFLIN SOCIAL STUDIES by Armento et al. Copyright © 1991 by Houghton Mifflin Company. Reprinted by permission of Houghton Mifflin Company. All rights reserved.

3.9: PHOTOGRAPHS: p. 125. I.N. Phelps Stokes Collection, Miriam and Ira D. Wallach Division of Art, Prints and Photographs, The New York Public Library, Astor, Lenox and Tilden Foundations (t); New York State Historical Association, Cooperstown, New York (r). From SEA TO SHINING SEA in HOUGHTON MIFFLIN SOCIAL STUDIES by Armento et al. Copyright © 1991 by Houghton Mifflin Company. Reprinted by permission of Houghton Mifflin Company. All rights reserved.

3.10: MAPS: p. 134–135. From SEA TO SHINING SEA in HOUGHTON MIFFLIN SOCIAL STUDIES by Armento et al. Copyright © 1991 by Houghton Mifflin Company. Reprinted by permission of Houghton Mifflin Company. All rights reserved. PHOTOGRAPHS: p. 134–135, © David Muench.

3.11: PHOTOGRAPH: p. 56. SCALA, Art Resources, New York. From A MESSAGE OF ANCIENT DAYS in HOUGHTON MIFFLIN SOCIAL STUDIES by Armento et al. Copyright © 1991 by Houghton Mifflin Company. Reprinted by permission of Houghton Mifflin Company. All rights reserved.

3.12: PHOTOGRAPH: Title page. From I KNOW A PLACE in HOUGHTON MIFFLIN SOCIAL STUDIES Armento et al. Copyright © 1991 by Houghton Mifflin Company. Reprinted by permission of Houghton Mifflin Company. All rights reserved.

3.13: PHOTOGRAPH: p. 1. © Will and Deni McIntrye, Photo Researchers, Inc.

3.14: ILLUSTRATION: p. 14–15. From I KNOW A PLACE in HOUGHTON MIFFLIN SOCIAL STUDIES by Armento et al. Copyright © 1991 by Houghton Mifflin Company. Reprinted by permission of Houghton Mifflin Company. All rights reserved.

3.15: ILLUSTRATION: p. 28–29. From I KNOW A PLACE in HOUGHTON MIFFIN SOCIAL STUDIES by Armento et al. Copyright © 1991 by Houghton Mifflin Company. Reprinted by permission of Houghton Mifflin Company. All rights reserved. PHOTOGRAPH: p. 28–29. © R. Perron, Nawrocki Stock Photo.

3.16: PHOTOGRAPH: NASA photo, p. 58–59. From I KNOW A PLACE in HOUGHTON MIFFLIN SOCIAL STUDIES by Armento et al. Copyright © 1991 by Houghton Mifflin Company. Reprinted by permission of Houghton Mifflin Company. All rights reserved.

3.17: MAP: p. 120–121. From I KNOW A PLACE in HOUGHTON MIFFLIN SOCIAL STUDIES by Armento et al. Copyright © 1991 by Houghton Mifflin Company. Reprinted by permission of Houghton Mifflin Company. All rights reserved. PHOTOGRAPHS: pp. 120–121, (flags) Stephen Kennedy, Copyright © (children) C. Lindstrom.

3.18: PHOTOGRAPH: p. 29. Earth Satellite Corporation/Science Photo Library, Photo Researchers, Inc. (t). From I KNOW A PLACE in HOUGHTON MIFFLIN SOCIAL STUDIES by Armento et al. Copyright © 1991 by Houghton Mifflin Company. Reprinted by permission of Houghton Mifflin Company. All rights reserved.

4.1: PHOTOGRAPH: p. T18. From SEA TO SHINING SEA Teacher's Edition in HOUGHTON MIFFLIN SOCIAL STUDIES by Armento et al. Copyright © 1991 by Houghton Mifflin Company. Reprinted by permission of Houghton Mifflin Company. All rights reserved.

4.2: MAPS: p. 135, From SEA TO SHINING SEA Teacher's Edition in HOUGHTON MIFFLIN SOCIAL STUDIES by Armento et al. Copyright © 1991 by Houghton Mifflin Company. Reprinted by permission of Houghton Mifflin Company. All rights reserved.

4.4: PHOTOGRAPH: p. 112. Nebraska State Historical Society. PHOTOGRAPH: Kansas State Historical Society, Topeka. From SEA TO SHINING SEA Teacher's Edition in HOUGHTON MIFFLIN SOCIAL STUDIES by Armento et al. Copyright © 1991 by Houghton Mifflin Company. Reprinted by permission of Houghton Mifflin Company. All rights reserved.

4.6: ILLUSTRATIONS: p. 114. Metropolitan Life Insurance Company, New York. *Thanksgiving With the Indians*, (t); p. 116. Pilgrim Society, Plymouth, Massachusetts, *Corne's Landing*, (b). From SEA TO SHINING SEA Teacher's Edition in HOUGHTON MIFFLIN SOCIAL STUDIES by Armento et al. Copyright © 1991 by Houghton Mifflin Company. Reprinted by permission of Houghton Mifflin Company. All rights reserved.

4.8: MAPS: pp. 117, 122, 135, 149. From SEA TO SHINING SEA Teacher's Edition in HOUGHTON MIFFLIN SOCIAL STUDIES by Armento et al. Copyright © 1991 by Houghton Mifflin Company. Reprinted by permission of Houghton Mifflin Company. All rights reserved.

5.2: ILLUSTRATION: p. 157. From I KNOW A PLACE in HOUGHTON MIFFLIN SOCIAL STUDIES by Armento et al. Copyright © 1991 by Houghton Mifflin Company. Reprinted by permission of Houghton Mifflin Company. All rights reserved.

5.3: ILLUSTRATION: p. T3. From SEA TO SHINING SEA Teacher's Edition in HOUGHTON MIFFLIN SOCIAL STUDIES by Armento et al. Copyright © 1991 by Houghton Mifflin Company. Reprinted by permission of Houghton Mifflin Company. All rights reserved.

5.4: ILLUSTRATION: p. T37. From SEA TO SHINING SEA Teacher's Edition in HOUGHTON MIFFLIN SOCIAL STUDIES by Armento et al. Copyright © 1991 by Houghton Mifflin Company. Reprinted by permission of Houghton Mifflin Company. All rights reserved.

5.5: ILLUSTRATION: p. 313A. From AMERICA WILL BE Teacher's Edition in HOUGHTON MIFFLIN SOCIAL STUDIES by Armento et al. Copyright © 1991 by Houghton Mifflin Company. Reprinted by permission of Houghton Mifflin Company. All rights reserved.

5.6a, b, c: ILLUSTRATION: pp. 186–187. From ACROSS THE CENTURIES in HOUGHTON MIFFLIN SOCIAL STUDIES by Armento et al. Copyright © 1991 by Houghton Mifflin Company. Reprinted by permission of Houghton Mifflin Company. All rights reserved.

6.1: ILLUSTRATION: p. 20–21. From SEA TO SHINING SEA Teacher's Edition in HOUGHTON MIFFLIN SOCIAL STUDIES by Armento et al. Copyright © 1991 by Houghton Mifflin Company. Reprinted by permission of Houghton Mifflin Company. All rights reserved. PHOTOGRAPHS: p. 20–21. Stephen Kennedy; p. 21, Smithsonian Institution (tl); Dennis Hamm, National Park Service (br).

6.2: ILLUSTRATION: p. 100. From A MESSAGE OF ANCIENT DAYS in HOUGHTON MIFFLIN SOCIAL STUDIES by Armento et al. Copyright © 1991 by Houghton Mifflin Company. Reprinted by permission of Houghton Mifflin Company. All rights reserved.

6.3: ILLUSTRATION: p. 454. From AMERICAN WILL BE in HOUGHTON MIFFLIN SOCIAL STUDIES by Armento et al. Copyright © 1991 by Houghton Mifflin Company. Reprinted by permission of Houghton Mifflin Company. All rights reserved.

6.4: ILLUSTRATION: p. 54. From ACROSS THE CENTURIES in HOUGHTON MIFFLIN SOCIAL STUDIES by Armento et al. Copyright © 1991 by Houghton Mifflin Company. Reprinted by permission of Houghton Mifflin Company. All rights reserved.

7.1: CHART: Jonathan Steuer, "Defining Virtual Reality: Dimensions Determining Telepresence," Journal of Communication, Vol. 42, no. 4, 1992, International Communication Association. Copyright © Oxford University Press.

Tables

Acknowledgments

Many people have contributed to the realization of this project. First and foremost is the community of historians at the UCLA department of History. It has been an exceptional opportunity to have participated in its academic program. Many individuals deserve special thanks. Gary Nash never failed to demonstrate his genuine interest. He made this book possible. Like Gary, Ed Berenson supported this project from the outset and always warmly expressed his solidarity. Many others at UCLA also provided stimulus to this project. Carl Weinberg impressed upon me the importance of aesthetic education in the curriculum. Nick Browne directed me to make the important connections between semiotics, culture, and power. Jeannie Oakes and Charlotte Crabtree who helped me sort out the larger political aspects of curriculum reform which shape the economy of the textbook. Dennis Lyday at UCLA read working drafts of the manuscript in its various stages and graciously offered his critical insight and editorial comments and greatly deserves my thanks. Robert Cleve spent many hours putting the manuscript in its final digital format.

For the concluding stage of this project I must gratefully acknowledge and thank the University of California Humanities Research Institute. Special thanks go to Pat O'Brien, HRI Director, Debra Massey Sanchez, the Assistant Director and all the HRI staff for providing a wonderfully supportive environment in which to complete this work.

Finally, a special note of thanks goes to Naomi Silverman at Lawrence Erlbaum Associates for taking on this project, and advancing it every step of the way, always showing great interest and keen insight. Also, thanks to Sondra Guideman of LEA, for helping to transform the working manuscript into a book. Last words are fittingly reserved for all those at Houghton Mifflin and Ligature (now IBIS), whose collective vision helped me map one small point of that great white space on both sides of the screen.

From Pre-face to Interface

Beginnings, like endings, matter. Would it be a surprise to anyone that this book began and ended in front of a computer screen? At the conclusion of this project, I am watching these characters emerge from the white luminescent ground of the writing space before me. I've always been mystified over just how this occurs. What's behind the screen? What worlds lie on the other side? My fascination with this viewing space is perhaps where the idea for this book first took shape. But I happened upon one of several such beginning places much earlier. I was doing field work for a study on video game players: "Gamers!" Picture a cavernous black walled space filled with flashing monitors and kids caught up in the game. Every time I entered that room I had the eerie feeling that this space was really just an outer hall to a digital labyrinth with each glowing monitor a portal inside.

In that study I thought my concern was with understanding the way in which video games had become a subculture for that generation of kids who came of age with a joy stick in hand. I wanted to understand them and their world in their own right, but instead, I was coming to terms with my own fear of computers and their power, cautiously building a bridge for myself into that virtual microworld.

In my observations I took note of the visual interface of the game screen. I became fascinated with how these presentations worked to hold a player's attention. But answers to this question were not easily gotten. Although I talked to players about why they moved in these microworlds as easily as they did in real life, the screen itself glowed in silence. Knowing about the global reach of the video game industry, and witnessing players who, now college-age, were first-generation gamers, I wondered, like many at the time, what cognitive impact such an intense visually kinesthetic experience might have on formal learning (Greenfield, 1990).

It is now commonplace to think of computers (a more sophisticated video game?) as a naturalized presence like television and film. All have contributed to creating an electronic cultural space saturated with images. And with the coming of the Internet this same space is now connected to the other side of the screen: cyberspace. We can see our writing space. The screen has the familiarity of the printed paper page. It's meant to. But it's just a metaphor, a transitional convention. Creatures of vision, we cannot yet *see* cyberspace, though we have small windows into its strange new dimensions and sometimes view it in part. So immersed in our visual culture, we often fail to realize that we do not just *see*. Our perceptions are largely structured by the present electronic media culture. These patterns of sight shaped by extensive acculturation, provide us with a complex set of visual filters aligning our sight to a shared body of meanings (Elkins, 1996). This seemed all too apparent while watching kids play video games. At the time I wondered if the games provided some new kind of informal curriculum in electronic visual literacy. Our visual acculturation starting with Sesame Street usually stops at the classroom door. Before and after school we are a society of viewers, yet in the classroom we do something else. And more often than not, it involves opening a textbook and listening to the teacher. Yet as these same glowing screens have moved out of that dark hall and into the classroom, I began to wonder how this viewing space and the space of the printed page might merge.

Not long after the video game study concluded, I was visiting a friend who was designing curriculum lesson modules at the National Center for History in Schools here at UCLA. On the table where she was working was a pile of large blue books. She took one and handed it to me, then remarked that her kids were likely to be using them in school next year. The book was from the Houghton Mifflin Social Studies Program recently adopted by the state of California. As I opened the book and began to turn the pages, something akin to that eerie feeling I had in that dark hall came over me. I turned to her and said, "These books were designed for children who watch MTV and play video games. I have to talk with the people who designed them."

Mapping that *somewhere* between page and screen, game space and cyberspace, now appeared possible, the "guidebook" still in material form on the table. Like the hyphen inserted into this Pre-face, the traditional beginning of a book, this project is an exploration of an in-between cultural and pedagogical moment. Is it a transition from printer's ink to pixels, or pixels into print? In postmodern terms a hyphen marks not so much an ending as a gap, an in-between where the stability of a traditional form of representation, in this instance, the textual world of the book, is called into question. But my sense is this gap is like that anteroom to the electronic labyrinth. In the *Visual Turn* the medium of the textbook is folded as it were into the medium of the screen. This in-between space may be one of transformation. The design and development of the Houghton Mifflin Social Studies K–8 textbooks seems to suggest that. This book is about a larger design of future possibility prefigured in their pages.

There is a wonderful title to a famous book which seemed to put the dynamic cast of terms like *transformation* in its proper perspective. In *The Coming of the Book: The Impact of Printing, 1450–1800*, by Febvre and Martin (1958), one can review the historical development of printing in European culture, economy and society as it evolved over several centuries. As an evolving cultural form, this "coming" unfolds over several centuries. Even without all the information society byte hype, we know that the digital era has arrived. Its coming is well upon us. But what it may mean for education not even the prime movers of the computer industry know. It should not go unnoticed that between the first and second edition of *The Road Ahead* (1995,1996), Bill Gates discovered the Internet. The power of distributed communication across electronic networks took many by surprise.

In this larger space of cultural change, mapping the transformation of the textbook may be just as difficult as anticipating innovative shifts in computer technology. If we could look back from even the near future, as we can along the timeline tracing the impact of print technology upon our culture, what changes would we see? What the present work explores is a vision for changing education. And strangely enough this begins with the most tradition bound object of instruction—the social studies textbook. For what these books suggestively represent is that the act of seeing is always beginning, and at every beginning.

Seeing comes before words. The child looks and recognizes before it can speak.

—John Berger, *Ways of Seeing* (1972)

Introduction:
Turning a Textbook Controversy
on Its Head

Graphic design is essentially about visual relationships—providing meaning to a mass of unrelated needs, ideas, words, and pictures. It is the designer's job to select and fit this material together—and make it interesting.

—Paul Rand, *A Designer's Art* (1985)

Apart from social studies teachers around the country who use the textbooks *this* book is about, few people may recall how controversial these books were when they came up for adoption during the summer and fall of 1990 in California. History textbooks seem to occupy a place in education that is similar to traditional religion's sacred books. Because they represent our past and the cultural heritage we transmit to our children, the question of whose story gets told has always been a delicate question of critical importance, as the annals of U.S. public education readily testify, and never moreso than now. The new Social Studies Program being considered by California certainly came to fit that pattern. Over the decades such controversies have largely become institutionalized rituals regulated by states, generally in the concluding stages of curriculum reform.

In 1987, California had just approved a new History-Social Science Framework mandating a shift to a multicultural approach in social studies. Certainly more radical than anything that had gone before, the new curriculum expanded the study of history to include greater coverage of ethnic and racial minorities, as well as the major world religions. The Framework boldly integrated inclusiveness with more traditional coverage of Western Civilization. Along with this wider historical scope, the Framework promulgated traditional citizenship education emphasizing America's unique "National Identity" over and above the country's multicultural diversity. Until the appearance of the California Framework, controversy about multiculturalism had largely taken place on college campuses. Yet with the Framework and similar reforms in other states like New York, America's culture war spread briefly to public school board meetings across the state of California, where the textbook's adoption came in question (see Cornbleth &

Waugh, 1995; Gitlin, 1995). Yet the struggle that ensued in California was less about the new textbooks, than over multiculturalism's place in the Social Studies curriculum as defined by the new Framework. And the controversy largely turned on the issue of unity *in* diversity, on how the U.S. symbol of *E Pluribus Unum* would now be defined.

In the checkered history of textbook controversies, opponents have usually tended to come from the right side of the political spectrum. Perhaps the most famous was a campaign waged against a series of textbooks authored by Harold Rugg. *Man and His Changing Society* was declared by the American Legion to be part of a communist conspiracy. In the 1940s this kind of red baiting was quite successful and effectively ended the use of his textbooks in classrooms across the country (see Rugg, 1941; Schipper, 1983).

However, across the intervening decades the only important connection these two controversies share is how each frames the notion of a national identity in terms of the Nation state. Nations are defined by a complex symbolic process of exclusion which inevitably resorts to that fatal dichotomy of Us versus Them. When a nation is preparing for war, as was the case when the attack on Harold Rugg's textbooks occurred (1939–1942), this campaign had only to tap into the defensive mood of the pre-war years to reach a critical mass of opposition, such that Rugg could be declared un-American. War psychology made it easier to presume that there is in fact a *true* national identity easily distinguishable from its un-American counterpart. In hindsight this is an important lesson, especially ironic for Social Studies, in as much as Rugg is considered by many to be the founder of the discipline.

With California, the same Us–Them dynamic was at play, but with a strange twist. Us in the new Framework for History-Social Science was conceived as a "National Identity," in which the multicultural identity of U.S. racial, ethnic, and religious groups (Them) would assimilate into an ideal "National" *Unum*. This assimilationist strategy muted, if not whited out, the perceived differences of particular groups who had objections to the Framework, and to how they were represented in the textbooks. The strongest opposition was mounted by a group of African American scholars who were at odds with the "moderate" vision of multiculturalism proposed by the Framework. Opposed to the Framework's conception of a "National Identity," and the state's control of the curriculum reform agenda, they countered with a populist Social Studies curriculum from below. Their proposal, which reflected a post-nation state view of cultural diversity that perhaps was ironically truer to the pluralist spirit of multiculturalism, sought to empower local school districts to develop their own curriculum materials (see King, 1995; Wynter, 1990).

Their opposition campaign was less than a Pyrrhic victory. The textbooks went on to be adopted by all but a handful of school districts in California. In one of the most accessible accounts of this controversy that appeared at the time, the books were described as being cast at the center of a "enormously complex and contentious political" debate over how the "teaching of history" should be conducted in a "polyglot" society (Reinhold, 1991). That "debate" is currently something of a stalemate. Multiculturalism's place in American education is certainly far from resolved.

Yet in California's textbook debate, there was another clash of cultures that was for the most part overlooked. Buried in the last line of a caption in the upper left-hand column about three pages into the *New York Times* article entitled "Class Struggle: California's Textbook Debate," which characterized the "political debate," is an oblique comment about the content of these books, which in a profound way turns the notion of a *text*book on its head. The caption boldly states that: "In the new textbooks . . . [the] graphics don't just explain the text, they *are* the text."

Still, the larger "graphic" implications suggested by this prescient caption did not go unnoticed by those in the field of graphic design or, for that matter, in Social Studies. Noting the recent appearance of "Class Struggle . . ." in the *New York Times*, an editorial commentary in *I.D.* magazine, a leading design trade publication, wondered why the format of "California's new history series" which is "suggestive of *USA Today*" is becoming "the national design ideal." Michael Rock (1992) direly observed that "the trend in typography is clearly toward a destruction of narrative text, with images increasingly responsible for carrying the content. . . . Something had to go, . . . and what went was the text" (p. 34). Closer to home, Gilbert Sewall (1992) of the American Textbook Council seemed to share Rock's iconclastic foreboding, though he does not name names.

> The expository nature of the social studies textbook has atrophied. In the place of a strongly written text, textbooks have substituted a nervous, fragmented, kaleidoscope, multivalent learning tool that seems designed, really for nonreaders. The gray no-nonsense history primer of the past is long gone. . . . A riot of colors and state of the art graphics may excite textbook buyers. Multiple typefaces and whitespace, photographs and sidebars, chart and boxes . . . create a shimmering mosaic. . . . But such books signal by their vacuous text that the epic stories of the past do not spark or cannot sustain student interest . . . (p. 28)

What angst animates these critics? Though it is somewhat ironic to hear a graphic designer portentously speak about the "destruction of narrative text" simply by images alone, nevertheless their shared conviction reinforces a widespread cultural assumption that is challenged throughout this book and that is: Visual information is inherently vacuous and deceptive, and images are without content. This animosity toward the visual is also widespread in education and now more than ever it needs to be challenged.

This is not to minimize the importance of multiculturalism in the social studies, an issue central to the future of public education in the United States. That issue is explored in due course, at least insofar as it concerns the power of images to represent multicultural realities. However, what may be of greater importance is understanding why this other less sensational "clash" that marked the appearance of these books may be key to how learning and instruction will be conducted in the 21st century. The future of the textbook is strangely connected to this fear of images. Rather than joining this chorus of dread, which senses the imminent "destruction" of the printed book, it might be more fruitful to view this alleged vacuousness as a space filled with creative possibility. For the cultural and pedagogical conditions that pit picture against text are no doubt radically changing. The high ground separating print from visual culture is now being seeded by another, more fundamental dichotomy set in the binary code of 0s and 1s.

The digitization of all information by the computer puts the question of content in a new light. This study follows the making of a textbook in all its stages at a time when the computer was just making its appearance in the culture of design. However, its entrance into the traditional process of book design in the particular textbook series studied here only served to enhance the design philosophy of its developers who intuitively had already grasped the computer's potential. It provided an electronic window to frame a vision already captured. Looking closely at this process not only brings a new appreciation of how instructional materials are actually made, it also prompts us to think about *how* and *why* we look at textbooks the way we do. In doing so the conventions that structure this act of seeing as reading, which are closely connected to the visual appearance of the book themselves, become visible. The graphic form which holds the text frames the picture. In this graphic opening, medium and message are drawn into a dialogue. Visuals, being nontext, placed on the printed page destabilize the text, drawing its existence into question. This unsettling format prompts the opening of a silent dialogue on the page. Why should the two be together? How can they, when they are not meant to be? But *how* and *why* are also intimately related to the computer. The digital medium accelerates this dialogue not only between image and text, but between page and screen. The shape that dialogue takes may also transform the textbook. This book is about creating a cultural space where image and word can become one, by revealing their potential to communicate together effectively.

Chapter 1 reconstructs the Social Studies design project from start to finish. These events are previewed with background information about Ligature. Ligature was the design firm responsible for the development of the Social Studies Program, and is the principle focus of this book. An account of how the company was formed, its mandate, and developments leading up to the project opens the chapter. It then renders a detailed account of the three major stages of project development: preplanning, planning, and production. The chapter explores the most interesting aspect of the development, which occurred during production, and involves the use of computer-based design to realize the goals of the project.

Chapter 2 concerns the in-house design practices evolved by Ligature. These are summed up in the Thumbnail Process. The design practices involved in this

Process reinvent a number of traditional publishing practices which are editorially driven. The larger significance of this Process rests with its re-definition of "content." In the design of a visual/verbal textbook all forms of visual information assume the same status as verbal text. This chapter examines the visual/verbal thinking behind this Process and the ways images and words can be effectively integrated to communicate by forming a "partnership of information."

Chapter 3 narrows the focus of the previous chapter to examine the unique features of the visual design conceived for the program. Two of the principal features looked at are the program "architecture," the graphical layout structures which organize the text presentation, and the visual/verbal Openers for unit, chapter, and lesson. The aesthetic quality of these features adds a realism to the presentation which complements basic social studies themes, and at the same time adds a new dimension to text.

Chapter 4 examines the major issues that arose during the development of the instructional design of the program. The principal question concerns how the visual design structures discussed in the previous chapter, like the program architecture and the Openers, may affect reader comprehension. The process and product of the Thumbnail, that is, the individual lesson, and the procedures followed in the making of the Pupil edition textbook are evaluated in terms of the "considerate" text principles derived from reading research. *Considerate* text structures embody a certain model of instructional design as well as certain standards of verbal literacy. The structure of a visual/verbal lesson presentation does not conform to either. Alternate principles regulating a visual/verbal form of presentation are considered here.

Chapter 5 continues looking at the issues surrounding the instructional design of the Social Studies Program by shifting focus to the design of the *Teacher Edition* instructional Margins. An overview of the formative influences contributing to the development of the instructional design for the Visual Learning strand is first considered. The use of visual information for instruction requires effective teacher support so that this visual content can be effectively taught along with the verbal. This support material found in the *Teacher Edition* is analyzed by looking at the structure of teacher/student discourse reflected in these scripts and strategies as it appears in the instructional sequence of a typical lesson.

Chapter 6 expands on the question of Visual Learning in the social studies curriculum by examining the multicultural audience's reception to several of the visual/verbal features heavily criticized during the adoption controversy in the state of California. Some of the innovative presentations called *A Moment in Time* and *A Closer Look* were even more controversial than questionable sections of text from the books. The inability, in these particular instances, of formal artistic expression to capture in visual form complex multicultural realities speaks a great deal about cultural boundaries and the different viewing positions of artist and audience. Such multicultural borders need to be crossed. The social studies curriculum needs to prepare children to critically interpret and evaluate visual information from our dominant culture. And, it also needs to provide critical interpretative models to deal with visuals from other cultures, less well known, and difficult to understand. The controversy surrounding these problematic visual representations recounted in this chapter provides a good lesson and starting point to discuss the most important Visual Learning issue: how children construct meaning of the world through images by being "active viewers" and not "passive watchers" (Stafford, 1996).

Chapter 7 shifts from the interactivity of audience and image to the formal and social dimensions of interactivity the textbook and computer interface afford as designed information structures. The essential features and correspondences between the two media as learning spaces are considered in light of larger advances in computer visualization tools for education and the electronic connectivity being introduced by the Internet.

In *Chapter 8*, these global trends provide the context for the concluding commentary on the Social Studies *place* in cyberspace. Apart from its more mythic associations, going digital poses a number of fundamental questions about how the emerging information society will transform American civil society, and consequently with it, basic suppositions and principles upon which the Social Studies edifice is erected. Some of the more interesting implications for the curriculum are discussed in this concluding section.

Social Studies for the 21st Century

This chapter chronicles the important highlights in the design and development of a social studies textbook. The product, Houghton Mifflin's K–8 Social Studies Program, was produced in partnership with Ligature, a R & D firm specializing in the design of instructional materials. The account focuses on Ligature's innovative role in this product development covering a period of time which runs roughly from the fall of 1988 to spring of 1990. It begins with a background profile of the firm. Pivotal to this account is the firm's unique mission to advance educational innovation through its evolving visual/verbal design philosophy.

Following this biographical synopsis, a broad overview of Ligature's first critical movements in planning for the Social Studies Program is discussed. Those opening investigatory movements are accounted for in the firm's internal planning document, "Social Studies for the 21st Century," or SS21 as it was called in-house. SS21 is more than just an initial market survey and research document. Although it provides the essential conceptual map of the key stages of product development for the K–8 program (a big picture of the project's trajectory), it more importantly situates all these in-house activities and procedures as fundamentally derived from Ligature's mission to advance a visual/verbal design approach in the creation of instructional materials.

Typically, the SS21 document can serve as a paradigm statement for the traditional stages of textbook development. Generally, development can be broken down into three successive stages: "pre-production, development, and production" (Young, 1990). Ligature generally adhered to this accepted standard and proceeded no differently. In presentation, this chapter will similarly follow this three-part process. Discussion of *Pre-production* will highlight development activities at this stage: Ligature's national competitive analysis and market survey (as found in the SS21 document), its national market testing of textbook prototypes, and its assessment of the impact the California State Framework for History-Social Science.

Consideration of the *Development* process, while initially focusing on basic in-house organizational planning and procedure, will show how these steps culminated in the Thumbnail Process, which reflects the essential tenet of

Ligature's visual/verbal philosophy. Finally, the central event of the *Production* stage, going to computer-assisted design with a Macintosh platform, technically provided the means to maximize Ligature's basic credo of visual/verbal design. Considering this advance, several related points animate the concluding discussion of this chapter.

Of first importance is the unsurpassed editorial and graphic capability the computer brings to text design. Not only does it call into question the traditional hierarchies and roles found in textbook publishing; but more fundamentally it requires a re-thinking of what presently constitute accepted conventions regulating textbook form and the presentation of content. That re-thinking begins simply enough with Ligature's own maxim reversing the order of operations in publishing implied by visual to verbal. Such a reversal poses wide-ranging questions beginning with the presumption of editorial privilege found in publishing. But, it can also quietly proceed to destabilize an entire culture erected on the production of text. Some of the more visible implications evident in this turn, for that artifact central to the curriculum, that is, the textbook, are explored in the chapters that follow.

LIGATURE: THE BINDING OF THE VISUAL AND THE VERBAL

Ligature was incorporated by Richard Anderson and Stuart Murphy in 1980. Then and now, the firm has had its principal offices in Chicago, Illinois and Boston, Massachusetts. For both partners, this step was preceded by over a decade working for Ginn & Company, the prestigious educational publisher located in Boston. The experience Anderson and Murphy shared was from different operational ends of that company. In tandem both men worked their respective ways up the company. While Mr. Anderson moved up the editorial staff ladder and eventually became head of math and social studies, Mr. Murphy became art director of the company. Being about the same age and at the same point in their careers, they naturally became colleagues.

This affinity was strongly reinforced by a shared view on how textbooks could be developed. Coming from the two most necessary (but always separate) areas of the publishing process, they came to share a perception of the inadequacy of that process. That perception inevitably forged a challenge to the prevailing model of text development in the field. Their view was based on the belief that the visual and the verbal development of a textbook (the editorial and design aspect) should be closely integrated, instead of segregated as they are traditionally. They felt that the traditional process, which involved the writing of the verbal text in isolation, and handing it over to the design department well into the writing of the manuscript, was incorrect and inefficient. Initially they weren't sure what their new notion meant in practice, but they decided to strive for its realization, believing it would lead to the production of better materials.

In the late 1970s they were given the opportunity to experiment. They came together to revitalize an important Ginn property—a social studies program that had defined social studies back in the 1940s that the company now wanted to re-publish. Given the opportunity to head up this project, but without company resources, the two men formed a collaborative effort with outside partners and managed to republish the product for Ginn. The re-issued and updated product went on to become a leading force in social studies for several years. It was this revitalized Ginn product that gave them the chance to try out their notion of visual/verbal product development in a very practical and demanding manner. This success spurred a move by both men to a partnership with a Chicago based firm, Edit Inc., that ultimately proved to be an unfulfilling venture, yet still provided them with the preparatory background and experience which propelled them to found Ligature. They took the name Ligature because it eloquently symbolized the defining mission of their new company. Stuart Murphy commented

> Ligature was a good visual/verbal name for us because it means a connection between two letter forms and a binding. So, we thought of it as a binding between the visual and the verbal. Our effort, [he said], was very much to promote this whole idea of visual/verbal product development as a way of developing higher quality educational materials.

The decade of the 1980s proved a successful "testing ground" for the new company's preamble. They produced a number of books in various subject areas that became "market leaders." And each was developed under their evolving visual/verbal hallmark. By the mid-1980s the company's revenues, staff, and reputation all had grown but its profitability was still minimal. They were looking for ways to leverage the success of their products to increase their profit. This problem led them to consider the notion of co-developing a program with a publisher, to be risk takers in a project, such that they could benefit in the sales if the product were successful. This strategy was reinforced by the successful effort they made in reviving the social studies program for Ginn; so it seemed natural for them to turn their sights to consider advancing an exploratory agenda for a new social studies program.

SS21: A Plan for Innovation

On October 17, 1988, Ligature circulated the first draft of an internal document (summarizing the company's strategy) that assessed the prospect of developing a new social studies program. The document, Social Studies for the 21st Century (SS21), revealed in broad detail a plan for a kindergarten-through eighth-grade program. This plan would guide the firm in its ongoing decision making for the next two years of product development, before they secured a partnership with a publisher to complete the project. A 30-page document, SS21 consists of a five-part outline organized in three programmatic thrusts. First, it presents a rationale based on its own research projecting national needs and trends in social studies programs in the U.S. market. Next, it examines the shortcomings of four major existing social studies programs in that market, and lastly, it proposes the innovative position they will take. SS21 conforms to standard practice in educational publishing. Squire and Morgan (1990) have observed that a "current characteristic" of all such development usually begins with a

> basic rationale prepared in advance, a detailed specification of the philosophy of the instructional design, and an indication of key instructional features. . . . These guidelines normally precede market studies that are often designed to check them . . . as are analyses of existing competitive products. (p. 115)

In the back section of the SS21 document entitled "Procedures and Responsibilities," a step-by-step breakdown is outlined. Ligature calls these three stages: Pre-planning: Conceptual Development, Planning, and Development/ Production. To assist in organizing the discussion of topics the steps appear below:

A.   Pre-Planning: Conceptual Development

1.   Competitive analysis of all major K–8 social studies programs (design, manufacturing, and instructional analyses).
2.   Marketing survey to determine K–8 social studies market climate and characteristics.
3.   Plan document for a K–8 social studies program (SS21).
4.   Prototypes (print and design boards) for Levels 6, 4, 2, and K.
5.   Conduct prototype focus testing and review and finalize all prototypes.

B.   Planning

1.   Scope and sequence plan of strands/skills, per level, across all K–8 levels.
2.   Table of contents to the unit/chapter/lesson levels.
3.   Develop chapter outlines and guidelines; identify, contract, and guide professional area specialists to critique, revise, and finalize chapter outlines.
4.   Establish and implement "Thumbnail Process" for editorial/design planning of visual/verbal interplay at the outline stage.
5.   Chapter writers: develop writer's guidelines; identify, sample, and contract writers.
6.   Establish color palette; identify illustration and photo style.
7.   Finalize development/production schedule.

C.   Development/Production

1.   Contract and coordinate all suppliers (design, editorial, production) during development/production activities.
2.   Manuscript preparation from writer's first draft through first and final edits; thumbnails; art and photo specifications; final markup.
3.   Complete final typographic specifications.
4.   Art direction: select and direct all personnel and activities related to photography, illustration, and all stages in layout of pages.

5. Proofreading and editorial review of galleys, page proofs, and film proofs.
(SS21: Social Studies Plan Document, 5/8/89, p. 29)

Generally following this outline, the activities of this initial conceptual development are now selectively reviewed, highlighting the more relevant occurrences. Important in this review is the fact that in all the company's activities adherence to its founding philosophy can be readily discerned.

SS21 and the Market Competition

Ligature's "competitive analysis" report scoping the national market in the fall of 1988 noted there were four major competing products. These social studies programs were published by:

- Harcourt Brace Jovanovich
- Silver, Burdett & Ginn
- D.C. Heath (now Houghton Mifflin)
- Scott, Foresman (now Harper Collins/Addison Wesley)

Because each of the publishers had developed and submitted their products to meet the current Texas adoption cycle, they had not similarly invested in developing programs for the new California History-Social Science Framework. Consequently, Ligature assumed that an entry into the West coast market could emerge as a "new leader." Ligature's analysis of the four products focused on program content and their components, evaluating each textbook's strengths and weaknesses in terms of each program's visual and instructional design. Apart from their evaluation of content coverage and the delivery components they found that the major strengths were in the instructional design component, and the major weakness in the visual design.

"None of the four programs exudes visual excellence," the report stated. Overall each program was characterized by varying degrees of "unengaging verbal and visual presentation." The weakness in the visual presentation is crucial, because Ligature would make an extraordinary effort to counter this lack of visual appeal by producing strikingly innovative visual displays. Some of the weak formats the report noted are: "low quality photographs and illustrations; hard-to-read and poorly rendered maps; a jarring mixture of sophisticated fine art and simplistic illustration; and a large percentage of nonfunctional, noninteractive, and merely illustrative art." Also noted about these visuals was the lack of integration with the verbal text. The market analysis concludes by stressing the overall inadequacy in each product's visual design. All, it stated, are "indistinguishable" and "look virtually the same."

SS21 Program Proposal

In the "Program Positioning" statement of SS21, Ligature envisions its visual/ verbal alternative by imaginatively voicing what teachers might say. Hoping to "set a new standard in social studies education," it exclaims, "teachers will say that this program is substantative, innovative, engaging, effective, and relevant." And they will say, it will be "substantive" because it "will develop in-depth understanding of history and geography," but the method of presentation will be "innovative and noticeably different." Ligature envisions "an instructional program that visually and verbally pulsates." Some of the outstanding attributes are:

1. Integrated visual-and-verbal presentation of lesson content that addresses a variety of learning styles.
2. History is presented as a well-told story through the use of "You were here" features to promote historical empathy.
3. Text and visuals that encourage students to discover connections between themselves and history, between history and geography, and between time and place.
4. Beautiful images and design make these books inviting to pick up and exciting to use.
5. Functional visuals not only illustrate but also teach historical concepts and facts and thus accommodate various learning styles.
6. Skills for visual learning are taught throughout the program and prepare students for a world in which visual technologies have increasing power.
   (SS21: Social Studies Plan Document: 5/8/89, pp. 14–15)

The explicit intention of every feature listed above, it should be emphasized, views the centrality of visual/verbal integration as the key innovative principle underlying Ligature's proposal.

The Five Environmental Conditions of the National Market

Influences shaping the national market also played a part in Ligature's thinking, making them believe the time was right for just such an entry. The current market is characterized as undergoing "significant economic growth (a 1.5 billion dollar market growing annually at 7%)." This growth, however, is taking place during a period of great national "unrest and criticism" over declining standards in social studies. Second, this growth is marked by the consolidation and merger of the major competitors who are more interested in "trading market share" than making an "innovative and creative response to market conditions." Third, "a stronger state influence" is making demands on this market, demanding higher quality textbooks which reflect standards of "excellence and equity." Fourth, a vast shift in market populations to more culturally and ethnically diverse groups is underway, and will "occupy the American educational system for the next twenty years." Finally, to creatively respond to these conditions, especially the conservative trend towards consolidation and merger, Ligature envisions "a shared venture" and partnership with a major publisher, in order to achieve the necessary convergence of factors conducive to innovation.

Together these conditions indicated that the next likely opportunity was with California. Next to Texas it was the largest and most important trend setting market. The state was already in the midst of wide-ranging educational reforms. And one major aspect of this change was instituting new curriculum frameworks. This reform, apart from the appeal to higher standards, was also a response to the rapid demographic expansion of ethnically diverse groups entering the state. Yet given the conservative inertia of the industry reluctant to take the risk of developing an entirely new product, Ligature assumed that such an entry required the creative potential of an independent developer allied with a major publisher. Such innovation, backed by a prestigious publishing house, could push industry awareness to an entirely new level.

PROTOTYPE DEVELOPMENT AND NATIONAL TESTING

The original SS21 document was written by an in-house editorial manager and senior editor who had "a particular interest in social studies." It then went through several revisions. Carolyn Adams, the senior marketing analyst, and Dan Rogers, senior editor, revised it on an ongoing basis. "Originally," Adams said, "they started with a text document [that had] just instructional descriptors and vision." Later the call for a "pulsating" visual/verbal program was added. The next major step was prototype development and national focus testing.

Stuart Murphy characterized this step as one of "cautious advancement." It began with just "our key group . . . putting feelers out there, trying to find out what was going on." In this group were Stuart Murphy, Richard Anderson, Carolyn Adams, Dan Rogers, and Joe Godlewski, the project art director, all senior partners of the firm, who had worked together on many projects before (see Appendix 1 for list of interview subjects). At this point the company still had two years of product development ahead without the backing of a publisher. The project quickly expanded to "a cluster of some fifty people." Progress was assessed first monthly, but then as the momentum accelerated, this key group planned their advancing strategy on a regular weekly basis.

The initial market testing began during the summer of 1988 and took place in two phases. The first sessions were done locally in Boston and Chicago, and the latter, done nationally in several states, involved an outside market researcher. Carolyn Adams and Dan Rogers described this first part as "informal," usually occurring on Saturday mornings and involving groups of 15 to 20 local teachers and sometimes in-house observers. These opening meetings were called "roundtables," although Dan Rogers also referred to them as "blue sky sessions." The discussion format was open ended and simple. Teachers would sit around tables and talk about social studies instructional materials. The general focus of these groups centered around "issues of a considerate text" and how to make a textbook more "lively and engaging." But, the more specific aim, Dan Rogers said, was to get teachers thinking about how social studies material could be presented "in nontraditional ways," particularly how content could be communicated "in a visual context."

As these roundtable sessions developed they "divided the group of teachers into three teams, one for third, fifth, and seventh grade." Prototype samples developed for feedback in these sessions were created to stimulate further thinking about the visualization of social studies content. The working premise of these early prototype boards was simple: that present "textbook conventions were extremely constraining to engagement of children." From this, they experimented with a series of prototypes that threw out the usual conventions of standard textbook size, typeface, and image to text ratios. "Some early prototypes," Joe Godlewski commented, had "huge photographs paired with maps . . . where the visual and verbal landscape was a 50/50 enterprise. . . . And people would step right into those landscapes and teachers loved it."

A typical prototype consisted of some 15 to 20 boards. A "board" (white faced illustration cardboard used in graphic design) was usually a two-page "spread" (a typical layout of facing pages complete with mounted text and visuals). The prototypes that were designed for national testing consisted of a sample unit, usually about 20 pages or 10 spreads. This prototype included "all the major elements of instruction: a unit opener, a complete lesson, the end of module review, and any special features."

Prototype development was the beginning of an experimental process. Godlewski characterized it as an attempt to engage the idea of "the beautiful book." Lessons presented in these prototypes were meant to be exceptional visually. The viewer was meant to enter "a strong visual landscape." Visuals were intended to be of such "high intensity" that the reader, it was hoped, "could really feel a sense of place and feel the people." Unit Openers always began by depicting "a setting and place." The reader could access verbal content by "stepping into" the visual.

Prototype development (which began in May of 1988) ran parallel to the second phase of formal testing, which took place at various sites in five states: California, Florida, Illinois, North Carolina, and Pennsylvania. This focus group testing began that fall and ran through 1989, even after the Thumbnail Process began in March of 1989. Whereas the informal testing was internal to Ligature's offices in Boston and Chicago (though for a time roundtables were held in several suburban school districts in Indiana), the national testing involved the contracting of an independent market researcher, who acted as a moderator or facilitator for the sessions. These sessions were held in rooms with a one-way glass so that Ligature staff could observe the groups. The "participants" generally consisted of teachers, because as Carolyn Adams remarked, they are the ones "who make the selection." In some cases curriculum directors or program administrators were included, but the inclusion of principals or school superintendents was as a rule not allowed inasmuch as their presence intimidated teachers. On occasion focus groups consisted of students, though this was a "much smaller effort," because, with students, Adams remarked, it was much "more a gut level check." Once the response was positive, as it usually was, "you don't need to keep testing." The primary reason for this, she said, was simply that children couldn't "dissect" the product or give the "precise feedback" that was expected from teachers.

The teacher focus tests were organized in two series involving the sample unit prototype. In the first series two sets of their own prototypes were put up on the walls of the testing room. This was done for comparison, testing "one against the other for feedback," to see which prototype was preferred. In the next series they tested Ligature prototypes against two of the "best" social studies programs already on the market. But both sets were mounted in such a way that neither product could be identified. Carolyn Adams commented that

> what a respondent is inclined to do is look at anything we test against (we always test against the current best seller) and say, "Well that's just like everything I've always had, same old thing." Some will say they're teaching with it, even though they may not be. They identify a different company [textbook] they're teaching with, but think that's it. Then they sort of turn their backs on that, look at ours and tell us what they like and what they don't like about it, perceiving it as the new one.

Gary Nash, the designated history author, also witnessed some of these focus groups. He saw the "elicited responses . . . as crucial." More often than not, the teachers selected the Ligature prototypes over the existing products. And the "feedback" was consistently "positive." Adams reinforced his observation. "It's true more than you can almost imagine." Response at the various sites around the country "was surprisingly much more uniform than we could have ever expected it to be." Nash felt that the "positive feedback" in these tests was a crucial factor in going ahead with the project. Without such feedback, further development, he suggested, "wouldn't have made good business sense."

THE INFLUENCE OF THE CALIFORNIA MARKET

On January 21, 1987 Ligature sent a delegation to California to explore possibilities for a new K–8 program. This was in advance of the formal release by the state of the new History-Social Science Framework (1988), which was approved by the state board of education the following July. In the opening section of SS21, one of the conditions duly noted was the "increasing state influence" on the national textbook market. Included in this section are the "upcoming state social studies adoption timetables." The opening paragraph of this section states:

> This Plan document outlines the rationale, positioning, and development plans for a kindergarten-through-eighth grade program scheduled for completion in time for the 1990 California social studies adoption. (SS21, p. 3)

Stuart Murphy regarded the new Framework as "an interesting phenomenon," because it seemed to "match" the proposed SS21 program. "The words weren't the same," he said, "but the degree of overlap of concerns was very close and supportive." Carolyn Adams, who went with that first delegation in January, characterized the response from Sacramento in positive terms, similar to the positive response they received for the national focus groups. But, according to Adams, "the real impact that California had . . . (where they clearly influenced us), was on the content decisions. . . . There's no doubt California was totally formative in what we did."

Such influence greatly reduced the innumerable curriculum decisions in devising a curricular scope and sequence for a K–8 program. But Sacramento was also positive about the visual/verbal prototypes. Carolyn Adams remarked that

> they thought it was just unbelievably attractive and beautiful. They were very proud that something of [such] high quality was the result of their Framework.

Initially though, Joe Godlweski was not so sure California would view a visual/verbal presentation so positively. He commented:

> We had interpreted the Framework to indicate that perhaps this really had to be a book that was a "good read," and that visuals and graphics could be considered interruptive and extraneous. And we weren't sure how that would fall. So we went to them with a very visual presentation, which is what we had. We couldn't do anything different. And the response from Sacramento was, "Do more of this."

John Ridley, Houghton Mifflin's editor for the program, seemed to think that Sacramento's response (to "Do more . . .") was of a more general nature. They were looking for "a break the mold program," that is, anything different than what was already on the market.

THE THUMBNAIL PROCESS: VIEWS OF DESIGNERS, EDITORS, AND AUTHORS

Following the success of their national testing and California's timely support, Ligature stepped up negotiations with various publishers to secure a partner. By the end of February 1989, Ligature and Houghton Mifflin had agreed to jointly produce the new program. Ligature had done design work for Houghton Mifflin before. John Ridley, who later took charge of the project, remarked that Ligature "had designed books for various Houghton Mifflin programs in English, Math, Reading, and Spelling. They now regarded the timing for such a collaboration as right."

At this point in the planning process, subject specialists had submitted "expert outlines" for units, along with writing samples in conformity with an in-house

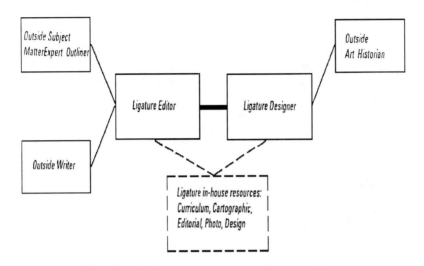

FIGURE 1.1. The Thumbnail Team.

Scope and Sequence that had been written using the California Framework as a content matrix. Using the earlier prototype experiments as visual/verbal models for page spreads, the intensive cycle of the Thumbnail Process began. By definition a thumbnail is a very small, brief, or concise sketch. Philip Meggs (1989) describes it as a form of notation designers employ and a process of problem solving.

> Thumbnails [rough page layouts of a spread] enable a designer to take a problem through a process of metamorphosis involving change, evaluation, and transformation. The solution evolves through a series of stages. (p. 157)

In principle, Ligature's Thumbnail Process moved along the same transformative trajectory. The major difference was that a graphic designer and an editor formed a team (Fig. 1.1). From March 1989 through September of the same year, the Thumbnail Process took place simultaneously at all three of Ligature's offices in Chicago, Boston, and St. Louis. The activity was intense. Rob Wittig, Team Coordinator at the Chicago office, recalls that there were "dozens and dozens of these sessions" going on at these offices. "Sixteen teams alone were at work in Chicago," he said. Approximately 70 Thumbnail teams were working at all three offices. Work on various books in the K–8 program was divided between the three locations. "The Kindergarten through Grade 3 texts were done in St. Louis. Grade 4 and 6 were [being] worked on in Boston, . . . Grade 5 . . . in Chicago." And, Grades 7 and 8 were worked on in both Chicago and Boston.

As a "series of stages" the Thumbnail Process took place over repeated 6 day cycles. Assuming the Thumbnail Process began on a Monday and ended on Saturday, then that 7 month period from March to September 1989 breaks down into about a 30 week period. If there were approximately 70 Thumbnail teams at work at the three Ligature offices, over 2,000 Thumbnail sessions took place. That gives something of the magnitude and intensity of the operation underway. This integration of editorial and design functions is reflected in the breakdown of steps each team would follow as they progressed through the cycle. The 6 day period was composed of 20 steps, 4 steps for preparation and 16 devoted to meetings. An in-house document illustrates the collaborative steps in this 6-day cycle:

Day 1: Preparation

1. Editor and designer gather and prepare research materials according to a schedule of chapters.
2. Read outline, check topic of chapter, and chapter research/idea files for related materials.
3. Receive Scope and Sequence outline analysis, which includes skill pages and building concepts assignments, and suggested number of pages per lesson. Find out from Editorial Director if a Literature selection has been decided on for the chapter.
4. Confirm availability of work room and equipment: research materials, easel, markers, paper, tape, etc. Establish daily check-in/review time.

Day 2: Meetings

1. Identify and refine chapter focus.
2. Mark the position of Lesson A Heads (Beginning Title) on thumbnail forms according to the Scope and Sequence analysis. Mark the lesson-opener timeline and include the dates. Mark the positions of the Skill pages, Building Concepts. Post these thumbnail forms on the wall.
3. Read lesson objectives aloud. Analyze them and formulate lesson concepts. List the lesson concepts on a separate sheet, establishing the logic of the transitions between lessons.
4. Write a list of chapter A Heads (Titles) and B Heads (subsection titles) on a large easel-sized sheet, based on the concept list, concentrating on the narrative flow from one head to the next (this follows that because).
5. Lesson by lesson, mark the B Heads and preliminary ideas for lesson-opening Hook on the thumbnail forms. Apportion visual/verbal space as needed to best convey the content of the chapter. Mark any visuals for which specific suggestions already exist. Reapportion pages among lessons if necessary.
6. Do a quick run-through of the entire chapter. Draft thumbnail forms, checking items off the expert's outline to make sure everything has either been edited out or put into a section under one of the heads.

7. At the daily check-in/review time: check-in/progress report/continued brainstorming with Editorial Director, Design Director and Thumbnail team coordinator. Compare working thumbnails to expert outline for chapter and lesson objective.

Day 3

1. Go through several more passes through the entire chapter to refine ideas on the thumbnail forms.
2. At the daily check-in/review time present first-draft thumbnails to Editorial Director, Design Director, Thumbnail team coordinator for review.

Day 4

1. Make further passes through the entire chapter thumbnails to reexamine, incorporate decisions made at the review and finalize.
2. Split up to do separate work: editor develops draft of Storyline document, designer creates schematic thumbnails of chapter for writer, works on refining/researching visual elements, building toward writing specs.
3. Storyline draft and thumbnails reviewed by Editorial Director, Design Director, and Scope and Sequence writer.

Day 5

1. Editor: revise Story Line per review comments.

Day 6

1. Send Story Line, Schematic Thumbnails, and Expert Outline to the writer.
2. Support: make and distribute copies of the final Story Line and the Schematic Thumbnails. Copies go to: Editorial Director, Design Director, Thumbnail team Coordinator, Chapter Editor, Chapter Designer, plus two copies for the file.
3. Write specifications for Photos and Fine Art, Graphic Organizers, and Maps.
   (Thumbnail Process for Editor/Designer Teams, 3rd Revision, 1989)

The importance of providing this day-by-day progression only becomes evident if the procedures are contrasted with a typical development model from publishing. Frank Loose, art director for Grades one through three at the St. Louis office, pointed out the difference with an anecdote about another joint Ligature project with Macmillan publishing company. Meeting with their representatives he used the term "visual/verbal," at which someone in the group immediately attempted to correct him asserting, "It's verbal/visual, *not* visual/verbal!" Implicit in this admonition are all the traditional divisions of authority, roles and procedure in standard publishing practice. Concerning that procedure, Stanley Rice (1978), a recognized author who has written extensively on the practice of publishing, related that, "only occasionally . . . is the designer required to decide what is to go in the book. . . . [Instead it is] the publisher [i.e., editor] who produces the manuscript with its accompanying visual material" (p. 1). Here, Rice is pointing to the accepted demarcation of roles and codes of practice, along with the usual developmental progression that begins with the author's manuscript.

The central relationship determining book form has always been between the author and editor, not designer and editor. "Words are, after all, the very stuff of the design of books," Rice stated (1978, p. 8). The editor only consults with the designer well into the process, generally when the formal appearance and editorial structures have to be specified before production. Though in terms of practice this is certainly not as rigid as it seems, nevertheless, the point is simply that editorial functions routinely take precedence over and determine design. Ligature instead attempted to integrate the two roles in a visual/verbal dialogue played out in the Thumbnail.

Step 5 of Day 2 subtly suggests how this simple change radically overturns publishing convention. This guideline for the thumbnail team states: "Apportion visual/verbal space as needed to best convey the content of the chapter." Implicit in this dispensing is that "content" is no longer viewed solely in verbal terms. Visuals now have parity with text. Together throughout the six days, except the fourth, when they split up temporarily to put together the respective components of the final product, the team has both elements in play in the page spreads of the projected lesson before them.

Normally, a chapter was constructed bottom up, lesson by lesson. A team would be assigned a room and on Day 1 begin. On Day 6 they would emerge with two items: a set of Thumbnail sketches, which were rough page layouts of every lesson in the chapter with the position of every visual and related text, and, the "Story Line," which was a summary of the "narrative structure of the lesson," in terms of its visual/verbal flow.

Perceptions of the Thumbnail Process were dependent on the role a person had in the process. Generally, these views were from two vantage points: observers and participants. For example, the daily reviews or "Check-Ins," which took place at 4:00 pm in the afternoon, were either overseen locally by a Team Coordinator and an in-house editor and art director, or by the program directors who traveled from office to office. John Ridley called this group the "Five Principals." Rob Wittig, Team coordinator at the Chicago office, described the process while standing in the original thumbnail room. This was a small enclosed conference room with no windows and bare white walls, with a pull down screen for slide or film presentations, and just enough room for a medium size table.

> This is the original thumbnailing room that we're in now. Basically, you'd be sitting around a table like this, the core group: one designer, one editor looking at this wall but it's covered with pieces of paper. Essentially, we'd

> start conceiving the chapter with pages up on the wall for every page of the unit, so that it's all up there. And then we'd work through a real structured pattern of gradually increasing detail . . . going through the whole chapter many times and gradually refining it. . . . So, it was quite a formula for that 6 or 7 days. . . . Everybody adapted to their own styles but they had to be out of that room. By the time they hit that last stage, there was another team waiting to use the room the next day. . . . So, it was just a matter of how do you get from nothing . . . from blank thumbnail pages in a coherent way to thumbnails that are detailed enough so that the designer can write the "specs" and the editor can write the storyline.

If one can imagine 70 teams queuing up on a weekly basis for 7 months, one team exiting, another entering, a scene of intense creative activity may come to mind. Such "transitions," Wittig noted, were marked by different stacks of books in the room; "60 books or 70 books would turn from Ancient Greece to Revolutionary North America overnight." This was generally how it worked at the local level. The critical moment of the process was the "check-in" on Day 4. As was said, these check-ins occurred with the resident art director and editor. But, sometimes attending were "the Principal Five." Moving between the three offices "literally on a fly-circuit," John Ridley said, they functioned in an oversight role evaluating the ongoing progress of the program.

This group consisted of Stuart Murphy, Dan Rogers, Editorial Director, Joe Godlewski, Design Director, Carolyn Adams, Marketing Director, and John Ridley, Houghton Mifflin Project Editor. Dubbed the "Principle Five" by Ridley, both he and Stuart Murphy stressed the jointly layered decision making aspect of the group:

> Wherever a decision was to be made we would bring to bear a marketing, editorial, and design perspective. So, we could layer that on to whatever the decision was. Whether it was a cover, a layout, or a scheme for handling the scope and sequence, it was a pretty remarkable synergy among those five people.

Presentations by Thumbnail teams were evaluated at two levels: first, from the threefold expertise brought by the "Principals," which Ridley referred to as "an evolving . . . shorthand vocabulary . . . that was mutually understood," and second, in Stuart Murphy's opinion, from the vantage point of knowing what "the bigger picture" was. Moving between the three offices over several months, "we got to a place where we couldn't see everything," Ridley said; "but, the lion's share, yes, we really did."

The subject specialists (who provided the "expert outlines" going into the process) in some cases observed and participated in check-ins, and at other points worked directly with the in-house editor and art director. Beverly Armento, the designated social studies author, participated in both roles. She spoke of being in constant telephone contact with the St. Louis office from Atlanta as the Thumbnail Process progressed with Grades 1 through 3 texts. She also worked directly with St. Louis.

> When I was up there the artist, editors, and I worked together. . . . We just knocked out the outline and did all the details. . . . Many ideas and decisions were laid out. But, in my experience, especially with the early childhood team, we kept changing those decisions day to day. The approach was constant. The content decisions and the visuals that were going to be used really did change as we worked together. I see the Thumbnail Process as a very dynamic evolution . . . between and among all the writers, editors, artists, and the main Ligature people. . . . So, I think there was a grand design but it changed.

The other function of the subject specialists began when the Thumbnail Process finished. They would receive a set of thumbnails and the storyline. But they didn't function as authors in the usual sense. More an architect than author, Gary Nash said his "main job" was organizing the pool of writers, "asking them to do what had then been divided up verbally/visually by the thumbnail teams."

If this dialogue between the editor and designer was innovative, the actual work done in the Thumbnail Process still was traditional, because it was done entirely by hand. However, when Ligature went to the Final Edits they moved to a Macintosh-based platform to finalize all the page layouts. With this move, the potential for "binding" the visual and verbal elements increased exponentially, and the focus of this dialogue shifted from the page to screen.

FINESSING AT THE BACK END: TEXTBOOK PRODUCTION AND COMPUTER-BASED DESIGN

The extraordinary result of going to computer-based design was that in one year Ligature went from prototypes to over 8,000 pages of camera ready text for the color separators and printer. This capability was made possible by re-tooling their production operation to a Macintosh platform using the desktop publishing software Quark Express. "Certainly this product could not have been produced . . . in that kind of time frame using conventional technology," Dan Rogers said. Production began with the completion of the first thumbnails and storylines in April 1989, a month after the Thumbnail Process started. An "immensely complex" production schedule began simultaneously at all three offices.

Ligature's production process went in two stages: First and Final Edits. First Edits ran from April to December of 1989. Final Edits began in July 1989 and ran to the end of January 1990. The target for this accelerated schedule was April 1, 1990. Ligature's production teams were attempting to meet the adoption requirements for California, which was that the K–8 textbooks of the Social Studies Program be available to State officials on that date. Given that deadline, the Teacher's Edition was printed during February 1990, and the Pupil Edition at the end of February and March.

Whereas the unit produced in the Thumbnail Process was the lesson, the basic unit that was "tracked" through production was the chapter. This tracking however ran along several paths, each of which corresponded to different types of production teams. There were teams for each chapter component: *Exploring Features, Decision Making, Skills, Chapter Reviews, Visual/Verbal Features*, like, for example, the Moments in Time, and Chapter Openers. Besides these teams there were also straight production teams who according to Sara Chavkin, a key production person at the Chicago office, "did whatever they were handed, literally doing production on any kind or part of the books." Chavkin and Wittig stressed that these teams always consisted of an editor and design person, thus at every level Ligature's visual/verbal approach was adhered to. The sixth-grade text, *A Message of Ancient Days* was the first book to make it through the First Edits at the Chicago office in September. Other books followed at about two-week intervals. Next was the fifth-grade text *America Will Be*, then the seventh, *Across the Centuries*, and finally the Kindergarten text, *The World I See*. Similar schedules were being followed in St. Louis and Boston for the remaining books in the program.

During the Edits a chapter went through a series of both content and design specification reviews. On any one day, Rob Wittig noted, perhaps 12 chapters could be passing through either of these two stages. At the conclusion of each Edit an ongoing ritual took place, where chapter layouts were presented in a special viewing room. This event usually involved the "Principal Five" and in-house staff. The first rough layouts consisted of page spreads with just text, the revised manuscript submitted by the authors. These roughs were more to be read and had no color or images. The Final Edit was a little more elaborate in presentation and occurrence. It was described as "the last formal ceremonial event in the life of a chapter." The page layouts were accompanied by color transparencies so that one could get a sense of what the end product would look like. These Final Edits would happen about every two weeks and usually consisted of large contingents of in-house staff along with Houghton Mifflin representatives.

After these Final Edits (which ran from September 1989 to the end of January 1990), each chapter was transferred (imported) into Quark Express. Once a chapter was on the screen the "back end" of production was reached. This final stage could run anywhere from five days to a week per chapter. This was the last chance to resolve any of the numerous problems that could arise with the final page layouts. Here any remaining editorial and design adjustments were made. Then, a chapter was "released" to the color separators in disc form and was converted into film and sent off to the printer. Once "released" the production process was over. Actually, Ligature was running about a month behind schedule in production. When all the books were at the printer by March they still were not far enough along to hit their target date. Consequently, for California, a certain number of books for the K–8 program were hand bound in order to make the April 1st deadline in Sacramento.

Moving to the Macintosh platform eliminated the most time consuming part of production. The quantity of camera-ready pages was directly related to the technical ease brought by the computer, which freed production staff from doing layout tasks manually. This was most evident with the problems associated with "modeling type" in the final page layouts. Ann Sievert, Production Manager at the Chicago office, commented that

> there's one major way in which the technology of computer-based design enabled us to function during SS21 different from the way we functioned before. And that is that once the pages were poured into Quark we could be copy fitting refinements instantly on the screen. . . . I think if anything we made changes that we wouldn't otherwise have made, because of the ease of doing it.

This enhanced capability eliminated the need for an outside typesetter. The usually frustrating cycle of sending copy out to a typesetter, getting the results, making changes, and then sending it back, simply was no longer necessary. With the computer all such changes were done right on the screen. To anyone who has experienced both, going to computer-based design forever changed the way text is designed and produced. Having started his career as a typesetter, Rob Wittig believed that the computer "can be the difference between something adequate and something extraordinary."

Before going to the computer, he said, "you had two or three chances to look at something." Basically typesetting was cost prohibitive. "Every change you made you paid for," Sara Chavkin remarked. In functional terms layout of type by hand, which was the way it was done, on the two dimensional surface of layout board, was both incalculably inefficient and prone to error. Getting type to fit the layout space accurately was nearly impossible on the first try, especially when every character and line had to be measured to fit the overall layout. This never happened the first time. Two or three trips to the typesetter were typical. Adjustments were often difficult to make, sometimes changing the entire design of the page.

With the computer the notion of a visual/verbal dialogue could be given full play. Commenting on the effect computers are having on publishing, Keith Smith (1992), an innovative book designer, points out how the present markedly departs from the past.

> The computer allows the writer, for the first time, to simultaneously compose the page as well as the text. . . . It gives the writer total control over the plasticity of the page, precisely as it will appear when it is published.

Smith's view is presently so germane to the field that it is nearly echoed word for word by Ligature. Rob Wittig remarked that, "as a word person, the Macintosh allows you to write to fit the space." Yet, what makes this observation by Smith less than prescient is that Ligature's Thumbnail Process manually applied in principle and practice what the computer now similarly does, but effortlessly. This release from the constraints of traditional layout techniques gives full play to the principle of visual/verbal dialogue underlying the Thumbnail. This "control over the plasticity of the page" corresponds precisely to the "modeling" Wittig describes, and gave Ligature the capability to realize their vision of a textbook that "visually/verbally pulsates."

Joe Godlewski noted that "the main difference" between the present and when they designed the Social Studies Program, was that Ligature did not have an in-house four color proofing system. Before, all the images for the Houghton Mifflin texts where put in at the color separator. Their software then only allowed them to scan in a rough black and white composite of the actual color transparency. But now these visuals can be instantly imported in full color and the program can be run to adjust the color ratios of the image, so as to fit the overall color combinations of the spread. Having this ability, Thumbnails are no longer done manually but on the screen. With a later project, a K–6 math program for Houghton Mifflin, Ligature produced test units, a series of actual lessons, which were then distributed to actual school classroom sites for trial instructional use to gain feedback as to their effectiveness. In effect two of the usual stages of development are superseded: market testing and prototyping.

However, the enormous difference in subject matter does not make for easy comparisons between the two projects. What made the Social Studies Program unique was the approach taken in its use of visual imagery as content, both in the enormous number of images that were researched and selected and in their quality. In addition to the exceptional production standards accorded visual design, what also set the Social Studies program apart from the usual textbook, were the innovative forms of visual display and presentation developed, which makes it an innovative marker for the field of social studies. Coming to a better understanding of visual/verbal design thinking (and its relationship to the computer) can only be approached by a deeper investigation of the Thumbnail Process. How Ligature engaged in this *recursive* dialogue of images and words on the graphic white space of the textbook page is explored in the next chapter.

When Image Meets Word

As described in the previous chapter product development culminated in an on-screen dialogue between images and words coming together to create a text. Though the computer allowed for the more creative juxtaposition and graphic resolution of these dichotomous elements, it did not provide a rationale or theoretical program to direct this work. Prior to going online with the Macintosh, the design thinking behind the Thumbnail Process emerged only during an in-house process of socialization and experimentation that brought together editorial and design personnel. This was intended to formalize a development process reflecting Ligature's visual/verbal founding principle. This in-house process of socialization is described here.

What words and images can do alone and together, how they communicate, is what the Thumbnail Process is all about. This chapter recounts the visual and verbal thinking that led up to the formalization of that process. The prototype phase of product development can be viewed as a period of active experimentation with novel graphic formats for text presentation and visual display. This preparation Joe Godlewski viewed as a series of "modeling exercises that we went through to kind of get ourselves up to the Thumbnail Process," exercises that were investigations about "how visuals work," and at the same time provided the basis upon which this "movement toward a visual/verbal philosophy began to jell." Through this "movement," Rob Wittig said, we "codified" a working set of visual/verbal principles. The Thumbnail actualized these principles.

The opening section of this chapter looks at the in-house setting that allowed Ligature's visual/verbal preamble "to jell," providing an inspirational basis through which accepted publishing procedures and presumptive hierarchies could be reconceived along visual/verbal lines. The "codification" of an evolving language of images and words is discussed next. This formal codification largely took place during the development of two innovative narrative and expository visual/text presentations called *A Moment in Time* and *A Closer Look*.

In the concluding section of this chapter, the theoretical and cultural context underlying this codification and the basis for a visual/verbal aesthetic at the heart of the Thumbnail Process is explored. How Ligature designers appropriated graphic communication standards from the larger design culture (e.g., advertising, news-

papers, magazines, technical illustration) to develop such visual/text presentations is considered. How such creative adaption of visual communication forms
was derived is traced to the professional and theoretical affiliations Ligature shares
with the work of other information designers, most notably Edward Tufte.

Situating the SS21 product design and development within the culture of
information design can serve to clarify Ligature's larger theoretical project to go
beyond the "text" book, to envision social studies learning and instruction beyond, as Joe Godlewski put it, a "discursive word-based delivery system." In the
field of graphic design advertising such a goal would hardly cause a ripple, but in
the context of textbook publishing, it becomes a fairly radical proposal. Any break
with the past may seem to be its own justification. For Ligature that break and
possible re-invention began with creating the esprit de corps, the mindset for
visual/verbal thinking. This process of socialization in the bringing together of
Thumbnail teams is considered first.

THE TEXTBOOK AND STANDARD PUBLISHING PRACTICE

> The textbook is an exposition of generally accepted principles in one sub-
> ject, intended primarily as a basis for instruction in a classroom or pupil–
> book–teacher situation.
>
> —Mauck Brammer (1967)

It is a widely acknowledged fact that the introduction of the computer to the
publishing industry is revolutionizing the field as well as changing the traditional roles and hierarchies in the production process (see *Print*, 1993, p. 124).
Perhaps a less acknowledged fact is the state of resistance within publishing to
the wider implications of this change. George Landow (1992) comments on this
resistance by observing that one of its effects is the publishing of a great number
of "appallingly designed books." This, he maintains, is principally because of a
near total lack of serious consideration for the "visual components" of a printed
text (pp. 49–50). Gary Nash, history author for the SS21 program reinforces
Landow's point with an anecdote about another textbook project he was involved
with. Nash noted that, "Never a word was said about visuals in five years." Only
at the "tail end" did the publisher even consider visual material, mostly because
of Nash's urging, and then only as an "add on" to a textbook that consisted of
2,000 unedited pages.

In the opening chapter Stuart Murphy remarked that he and Richard Anderson had come, through experience, to regard the traditional separation of the
editorial and art director in the development of textbooks to be an "incorrect
method." Yet that method is standard practice. Confirmation of this came surprisingly from the same publishing company that they left to start Ligature. James
Squire (Squire & Morgan, 1990) of Silver Burdett & Ginn (Murphy's company in
Boston) and Richard Morgan, of Macmillan/McGraw, state that, "The visual design of a textbook program [should] follow, not precede, the content and instruc-

tional design" phases of development (p. 117). Such a conservative view properly reflects a long arc of economic and technological development that has institutionalized a culture for the rational and efficient production of the printed book, though such conventions, demarcation of roles, and procedures may seem now overly determined in a postindustrial era.

Still, this view generally tends to be the accepted one. "Conventionally," John Ridley commented, "an editor has crafted a manuscript, but with the visuals in mind, in fact writing the art specifications. . . . So the text has never been done in a vacuum. . . . The big difference, with Ligature, was that the editor (in the editorial process) brought to bear the visual at the same time. . . . The operative thing is not, *and then*, but rather, *at the same time*."

In one sense Ridley's statement seems prescient. Although "same time" refers to the dialogue of images and words, it also suggests a suspension of the terms in Squire and Morgan's linear proposition. By collapsing the industrial logic of its steps into a "same time" simultaneity it provocatively alludes to the online "plasticity" going to the Macintosh platform provided Ligature production teams. Yet, he also recognized that, until the SS21 project, such a collaboration with Ligature, where their visual/verbal approach was fully brought to bear on the development of an entire textbook series, was not considered feasible by the industry. Because, he said, it was "a very different model for publishers to work with."

To a greater and lesser degree both Nash's and Ridley's commentaries make clear the central role of the editor in a manuscript-driven process. Reflecting this view held within the profession, Stanley Rice (1978) aptly noted that, "words are, after all, the very stuff of the design of books." And so it follows he says that the basic "editorial structure" is the sentence (p. 8). As the SS21 project development converged on the Thumbnail Process, Ligature had already established an additional role and structure. While Rice views the designer actively consulting with the editor, ultimately the editor directs the process. In the Thumbnail Process editor and designer become a team, the parallel structuration of visual with text drives development. With Ligature words and images become the "stuff" that books are made of; visual and verbal "sentences."

THINKING BEYOND THE BOOK

As with "a lot of industries," Stuart Murphy observed, "educational publishing has an inbred aspect to it." This self-reflexiveness tends to "re-create . . . the same thing . . . with minor improvements." To counteract this tendency, Murphy had a twofold strategy: creating visual/verbal teams and task-oriented brainstorming sessions. From Murphy's perspective, one potential problem with the SS21 project early on, was that "people were already thinking in book forms, when we were well away from being in a book yet." To correct this they tried to put together "people that wouldn't necessarily choose to sit next to each other at lunch, or wouldn't necessarily choose to be working with each other on a project." Since editors and designers tended to "cluster" with their own kind, these brainstorming teams were deliberately mixed; the usually separate areas of publishing expertise were brought together. Then, they were told, Murphy relates, "Okay, you're the group and you've got three days to come back to us with an idea! You can devote all your resources for those three days to that idea, and then be ready to present it. And so suddenly, we put these people together who weren't accustomed to working together."

Rob Wittig recalls that Murphy told the three assembled teams, "to cast the net really wide to make sure they were not getting traditional too fast. We want to have one more completely different thing!" Murphy's intent was to "break down barriers," social as well as conceptual. "I remember him sort of gesturing toward the ceiling," Wittig said. "It can be any size, shape, anything, just come back with it." These exercises, he felt were very "influential." They got "us off columns and linear things." This was "crucial" to visual/verbal thinking. And it resulted in some exceptionally creative prototype designs.

The "Banana Boat" was an illustrated timeline "which traced the banana from the tree via all the people that touched it, until it had got to a North American kid's table." Another, was "Olympics Then and Now," Wittig added. It was a "spin game" that allowed students to imagine competing in ancient or contemporary Olympic sporting events. And, one other result of this collaboration was a poster called, "Where Would You Be?" It was a chart that showed the student what it might be like if they chose to live in either Europe or America at various points along a timeline that spanned the past three centuries. "These things," Wittig remarked, "were brought up over the course of development of the program many times, to kind of push that energy into, 'It's getting kind of flat, it's getting traditional. So, think of the banana!'"

Another social aspect of this in-house "self-education process" was the example set through role modeling. Wittig noted that new staff confronted the principle of visual/verbal thinking in the status accorded Ligature's senior members. The "power structure" of the organization constantly reinforced this principle. In the work-a-day operations the fact that the senior art director and senior editor are given equal voice in meetings where editorial and design decisions are made, clearly has "immense influence" Wittig felt. "I've seen that moment happen where you can just see people thinking, 'Wow, they're really serious about this, they really believe it.'"

Content Is Everything

This ongoing visual/verbal acculturation had to be rhetorically appealing and persuasive enough to convince the editorially minded. A double axiom informed in-house conversation and acted as sort of "a litmus test." Rob Wittig recalled that, "During the course of making these books . . . we got in the habit of catching others from opposing, as is traditional in educational publishing, '*pictures*' and content. . . . When and if people say, '*content*,' do they use it interchangeably with words (or does it mean only language)." Against this standard, Wittig exclaimed, "we had to constantly insist that, 'Content is everything . . . including all forms of visual information.'. . . And the other banner throughout the process was, 'No gratuitous images! No gratuitous images . . .'" At a pragmatic level one key conceptual "wedge" used to deconstruct word bound notions of content was the typical social studies map. Wittig recalls that staff were asked to consider the distinction between history as writing, and history as maps. "The map," he said, "is the proof-a one line proof. Is a map content or not?" Here, Wittig probably means that maps are composed of single lines which conform to a conventional set of highly naturalized visual codes that convey information about historic events through shape, pattern, and form, rather than through written text. Because the map inhabits something of a graphic intermediate zone, integrating visual and verbal information, it prompted people, Wittig believed, into the Thumbnail frame of mind. Maps were considered to be the "conceptual centerpiece" of the design for the Social Studies Program because they exemplified Ligature's most basic principle. "Structurally," Wittig said, "maps are random accessed and layered." A map can be read in an all over fashion or studied point by point, area by area. It was the structural features of maps that became "foundational" in the training of Ligature's teams. Maps were a key example indicating that history content has always had "a visual track."

A Partnership of Information

Beyond the conversion factor of persuading staff to seriously look upon visuals as content was the fine line of another conceptual threshold. Beyond this "education process," Stuart Murphy stressed that it was best "to put a little less emphasis on the idea that the visuals are content . . . in that it almost sounds like it's a replacement . . . to the text." Rather, in his mind, the more appropriate analogy was one of "partnership." The visual was to be looked upon as "a colleague or partner . . . working with the words to create a text."

So, the next theoretical hurdle or threshold to pass was to simply look at words and images as equally "legitimate," but distinctively different forms of representation through which "information can be conveyed." On this point, Joe Godlewski concurred. In visual/verbal terms, resolution to a design problem, he said, simply "came out of the information." With this approach, "the extent to which you can visualize information is really . . . not to replace text, but to present certain information that is more conducive to receiving it." Or, in simpler terms, "to present information in either a visual or verbal form that is 'more' appropriate to what content is being presented." This is especially interesting because Godlewski refers to the Thumbnail Process as a "dialogue liberating text and visuals." But taking this position which views words and images as information was a necessary precondition for this "dialogue" to occur.

Inside the Thumbnail Room

The six-day process described by participants in the first chapter can be divided into three overlapping stages: Preparation, Apportionment, and Refinement. The first and second days were involved with preparing all the assembled materials for the chapter by reviewing it within the context of the story outline and analysis. On the second day the chapter focus would be identified and refined in light of the lesson objectives. From these concepts a list would be drawn up "establishing the logic of transitions between lessons." This information was marked up on a standard thumbnail form (Fig. 2.1). Basically, this form was a series of computer generated page layouts including every two-page spread for each lesson in the chapter. The forms were numbered by line copy (text lines per page) and columns.

On the thumbnail form the team first entered the positions of all Lesson A *Heads* and B *Heads* (title and subtitles), the lesson opener-timeline, and the position on the spread of the skill features. Next the concept map for each lesson in the chapter would be sketched out on large easel size blank paper so that "the narrative flow" from one head to the next could be viewed in its entirety. This conceptual map was then entered on the thumbnail forms marking the corresponding position of each *A Head* and *B Head* in the lesson sequence.

The crucial moment in this second day came when the team "apportioned the visual/verbal space as needed, to best convey the content of the chapter." Days three, four and five involved a progressive refinement of these decisions, which included presentation and evaluation of the product. On the sixth day these results were circulated to supporting staff who would ready the lesson(s) for production.

The Terms of Apportionment

> Images require analysis in relation to their text. How, then, is this done? The designer, in consultation with the editor or the author, must ask questions.
> —Stanley Rice, *Book Design* (1978)

In the original Thumbnail room, with slides of "a few thumbnails" that Joe Godlewksi "was able to find," projected on the same wall where thumbnail forms and sketches went up, Rob Wittig described the images "up there as a record [reflecting] a lot of thought, study, and negotiation on the part of the editor and designer." On the first day, he said, the team reviewed the "pool of information" covering all the preparation done for that lesson sequence, until both members of the team "have ownership." On the second day, the team would "start conceiving the lesson, with every page up on the wall, so that it's all up there." Then the team would begin "working through a real structured pattern going through the whole lesson many times, gradually refining, gradually increasing detail."

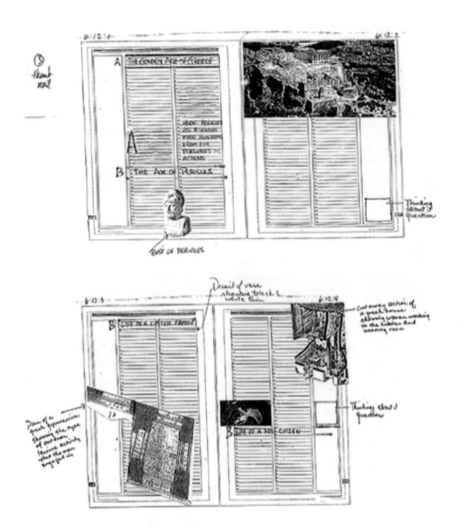

FIGURE 2.1. Thumbnail Forms.

But as the overwritten and sketched on thumbnail forms may indicate, "the pages were like a platform of negotiation." Here the team "had to get to the point" when it had to be decided "where the information was going to fall as a total page." Agreement on "what was the very best way to express" chapter content, whether an image or a visual/verbal combination, could only result through an intense working dialogue between editor and designer with the materials before them on the wall. "The question," Wittig exclaimed, "would constantly be, 'Why is that image there? What is it doing or showing? What kind of explanation is there for it, and what concept is it trying to get across?'" Elaborating further, while pointing to the projected images showing gold artifacts from the African kingdoms of the south Saharan desert, Wittig commented that "the notations on this page are really indicative of that process." The question, he felt, was whether the image was meant to be simply didactic, "Just [an image of] gold artifacts," or something more integral. Wittig continues:

> Well, gold artifacts are pretty, but what are they for? What are they show-ing? And, a lot of the choices on images would be well, "I know this is nice but it doesn't really add to the . . . concept. Remember you'd be asking [referring to Joe Godlewski, the senior art director], "What's the concept on this? What are we trying to get across? Is there something else that would show it?" There had to be a reason.

The crucial problem during this Apportionment phase for the Thumbnail team was deciding to what extent the information should or could be visualized. This could only be resolved, as Wittig demonstrates, by going to the conceptual core of the lesson through this ongoing questioning process; but there were also a num-ber of other factors. Another example points to the degree of complexity entailed in this decision-making process.

> Joe: The "Battle of Salamis" (Fig. 2.2) was an extravaganza, which was to show how the Greeks outwitted the Persians. We went through a lot of changes with what was actually going to be shown in the actual spread.

> Dan: But that was an example of where we got a tremendous amount of research on that battle and that is what really spurred us to take a different approach to that spread. Because the intricacy of the strategy involved simply couldn't be shown in one landscape. You needed a series of differ-ent individual spreads.

> Rob: Yes. And on this spread too it is worth noting that we were way above the 60/40 art to text ratio. But you can see that if the point of the spread is to communicate the issues of the battle, how warfare was fought at that time, and how they used geography to win the battle, then the decision was made that the images were a much better way of dealing with that on the spread than to try to write a description.

> Joe: Yes. It's a good example of how we approached this decision making. Confirming that sort of question: How did you come up with the design for this thing? Oh, it really came out of the information.

During the Refinement phase "these working sketches . . . would be redrawn many times," until the team split up; the editor to write up a "storyline," and the designer to work up a "set of thumbnails." At that point the decision making on the final shape of the lesson moved to a higher level. The team would make a presentation, making a defense of the results, before the in-house project editor and art director, which in some cases was reviewed also by the "Principal Five," as John Ridley of Houghton Mifflin called them in the last chapter, who were moving between the three offices.

While determining which mode of depiction (in terms of information) would better suit the conceptual requirements of the lesson, the actual work was evaluated in terms of how it seemed to reflect the degree to which the team had integrated the in-house visual/verbal ethos into their decision making. Stuart Murphy felt that the extent of this assimilation could be observed during these final check-ins.

> We had certain code phrases for the way we worked. For example, it was a negative thing for someone to say, "That's a design decision." Or, "That's an editorial decision." That would be a very negative response, because that's not true. It's a product decision, that everyone [on the team] is affected by. A very positive thing was when we'd go into some of these check-ins at the Thumbnail meetings, and the people started presenting the program, and we couldn't tell whether it was the editor or the designer who was talking. [From this], you can get a kind of sense of the spirit we were looking for.

In the end the approved results, according to Dan Rogers, represented less a product than the completion of another "stage" in development. The set of thumbnails and the storyline which emerged from the process "we saw as sort of the blueprint stage, [where] we tried to get it to a point where those parallel tracks could then go on: writing, image development, and photo research."

Stanley Rice (1978) characterizes illustrations as "extensions of the text . . . its tone and intention" (p. 21). When Rice speaks of a "text," he is referring to a manuscript, already written. Though Wittig raises the question whether the image adds to the concept, he is talking only about a lesson outline. The manuscript was written after the Thumbnail Process on the basis of the storyline. The purpose of the storyline was to give "the writer directions in terms of how [the team] would like it structured and how much space they had to work with, so they knew that they were writing in the script." The inverse of visualizing information is, of course, the manuscript driven book. The contrast then should be fairly obvious. In effect the visuals were structuring the story, the text was "to play off the images."

Yet, when Wittig speaks about the use of visuals in the Battle of Salamis example as a "better way" than doing a "description," it is necessary to point out, that the spread still very much relies on verbal description. If one looks closely, there are four colorful cutaway topographic tableaus showing the progression of the Battle, and each is numbered and captioned. None of these individual 3-D diagrams would even be comprehensible without the captions that describe and explain the battle sequence. Though, it should also be pointed out that the photograph above the four 3-D diagrams shows what the tiny ships would look like to scale. Without it the shapes are of little significance. In visual/verbal terms, both depictions can reciprocally extend or add to the text in its entirety, when necessary.

In this sense writing involved not only composition of the main running verbal text (the "script" to be written in), but also these captions, under which the *Heads* (titles and subtitles) can be included. It is the design of this verbal text structure that is in some ways even more integral in this visual/verbal equation of the "total page," than the apportioning of the graphic space central to the Thumbnail. The design of this relational structure initiated with the Thumbnail Process continues the dialogue of images and words.

HOW IMAGES AND WORDS WORK TOGETHER

> Any attempt to grasp "the idea of imagery" is fated to wrestle with the problem of *recursive* thinking, for the very idea of an "idea" is bound up with the notion of imagery. . . . A productive way of dealing with this problem is to see ideas as images. . . . This involves attention to the way in which images (and ideas) double themselves: the way we depict the act of picturing. . . . These double pictures, images, and figures are strategies to see ideas as images and to allow the recursive problem full play.
> —W.J.T. Mitchell, *Iconology: Image, Text, Ideology* (1986)

In discussing the fairly recent shift in focus away from a behaviorist model of research on teaching social studies, to a more constructivist approach, Beverly Armento (1986) observes that such a shift raises the question whether the teacher can "influence the student to construct images and meanings of the social world" (p. 946). In the *About Your Book* section of the first- and second-grade text, which basically describes and explains how to use the special recurring visual/verbal features that are found therein, the first relevant instructional statement closely follows this constructivist approach. It states simply, "Pictures and words work together. Together they help you learn" (p. xii). The repeated emphasis on "together" recalls Stuart Murphy's notion of "partnership" when he stressed the complementary aspect images and words should take in successful visual/verbal presentations. As has been shown so far, visuals in the SS21 program, were oftentimes introduced to carry the meaning of the lesson. In fact the ongoing flow of the storyline was a construction of images so interwoven with its textual counterpart, that any meaning could only be seen in visual/verbal terms. Because, in one respect, the goal of social studies is to construct a normative picture of the world, the way meaning, through the design of verbal text structure, is imputed to pictures, is the key design problem after the Thumbnail apportions the basic area of graphic space to each.

Images Real and Unreal

Because the SS21 program development agenda acknowledged that "children live in an increasingly complex and highly visual society" (p. 25), it purposefully set

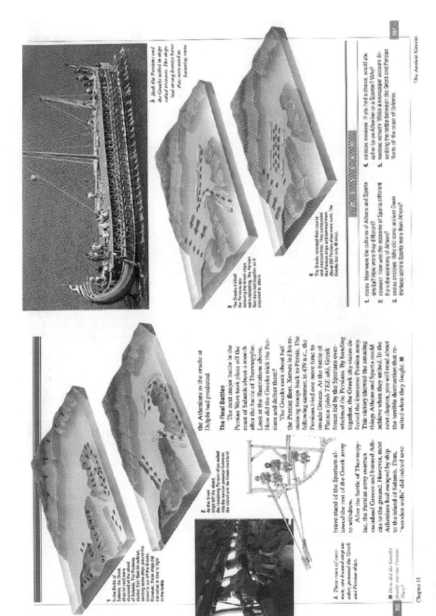

FIGURE 2.2a. The Battle of Salamis, Grade 6, pp. 356–357.

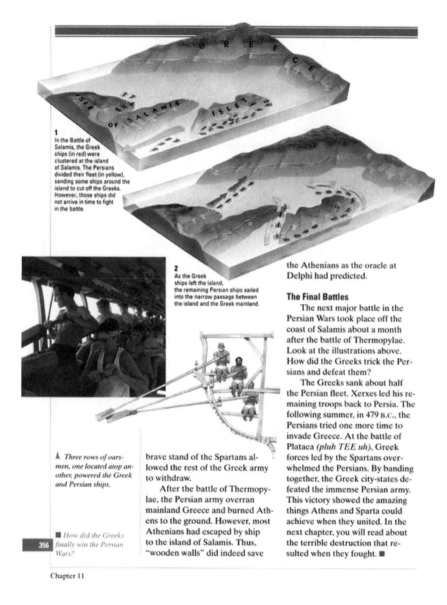

1
In the Battle of Salamis, the Greek ships (in red) were clustered at the island of Salamis. The Persians divided their fleet (in yellow), sending some ships around the island to cut off the Greeks. However, those ships did not arrive in time to fight in the battle.

2
As the Greek ships left the island, the remaining Persian ships sailed into the narrow passage between the island and the Greek mainland.

▲ *Three rows of oars-men, one located atop an-other, powered the Greek and Persian ships.*

■ *How did the Greeks finally win the Persian Wars?*

brave stand of the Spartans al-lowed the rest of the Greek army to withdraw.

After the battle of Thermopy-lae, the Persian army overran mainland Greece and burned Ath-ens to the ground. However, most Athenians had escaped by ship to the island of Salamis. Thus, "wooden walls" did indeed save the Athenians as the oracle at Delphi had predicted.

The Final Battles

The next major battle in the Persian Wars took place off the coast of Salamis about a month after the battle of Thermopylae. Look at the illustrations above. How did the Greeks trick the Per-sians and defeat them?

The Greeks sank about half the Persian fleet. Xerxes led his re-maining troops back to Persia. The following summer, in 479 B.C., the Persians tried one more time to invade Greece. At the battle of Plataea *(pluh TEE uh)*, Greek forces led by the Spartans over-whelmed the Persians. By banding together, the Greek city-states de-feated the immense Persian army. This victory showed the amazing things Athens and Sparta could achieve when they united. In the next chapter, you will read about the terrible destruction that re-sulted when they fought. ■

Chapter 11

FIGURE 2.2b. The Battle of Salamis, Grade 6, p. 356.

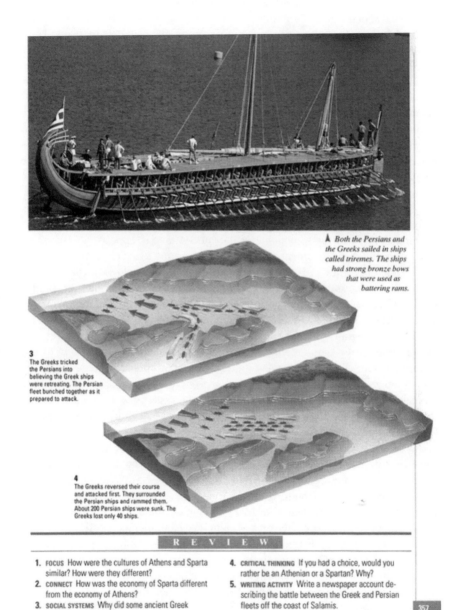

▲ Both the Persians and the Greeks sailed in ships called triremes. The ships had strong bronze bows that were used as battering rams.

3
The Greeks tricked the Persians into believing the Greek ships were retreating. The Persian fleet bunched together as it prepared to attack.

4
The Greeks reversed their course and attacked first. They surrounded the Persian ships and rammed them. About 200 Persian ships were sunk. The Greeks lost only 40 ships.

R E V I E W

1. **FOCUS** How were the cultures of Athens and Sparta similar? How were they different?
2. **CONNECT** How was the economy of Sparta different from the economy of Athens?
3. **SOCIAL SYSTEMS** Why did some ancient Greek thinkers admire Sparta more than Athens?
4. **CRITICAL THINKING** If you had a choice, would you rather be an Athenian or a Spartan? Why?
5. **WRITING ACTIVITY** Write a newspaper account describing the battle between the Greek and Persian fleets off the coast of Salamis.

357

The Ancient Greeks

FIGURE 2.2c. The Battle of Salamis, Grade 6, p. 357.

out to advance a more sophisticated approach to visual learning skills, which in the typical social studies curriculum usually only involved map and globe skills. To the Ligature developers one of the most important "elements of a sound citizenship education," in the present, obviously meant being highly visually skilled, since students largely constructed their meanings of the "social world" through visual information (Marker & Mehlinger, 1992, p. 835).

In the *About Your Book* section, the intent of the designers was to start students off right at the beginning by showing them how "pictures and words" are meant to "work together." In terms appropriate to a first-grade audience constructing a meaningful image of the world means first to distinguish between real and unreal. In the *Starting Out* spread of this section (Fig. 2.3), a simple comparison is made between two types of visual information: a drawing and a photograph. A cartoon drawing of a talking ear of corn is compared to a photograph of corn being harvested on a farm. The caption tells the student which is real and which is not. On the next page, students are asked by the caption to distinguish for themselves which is real or not. Above it, appearing in the most basic of terms, the fundamental visual/verbal learning principle appears, which states, "Pictures and words work together. Together they help you learn."

In the *About Your Book* section of Grades 3 through 8 a similar, but slightly more sophisticated, statement appears. It states that, "A picture is worth a thousand words. But just a few words in a caption can help you understand a picture, a map, a photograph, . . . an illustration, a painting, a cartoon." However, the first definition of a caption appears only in the Teacher Edition Margin of the third-grade text (Fig. 2.4). It states: "a caption is a brief description or explanation of a picture or photograph and often appears just below the picture." Of far more instructional importance is that students are asked "to write captions for the pictures they draw." This is modeled by the visual of a child reading from the finished copy of her handmade book. Handwritten captions describing the masks made by a Cherokee Indian tribe appear at the bottom of the spread. Whereas caption writing exercises like this are initially found in the third-grade text, in Grades 1 and 2, there is a Visual/Verbal Glossary (Fig. 2.5). With the help of the Glossary the student can build vocabulary skills by word and image association. Each word listed in alphabetical order appears in the main text as a Key Word in the Thinking Focus of the Scholar's Margin. For example, the word "ancestors" appears on page 44 in a lesson titled "Learning About Ancestors." For this grade level, the Lesson and Glossary appropriately reinforce the key word in visual and verbal terms. This complementarity of showing and telling reflects the intended working relationship of pictures and words for the overall design of the program.

The *Caption* along with the *Heads* (titles and subtitles) provide the basic structural framework to properly contextualize the various kinds of visual information presented. According to the captions found in the *About Your Book* opening section of each grade level text:

FIGURE 2.3. The Talking Ear of Corn, in the About Your Book section, Grade 1, p.xi.

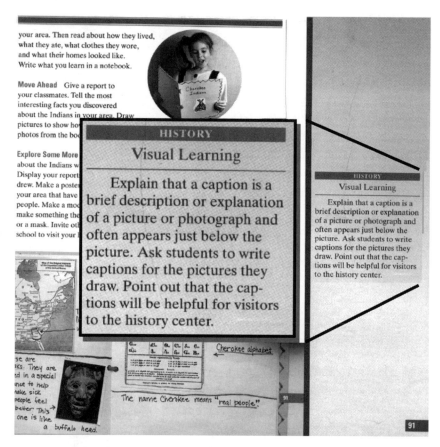

FIGURE 2.4. Definition of a Caption, Visual Learning, Teacher Edition, Grade 3, p. 91.

> *Titles* "tell what the lesson is all about, . . . outline [it], . . . giving the main points . . ."
>
> *Captions* "help" the student "understand" what they are seeing . . .

The functional importance of captions in the design of a textbook that involves such a wealth of visual information cannot be overestimated. As it states in the *About Your Book* section, they can be likened to "road signs" telling the student where they are in the text and what they are seeing. Appropriately designed and worded captions are meant to name, identify, describe, and explain the visual presented. In short, captions provide the verbal frame which sets the proper boundaries of the visual frame; a conceptual template through which the teacher can assist the student to understand what is seen.

ancestors Members of your family, starting with your parents, who were born before you. Page 44

citizen A member of a country. Page 104

country A land with its own laws, symbols, and people. Page 16

athlete A person who is trained in sports. Page 144

colony A community of people ruled by a country far away. Page 109

crops The plants farmers grow to sell or use. Page 9

author A person who writes books. Page 166

compass rose A symbol showing the directions of north, south, east, and west. Page 6

custom The special way a group of people does something. Page 168

ballot The paper on which people mark their votes. Page 115

consumer A person who buys things. Page 38

depend To need someone. Page 3

celebrate To honor or remember a special day, event, or person. Page 106

continent A large area of land with water around it. Page 15

diagram A drawing that shows and names the important parts of something. Page 34

FIGURE 2.5. Visual/Verbal Glossary, Information Bank, Grade 2, p. 187.

Such a structure, though secondary to the main running text (yet only in the amount of actual space it takes up), is just as integral to the overall graphic structure of the total page, since its purpose is to directly link the visual to that main section of text on the page. Consequently, the design of this text structure was of great concern and involved some of more interesting typographic experiments made during prototyping. The design thinking behind captions is considered next.

Familiar Graphic Forms For Unfamiliar Purposes

One example of an idea that carried over through the successive stages of the SS21 development to become one of the visual/verbal centerpieces of the Social Studies Program was *A Moment in Time*. It also served, according to Rob Wittig, an important role in "the codification of Ligature's thinking," in regard to finding "different ways . . . to dispose of words and images . . . other than a boxed image [with] a caption underneath." Departing from the standard definition given earlier that appears in the third-grade Teacher's Edition, Wittig recalls that in their prototype explorations, two "graphic forms . . . rarely seen in history textbooks," inevitably developed into the "paradigm" for the caption design which became *A Moment In Time* and *A Closer Look*.

These were technical illustrations and mail-order catalogues. The exploded diagrams, usually found in "model kits and repair manuals" with captions (called callouts) arrayed around a central image became one adapted form of caption strategy. Another "really big influence throughout the Social Studies Program were catalogues." Both graphic forms, Wittig felt, allowed for "nonrectilinear forms" for visual/verbal presentations. In his mind these forms made for a "more visually pleasing page." These "free-floating formats," where "you can put words anywhere, matching them to items," were first systematized, by Wittig, in the *Exploded Knight* (Fig. 2.6). Originally, this idea came out of one of their early "blue sky sessions," where the problem was to think of ways to visualize a typical history narrative. Then, Wittig and Rogers came up with the idea of showing a crusader knight in battle. The key word for understanding Ligature's evolving thinking regarding captions is in the bracketed term "annotated." The caption is an annotation on the visual *Moment*, rather than on a particular text passage.

In the visual/verbal display of an exploded diagram, captions are referred to as *Callouts*, like the ones showing the parts of a carburetor. Adapted from a book on Japanese technical illustration, Wittig noted that the callouts were intended to create a "field of pointed visual/verbal details." With the *Exploded Knight*, the callouts fan out from the central dramatic image of a crusader in battle (Fig. 2.6). Starting from a clockwise position each callout is listed below; the title of each implies their intended verbal function. Generally, each callout was meant to build up an array of descriptive and contextual "details" which added to and embellished the single visual image. This list provides the essential "codification" for

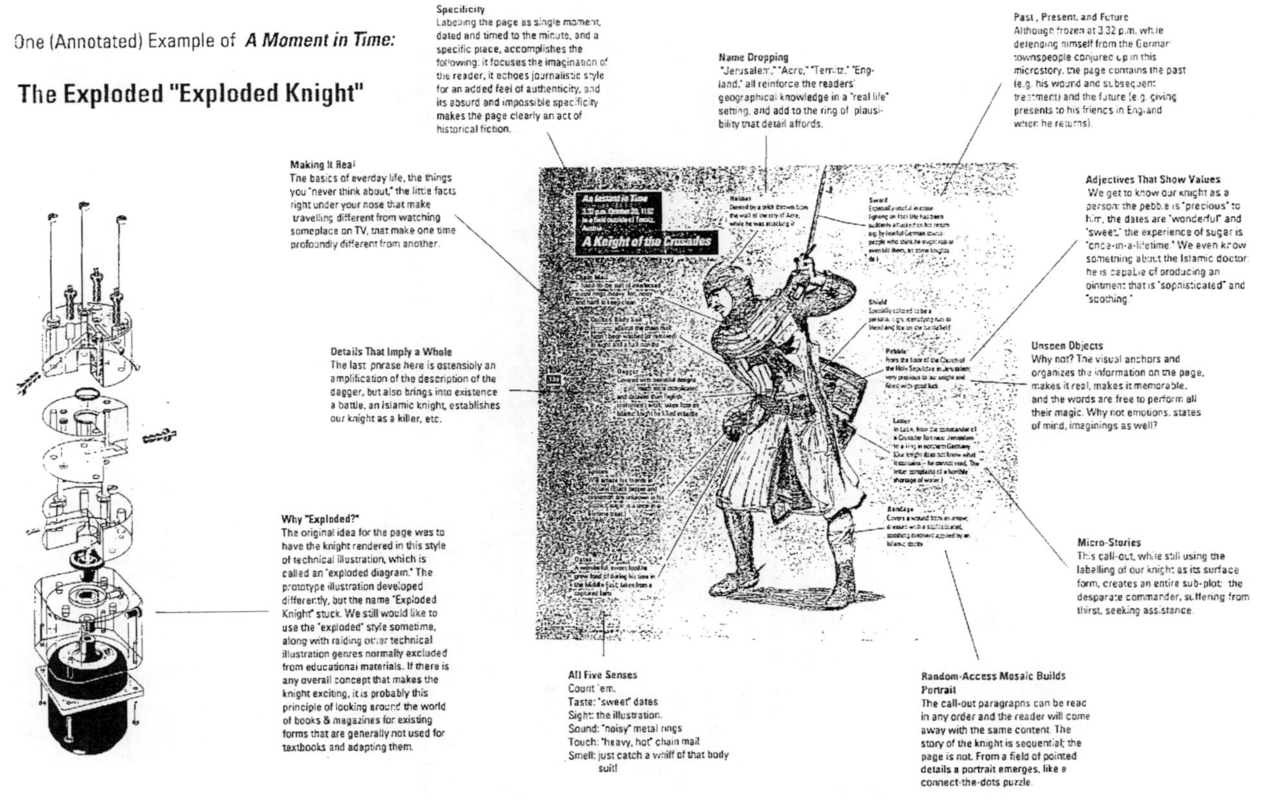

One (Annotated) Example of *A Moment in Time:*

The Exploded "Exploded Knight"

Specificity
Labeling the page as single moment, dated and timed to the minute, and a specific place, accomplishes the following: it focuses the imagination of the reader, it echoes the journalistic style for an acted feel of authenticity, and its absurd and impossible specificity makes the page clearly an act of historical fiction.

Past, Present, and Future
Although frozen at 3:32 p.m. while defending himself from the German townspeople conjured up in this microstory, the page contains the past (e.g. his word and subsequent treatment) and the future (e.g. giving presents to his friends in England when he returns).

Name Dropping
"Jerusalem," "Acre," "Terror," "England," all reinforce the readers geographical knowledge in a "real-life" setting, and add to the ring of plausibility that detail affords.

Adjectives That Show Values
We get to know our knight as a person: the pebble is "precious" to him, the dates are "wonderful" and "sweet," the experience of sugar is "once-in-a-lifetime." We even know something about the Islamic doctor: he is capable of producing an ointment that is "sophisticated" and "soothing."

Making It Real
The basics of everyday life, the things you never think about, the little facts right under your nose that make travelling different from watching someplace on TV, that make one time profoundly different from another.

Unseen Objects
Why not? The visual anchors and organizes the information on the page, makes it real, makes it memorable, and the words are free to perform all their magic. Why not emotions, states of mind, imaginings as well?

Micro-Stories
This call-out, while still using the labeling of our knight as its surface form, creates an entire sub-plot: the story of the knight as desperate commander, suffering from thirst, seeking assistance.

Details That Imply a Whole
The last phrase here is ostensibly an amplification of the description of the dagger, but also brings into existence a battle, an Islamic knight, establishes our knight as a killer, etc.

Random-Access Mosaic Builds Portrait
The call-out paragraphs can be read in any order and the reader will come away with the same content. The story of the knight is sequential: the page is not. From a field of pointed details a portrait emerges, like a connect-the-dots puzzle.

Why "Exploded"?
The original idea for the page was to have the knight rendered in this style of technical illustration, which is called an "exploded diagram." The prototype illustration developed differently, but the name "Exploded Knight" stuck. We still would like to use the "exploded" style sometime, along with raiding on our technical illustration genres normally excluded from educational materials. If there is any overall concept that makes the knight exciting, it is probably this principle of looking around the world of books & magazines for existing forms that are generally not used for textbooks and adopting them.

All Five Senses
Count 'em.
Taste: "sweet" dates.
Sight: the illustration.
Sound: "noisy" metal rings.
Touch: "heavy, hot" chain mail.
Smell: just catch a whiff of that body suit!

FIGURE 2.6. The Exploded Knight

captions which served as guidelines for all the Moments in Time throughout the program.

1. Past, Present, and Future
2. Adjectives That Show Value
3. Unseen Objects
4. Micro-Stories
5. Random-Access Mosaic Builds Portrait
6. All Five Senses
7. Details That Imply a Whole
8. Making It Real
9. Specificity
10. Name Dropping

In the final version of the Crusader knight, as it appears in the seventh-grade text, *Across the Centuries,* the specific time is 3:32 P.M., on October 20, 1192 in a field outside Temitz, Austria (Fig. 2.7). The past and future are indicated in other callouts. A bandage covering an arrow wound on his leg, alludes to the previous battle for Jerusalem. Another caption describes his side pouch in which he carries a pebble from the floor of the Church of the Holy Sepulchre in Jerusalem, and the spices black pepper and sugar. The caption tells that he has saved these as gifts for a future reunion with friends back in England. The unseen pebble is described as "precious." Such layering of imaginatively concrete "little facts," arrayed around the image is intended to engage the reader.

Other callouts take the form of "micro-stories," potentially stimulating mental images adding further historical context. Supposedly, the knight carries a letter from a commander of a crusader fort near Jerusalem to a king in northern Germany. The cumulative effect encourages "random-access" into the narrative of the Moment. This recalls Wittig's earlier comments about the reading of maps. This imaginative reconstruction by suggestion (a fictive history of rhetorically charged details) Wittig thought would viscerally connect the student to social studies content in an entirely new way.

> The key to the whole issue of historical empathy and how to help kids contact people in history, and feel that they're real life people and not just names and very abstract entities was to . . . try to get to this personal level of detail, particular things like the smell of his suit of armor. Essentially, if we could infer that detail: that the knight might not have been the most fragrant fellow, which was not likely found in all the details of regular sources you get, it would be a big achievement.

Here Wittig is referring to the lower left-hand callout which suggests that a knight's quilted body suit quite reasonably might not smell very fresh, since the callout states that it has not been "removed in eight and a half months." This reiterates the point made in the callout of the "Exploded Knight" prototype that suggests using a verbal hook to appeal to the reader's five senses. In building up this

A Crusader

3:32 P.M., October 20, 1192
In a field outside Temitz, Austria

Sword
This weapon is useful for fighting on foot. On his return trip, he has been attacked by German townspeople who think he might rob or kill them, as some knights have.

Chain Mail
The knight's head-to-toe suit of interlocked metal rings is heavy, hot, noisy, and hard to keep clean.

Pebble
He picked this stone off the floor of the Church of the Holy Sepulchre in Jerusalem. Filled with good luck, it's very precious to our knight.

Shield
Designed as a personal sign, his shield identifies him to friend and foe on the battlefield.

Spices
These gifts will amaze his friends in England. Black pepper is unknown in his district; sugar is a once-in-a-lifetime treat.

Letter
A commander near Jerusalem wrote this letter to a king in northern Germany. Our knight cannot read the letter, which complains of a water shortage.

Quilted Body Suit
Protecting him against the chain mail, this suit hasn't been washed or removed in eight and a half months.

Bandage
The knight's arrow wound is dressed with a sophisticated, soothing ointment, applied by an Islamic doctor.

298

FIGURE 2.7. A Moment in Time: A Crusader, Grade 7, p. 298.

annotation or gloss on the visual the potential of carefully crafted and well-written captions to expand the "story space" through the layering of mental images is suggested.

Such figures of speech (metonymy) can be employed to suggest a larger narrative, for example, the pebble as an artifact of battle, a metonymy for the retaking of Jerusalem by the Crusaders during the first Crusade (Monaco, 1981, p. 135). This recursive strategy is also one of economy and compression. A few simply written lines in the callout utilizing the least amount of graphic space can render a larger imaginative storyline further contextualizing the image and still leaving the page relatively uncluttered so that it does not look busy, and hence difficult to access. Again, this strategy could be employed both verbally and visually.

Say What You Cannot See

Concerning this issue of empathy being somehow triggered by a caption's rhetorical resonance, Rob Wittig felt that what made some of the Moments in Time more effective than others, was generally "an aesthetic thing," where the specific detail, for instance, the smell of the knight's armor, intersected and connected with the life experience of the reader. In verbal terms, Wittig regarded *The Samurai*, which appears in the seventh-grade text *Across the Centuries*, as an exceptional example (Fig 2.8). Wittig noted that in supervising the people "composing and editing the callouts, it was necessary . . . [to] check their first impulse . . . to say what you could already see." With the Samurai there were two seen visual elements to which the callout adds three powerful verbal suggestions, "designed to create an image in your mind." Noting the samurai's headdress, which is obviously seen but not elaborated on in any callout, Wittig asks, "What do they tell you about the mask?" In two terse lines the callout effectively creates a powerful mental image: "It was designed to terrify his enemies, and it will. The polished iron face is strong enough to stop a spear." This, he says, "is something you could not tell by looking at it, [such that], in an oblique single sentence you posit the whole scene that he's going to be hit in the head with it."

Similarly, the callout for the Helmet describes a sensuous detail not seen. Here, the "lacquered metal smells of incense." Incense, it explains, is burnt "so that if an enemy cuts off his head, it will smell sweet." That, Wittig remarks, really "goes for the jugular with the kids because that's a very powerful image. It implies . . . the whole horror of battle in a very real sense." Here he seems to be invoking Joe Godlewski's maxim for presenting information in the form that is "more conducive," or rather appropriate, to what is being conveyed. Obviously, presenting a visual of decapitation is in poor taste and out of the question. But neither can "the smell of incense" or the "lacquered metal" be adequately presented through a visual. Therefore a concise highly suggestive verbal description layers a charged mental image onto the pre-battle scene of the Samurai dressing.

FIGURE 2.8. A Moment in Time: A Samurai, Grade 7, p. 233.

Consequently, Wittig adds, "You tell what it's made of, because you cannot show it. . . . You point to things that you simply could not see." In doing so, he says, "You use the visual as the beginning of a path that ideally leads as far away from the visual as possible."

As with the unseen pebble from the tomb of the Holy Sepulchre in the Crusader's pouch, the callout indicates that the Samurai possesses a note from his lord informing him of tomorrow's battle, which alludes to an event of great national importance in Japanese history, the sinking of the Mongol Kublai Khan's invasion fleet in an unexpected storm off the coast of Hakata Bay on the Sea of Japan. With these three callouts, the *Mask*, *Helmet*, and *Note*, the expressive range of the single image is increased. And in this layering of doubled images, mental over visual, the potential of words and pictures to form recursive relationships is indicated through the creative use of captions. This *recursive* (nonlinear) visual/verbal layering of meaning was also explored in another visual/verbal display called *A Closer Look*.

History in the Details

While the exploded diagram adapted from technical illustration provided the inspiration for *A Moment in Time*, Frank Loose, the design manager for Ligature's St. Louis office, related that the imagined surface of a scholar's work table found in the "greatest library/museum in the world" was the "conceptual model" for its companion feature *A Closer Look*. Loose recalled that the idea for it originated with an in-house memo circulated by Joe Godlewski, the senior art director at the Chicago office. The memo referred to as *Looking Down* became, like *A Moment in Time*, a major visual/verbal feature for the program.

Whereas *A Moment in Time* was conceived as a single image with callouts showing a person or object frozen in an imagined historical moment, *A Closer Look* consisted of multiple images and captions that focused on "the analysis of a real place or object," by "taking a closer look at the different parts." Just as callouts were intended to verbally layer the single image of *A Moment in Time* placing it in a larger narrative, with *A Closer Look* the presentation was built up by the layering of different detailed views of the subject or object under analysis. Rather than a frozen moment lifted out of a larger story narrative, *A Closer Look* was more "expository" in its presentation (Singer & Donlan, 1989, p. 114).

Because of the visual complexity of *A Closer Look*, the link between caption and visual was particularly important. In principle, "the presentation should integrate text and visuals so that one could not be understood without the other." Visual/verbal information was intended to link at three levels:

Verbal	Visual
1. Title	1. Background Image
2. Introductory Paragraph	2. Central Image
3. Captions & Callouts	3. Detail Images

Following the memo, a set of guidelines similar to the *Exploded Knight* was circulated to the editor/designer teams. In *A Closer Look at A Closer Look* (Fig. 2.9) guidelines were provided to give the teams a framework (referred to as "the order of reading") so that all the "images/copy [would] support the concept" of the presentation. Because it is a more expository format, *A Closer Look* is analytic and explanatory in approach, the callouts, especially the ones concerning verbal elements, in a sense almost recapitulate the basic questions of the Thumbnail Process involved with the selection of visuals. The Title and Introductory Paragraph "serves as a caption" to identify the subject of the central image and inform the student about "the approach being taken to it." In the final version of *A Closer Look* feature *Mohenjo-Daro* (Fig. 2.10) the introduction asks that the pictures be looked upon as "clues" to an archeological puzzle.

Following this investigative approach, there are three kinds of guidelines found in the callouts for the verbal complement connected to the detail images: Sentence strategies, Bold Beginnings, and Captioning Tabletop Items. *Sentence Strategies* suggest gaining the attention of the reader by posing rhetorical questions ("What's for Dinner?") about the object followed by explicit answers. "Use exhortations! Tell the reader to look at this, consider that, and wonder about one thing, and imagine the texture and fragrance of another." At the same time captions can provide "intriguing" descriptions of the object (through combining several adjectives), which can evoke its physical qualities. In the final version "thin, light, and strong" describe the pottery on the lower right of the spread.

These "information poems" (as they are called) differ from the caption sentences in *A Moment in Time*, insofar as they don't direct the reader away from the object, but instead ask the reader to focus more closely on the qualities of the object. In this sense the question/answers recapitulate the questioning found in the Thumbnail Process concerned with the selection of images. Here, the images are already found, and the questions are posed for the reader to learn more about what is before them.

The bottom center-right callout *Bold Beginnings* recommends that these "intriguing, dynamic, detailed sentences" can be made to visually speak by graphically altering the first few words of the callout in bold typeface. In the final version of *Mohenjo-Daro* all of the first few words in the callouts begin in bright red. The answer or description follows in black. "This [it states], is a tool to develop a lively rhythm within the caption." These "rhythms" can be in the form of either a "question/answer, description/subject, [or] topic/development."

In the top right callout, *Captioning Tabletop Items*, suggestions for deciding whether an object needs to be explicitly identified are determined by the context in which it appears. The general "rule of thumb" calls for naming the detail image if it cannot be recognized by the reader, or if other information on the page (captions and visuals) does not refer to it "directly or indirectly." The callout notes that the "What's For Dinner?" caption appears above the grain, "but does not refer to them directly, becoming a caption by association."

A Closer look at *A Closer Look* at *A Closer Look*

Captioning Tabletop Items

Tabletop items maybe explicitly captioned (if necessary. Rule of thumb: if a kid will be able to identify the object or substance, and there is a reference (direct or indirect) to it on the page, it does not need a separate caption. But, if there are references to the agricultural life of Mohenjo-Daro (the plants), and an exhortation to the readers to imagine they are archaeologists (the dirt, the brush, and the plants). Note that the "What is for dinner?" caption, e.g. is positioned next to the piles of grain on the tabletop, but does not refer to them directly, becoming a "caption by association."

Leader Lines, Frames, Color Shapes

Squared-up photos & fine art have a border around them as shown. Leader lines are long, solid, angles of bright color as shown. If added color is needed for the composition, color shapes (matching the leader lines) may be added, as shown.

Text Needs Some Room of Its Own

As a guideline, there should be no lightened areas behind the text blocks as shown here. The text blocks should all fall within the empty areas of the background tabletop photo. However, if absolutely necessary for legibility, text can be placed on textured, torn, neutral-color paper backgrounds.

Sentence Strategies

Why not use questions? As long as they are answered explicitly it's fine. Use educational. Tell your reader to look at this, consider that wonder about one thing, and imagine the texture and fragrance of another intriguing, dynamic, detailed — sentences begin with three adjectives can be all these and more. These are information poems.

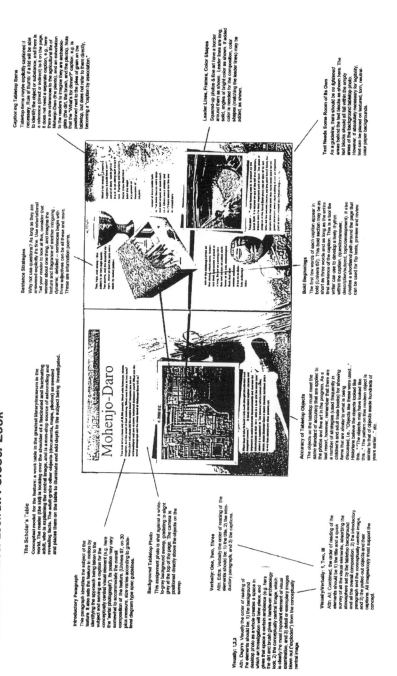

Mohenjo-Daro

c. 2000 B.C.

The Scholar's Table

Conceptual model for the feature: a work table in the greatest library/museum in the world. The reader (the kid) is looking over the shoulder of a fascinated and fascinating adult, who is explaining the central image, and is a non-stop source of astounding and revealing facts. The adult grabs other objects (documents, maps, photos) as needed and places them on the table to illuminate and add depth to the subject being investigated.

Introductory Paragraph

This paragraph identifies the subject of the feature. It also sets the feature in motion by identifying the approach taken to the subject and serving as a caption for the conceptually central visual element (e.g. here the "aerial photograph"). Its position may be somewhat to accommodate the overall composition of the feature. (Univers 67, on 30 pica measure. Leader text varies according to grade-level diagram type epic guidelines.

Background Tabletop Photo

This assignment photo is shot against a whole-to-grey background sweep, gradating to a slight grey at the top of the page. The camera is positioned directly above the objects on the sweep.

Verbally: One, Two, Three

Attn. Diagrs. Verbally the order of reading of the elements should be: 1) the title, 2) the introductory paragraph, and 3) the captions.

Visually: 1,2,3

Attn. Diagrs. Visually the order of reading of the elements should be: 1) the background desktop photo as a whole creates a space in which all the visual elements, establishing the atmosphere set by the tabletop background and the overall composition, 2) the introductory paragraph gives a hands-on archaeology look, 2) the conceptually central image, which is clearly the most important element of visual examination, and 3) the pulled-out objects and their blown out ("exploded") from the conceptually central image.

Visually/Verbally: 1, Two, III

Attn. A:I. Combined, the order of reading of the elements should be 1) the title and a quick survey of all the visual elements, absorbing the atmosphere set by the tabletop background and the overall composition, 2) the introductory paragraph and the conceptually central image, and 3) the pulled-out objects and their captions. All image/story must support the concept.

Accuracy of Tabletop Objects

The objects on the tabletop must meet the same standard of accuracy that are applied to the photos and fine art in the program. As a last resort, however, remember that there are a number of strategies (used frequently in children's and adult trade books) for showing items that we are not sure of being discussed. (i.e. "Objects like these were used . . ." "The objects may have looked like this . . ." The pattern on this modern object is similar to that of objects made hundreds of years earlier . . ." etc.

Bold Beginnings

The first few words of each caption appear in bold (Univers 67). This bold section may be as short as three words and as long as the entire first sentence of the caption. This is a tool the writer can use to develop a lively rhythm within the caption. (question/answer, description/verb/verb, topic/development). It also creates a shorthand path around the page that can be used for flip tests, preview and review.

· FIGURE 2.9. A Closer Look at A Closer Look

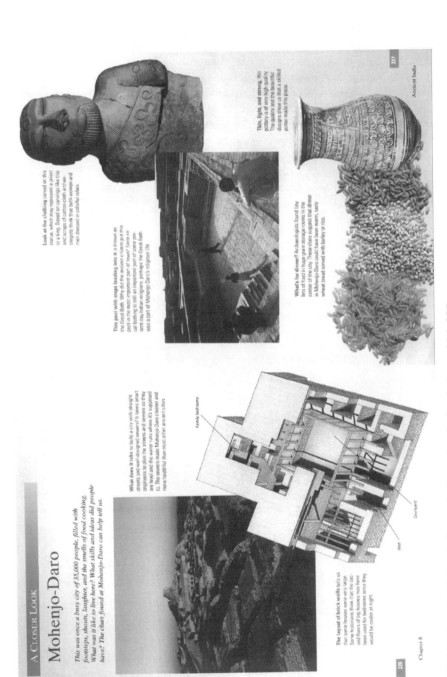

FIGURE 2.10. Mohenjo-Daro: A Closer Look, Grade 6, pp. 226–227

Overall the functional purpose of captions and callouts in *A Closer Look* is expository in nature. The visuals show the reader different views of the same object, and the captions/callouts explain these selected views, drawing attention to it through questions and description. Like the Knight, *A Closer Look* presented social studies content in a "recursive nonlinear way," said Joe Godlewski. Both features sought to gain a reader's attention and empathy by imaginatively depicting history through the heightening of visual and verbal details. As with the Thumbnail Process or the memo, *Looking Down,* which evolved into the feature *A Closer Look*, Godlewski always emphasized the "constructive tension" of this recursive process. "A richer pool of . . . visual references would spark ideas" for the Thumbnail teams he said, and inevitably presented the "opportunity to write a more engaging narrative" for the writers. This visual/verbal "synergy" was active in the evolving design of *Mohenjo-Daro.*

> We were fascinated with this idea of primary sources and archeological fieldwork. And that students could become engaged in the idea that history is ongoing, historians work today. So that it would be great to get involved and go actually look at a site, the dig, get a sense of the geography, the sophistication of the architecture. This kind of high impact combination of things that really pulled out from this notion of place and this time was analogous to the knight. We felt this table-top approach gave the kids the sense that they could touch and feel the thing. [And here he pauses] They could feel the thing willing to break the "*flatland*" of the page.

With this cryptic comment, one notable source of inspiration guiding Ligature's approach to visual/verbal relationships has been reached, the work of Edward Tufte.

WORDS AND PICTURES BELONG TOGETHER

> The world portrayed on our information displays is caught up in the two-dimensionality of the endless flatlands of paper and video screen. All communication between the readers of an image and the makers of an image must now take place on a two-dimensional surface. Escaping this flatland is the essential task of envisioning information.
> —Edward Tufte, *Envisioning Information (1990)*

Rob Wittig recalls that "at the time we were doing this (SS21 program development), Tufte's first book had only come out, which is titled, *The Visual Display of Quantitative Information*" (1983). Though this book is concerned with the presentation of statistical information, its basic working principles for the display of "data" bear strong resemblance to Ligature's conception of visual/verbal integration, as it shapes and influences book design production.

In this first book, Tufte reached the same conclusion as Stuart Murphy concerning the institutional constraints in publishing that have separated editorial and design functions. But he also made a strikingly similar statement, which echoes the guiding pedagogical purpose of the Social Studies Program, found in the *About Your Book* section of Grades 1 and 2 noted earlier.

> Explanations that give access to the richness of the data make graphics more attractive to the viewer. Words and pictures are sometimes jurisdictional enemies, as artists feud with writers for scarce space. An unfortunate legacy of these craft-union differences is the artificial separation of words and pictures. . . . What has gone wrong is that the techniques of production instead of the information conveyed have been given precedence. *Words and pictures belong together.* Viewers need the help that words can provide. (p. 180)

Joe Godlewski felt that Tufte's work had "tremendous" influence because it provided theoretical common ground, confirming mutual insights about the design of information. Rob Wittig felt Tufte to be "more a general mentor," who provided "aesthetic influence expressed through simply his taste. His books are full of good and bad examples," he said. But it is neither a question of degree or attribution, rather more like the common ground of shared insights found at the cutting edge of a discipline in transition. Actually, Wittig's allusion to the fact that Tufte's (1990) later work, *Envisioning Information,* only appeared after the Social Studies Program was finished, lends credence to the view that Ligature had already presciently put into practice insights Tufte later synthesized and wrote about. One of the more powerfully circumspect observations Tufte makes concerning progress in the field of design, which bears upon the notion of shared insight at the cutting edge, may be this one:

> All the history of information displays and statistical graphs . . . is entirely a progress of methods for enhancing density, complexity, dimensionality, and even sometimes beauty. Some of these methods . . . include micro/macro readings of detail and panorama, layering and separation of data, multiplying of images, color, and narratives of space/time. (p. 33)

This synchronicity of thinking is apparent if another look is taken at the design for *Mohenjo-Daro*, because the visual/verbal display closely corresponds to these methods Tufte suggests. Reading it means moving across a page of micro/macro images, with multiple detail and panoramic views of the site. A panoramic photograph of the present site on the left is matched with a detailed (and panoramic) view of the Great Baths on the right. Both striking color photographic images are connected by a detailed cutaway illustration of the floor plan of a typical brick house that might have been found there. The drawn bricks from this imaginatively reconstructed house from the remote past are layered over the actual bricks of the present site in the opening panoramic view to add contrast. Other multiple images of pottery and food grain, layered together, hint at what inhabitants ate and how they stored their food. A statue in the top right side of the layout layered behind the Great Bath may indicate how people dressed. The colorful seeds of grain (so visually tactile they seem touchable) match the lined shapes of the adjacent pot. This matching of visual elements from the present and imagined past suggest, in archeological terms, a grand narrative of space and time. Change, disappearance, and mystery are implicit in the assembled artifacts for the viewer to consider.

AT THE INTERSECTION OF IMAGE, WORD, NUMBER, ART

In the Thumbnail Process "the feud for scarce space" ends. The "artificial separation of words and pictures" is transcended. The dialogue of designer and editor is a means for "escaping flatland." The apportioning of page space sets up a definite area for visuals, the other for text. The codification of verbal strategies through captions, etc. provides a means of integrating the two respective areas of the total page, such that it can no longer be regarded in two-dimensional terms as a linear text. The reader moves through a multidimensional "storyspace" constructed of visuals and text (Chatman, 1978).

Tufte's expression "envisioning information" appealed to Joe Godlewski because it reflected the essential recursive principle underlying Ligature's visual/verbal design thinking. It also reinforced their intention with the SS21 project to imagine a different kind of social studies textbook. Such an imaginative move is definitively indicated by the presentation style conceived for *A Moment in Time* and *A Closer Look*, because each format decisively moves away from a straight linear text presentation. By apportioning part of the page to visual information, text intersects with those "micro/macro" graphical dimensions Tufte describes. It was the intent of Ligature to make their program so visually compelling that the reader could "escape from [the] flatland" of the typical social studies textbook. But does such an "escape" mean moving beyond the textbook? In the next chapter on visual design the aesthetic move to spatialize text is examined. This spatialization through images represents a significant step beyond text, and alludes however faintly to the potential for design in the virtual dimension of cyberspace now being introduced by 3-D computer graphics.

Making the Beautiful Book

Children live in an increasingly complex and highly *visual society*. Some children spend many hours with visual media such as television, video, and computers. (SS21, 1989, p. 25)

Social studies provides the primary *place* in the curriculum where American children are taught what it means to be an American, with all the complexity that it implies. (Marker & Mehlinger, 1992, p. 845)

Reinforcing the observation of the SS21 document concerning the necessity of visual learning, Joe Godlewski believes that "history and social studies should be visually compelling." As instructional designers with the objective to create "a beautiful book," the Ligature team's reasoning was complex. In this chapter the visual thinking behind that objective is examined. This review can provide the proper context to discuss the most prominent examples of that vision. "Typically," Godlewski stated, "no one develops a book in this way. Our design process is informed by the interactivity of working with the computer. . . . Media really affected our perception of [those] development procedures."

The technology influencing Ligature's mode of production also shaped the form their product took. When Godlewski says that "no one develops a book in this way," he is also referring to their move to spatialize the text by including a "parallel visual track." Actually, the notion of a visual/verbal textbook is not new. In the opening section of this chapter this historic precedence is briefly sketched in order to frame the more pertinent issues determining the visual design of textbooks in the present.

The crux of these issues basically reiterates the problem in the last chapter regarding visuals as "content." Unfortunately, if the discourse concerning the visual design of textbooks is any indicator, the question primarily seems to focus on an irresolvable dichotomy which tends to privilege verbal text over visual information. The debate rarely seems to go beyond the perception that attractively designed textbooks are tantamount to "coffee table books," slickly produced, very pleasing, all surface and little serious content. This opinion holds that as the number of illustrations goes up, the supposed quality of instruction goes down. Visual design is seen "as a proxy for textbook quality" (Woodward, 1993, p. 132).

The crucial issue, whether visual information, that is, page layout, typography, and illustrations "facilitate comprehension and stimulate effective learning" is often correctly posed, but it largely stalls at the critical level noted before: aesthetic quality viewed as packaging, a selling device for market-driven publishers to obtain "customer acceptance" (Chall & Squire, 1991, p. 128). In the second part of this chapter, the visual "architecture" (page layout and typography), and the visual Unit Openers will be considered in light of these crucial issues, especially as they were understood by Ligature designers.

With Ligature, aesthetics is another means to represent knowledge, that is, to "envision information." Working within the culture of design, the notion of a "beautiful book" was not necessarily in contradiction with a textbook designed to be an effective instructional tool. Certainly, as the first chapter makes clear, Ligature did extensive market research with highly attractive prototypes, which no doubt enhanced their marketability by being so visually appealing. However, their thinking went beyond a surface design suitable to pass a marketing "thumb test" (Chall & Squire, 1991, p. 128).

In the concluding section of this chapter the aesthetic strategy to spatialize the textbook is discussed in terms of how it complements the most fundamental themes in the social studies curriculum. In constructing the "beautiful book," Ligature built up an Image of the world. In so doing they were providing a learning platform where the student could most easily view that "Place" they already see and know.

THE COMENIUS CONTINUUM

Educational historians generally attribute one of the earliest textbooks with pictures to the German churchman, Johann Comenius. Orbis Sensualium Pictus (The Visible World in Pictures) was a basic Latin primer that was printed in 1658 and was widely used in England, Europe, and America for the next 200 years (Reiser, 1987; Venezky, 1992; Westbury, 1990). Of greater importance, although having little pedagogical influence at the time, was the learning theory of Comenius. Reiser (1987) notes that Comenius believed "that we initially learn about things through our senses and therefore real objects and illustrations should be used to supplement oral and written instruction." Such a "proposition" did not have educational currency until the early 18th century when the work of Johann Pestalozzi, a Swiss educational reformer, became quite popular. The influence he had in America largely peaked "during the 1860s" (p. 13). Like Comenius, Pestalozzi held "that words have meaning in relation to concrete objects." Consequently, instruction should have a visual component to assist in the comprehension of objects and the initial stages of conceptual thinking (p. 13). The expanded educational use of the illustrated textbook in America during the later part of the nineteenth century rested principally on three developments: the growing influence of Horace Mann, who was a firm advocate of the Pestalozzian method, the growing sophistication of print technology, and the artistic production of children's storybooks. The latter which were published solely for enjoyment used extensive color illustration. Inevitably this development led to the greater use of color illustration in textbooks (Mulcahy & Samuels, 1987, p. 40).

In fact, each successive decade of the twentieth century in the American publishing industry saw the "technological advances" in print and color reproduction, similarly advancing the "quality and quantity of illustrations in schoolbooks" (Mulcahy & Samuels, 1987, p. 43). Technically, these "advances" contributed to radically altering the form and content of the textbook, such that by the 1980s four-color reproduction print formats were the norm. According to Mulcahy and Samuels (1987), the technical implications of this change to full color has had three profound effects which bear upon the design of visual/verbal text presentation:

> First, the growing use of color pictures is creating the need for a visual literacy for illustration as well as for text. Young students need to use their background knowledge to answer questions about the illustration and to supplement information in the text. Second, one theme prevalent throughout the history of illustration in American textbooks is *realism*. The advent of color helped improve that sense of realism. Color photography further increased semantic text parallels and contributed to realistic interpretation of the text. Third, the use of color increased the appeal of schoolbooks to both young and mature readers. Increasing the illustration's aesthetic value, color lends additional significance to the truism that the book is a work of art. (p. 43)

Of their three points the latter two are relevant to the topic under discussion. As this chapter develops it becomes clear that the "theme of realism" is both key to the visual design of the SS21 program, and fundamental to the presentation of social studies content. In envisioning a "beautiful book," Ligature introduces the category of beauty into the instructional design process. By doing so, certain basic aesthetic criteria have to be considered. Consequently, line, color, form, texture, proportion, rhythm, tone, all those elements synonymous with the pictorial sense, become essential for understanding the visual design. Following Tufte, beauty, along with density, complexity, and dimensionality, all figure into this notion of realism as it applies to the spatialization of text. To think in aesthetic terms means to think of representing space; to create through the technical means available a virtual three-dimensional space on the page. By enhancing this visual sense of the real, Ligature designers found this approach more suited to the California History-Social Science Framework than they had originally imagined. Joe Godlewski commented on this issue:

And the question was raised: Were we interrupting this concept of "a story well told" with a very strong visual poster-like component, from a steady print to the visuals. And she (Diane Brooks) said, "Oh no no no, you can't do too much of that, because its very much a part of this way of communicating more effectively to children." They felt that it brought this *realness* of history.

Bad Books/Captive Audience

In their turn to Tufte, Wittig noted, Ligature found "a general mentor" whose "great value is as an anthologist. On a case by case [basis], . . . his books are full of good and bad examples" of book design, which are "so expressive of his taste." This "aesthetic influence" provided one frame of reference during their prototype investigations; discriminating the ideal from the real in the current social studies textbook market. As their market research indicated, the visual design of existing programs was a mixed bag. Some had good visually conceived elements, but overall the programs reviewed had an "unengaging visual presentation," which "looked virtually the same," and generally "conveyed an impression of imitation, timidity, and perhaps even mediocrity" (SS21, 1989, pp. 12–13).

Rob Wittig felt such production values showed a disrespect for the students who had to use them. "Whoever put this thing together is extremely aware that they have a captive audience, because they need to make no effort to pull kids along, . . . to please them or draw them into it." The general in-house consensus was that the traditional social studies textbooks were "dry, sanitized, and uninteresting, the dullest of presentations." The text was "written in a very stilted choppy manner . . . with visually ugly dense grey walls of justified type." The usual ratio of visual to text was low: "10% to 15%." And, the images that were used were "add-ons, always squared-up (boxed), poorly positioned on the page, and usually very muddy, poor [quality] reproductions."

Another problem with the quality of visual information presented was in its prior selection. Godlewski remarked that publishers often simply relied on outside professional "agencies that handle just art." The images found there "might be what you're looking for, [but usually] have been duplicated many times, and it is a very limited universe of possibilities." One major consequence of such uncritical selection was that the image often inappropriately connected with its textual reference. This was especially problematic for historical source images which might inaccurately represent a past person, place, or event. "No distinctions are made between images contemporary to the period they're talking about, or images done later," Rob Wittig said. To elaborate, he mentioned two "classic examples."

> There was a photograph of a model of ancient Rome at some period, very lavishly done so it looks realistic. Taken from above, it looks like an aerial shot. And the book identifies it as Rome at such and such a date, with the implication being that this could in fact have been an

aerial shot of Rome at that date. Also, the constant picture of Julius
Caesar. But just any old picture. Some Victorian era painting is just
captioned: "Julius Caesar," with no regard for the fact that he lived
many thousands of years before.

With Ligature, the solution to the problem of selecting images that carefully reflected their textual source lies in not relying on such agencies, and having photo
researchers work closely with the Thumbnail teams. This meant they had "runners
and interns going to libraries, bookstores, and various local universities" to find
visual material.

One result of such intensive research was a "richer reference pool" of images,
which Godlewski felt contributed to "better the opportunity to write a more engaging narrative." With the SS21 project, in-house researchers sometimes made
extraordinary efforts to acquire appropriate images. Sara Chavkin, a production
manager who supervised these searches, related that "we were calling all over the
world trying to get pictures: Turkey, England, Africa." Oftentimes there were "de-
lays of three to four weeks before you could actually see what something would
look like, and . . . if it could be used." However, such sensitivity to visual design is
not typical. Research on social studies textbooks generally tends to focus on verbal content issues and matters of textual inadequacy (Marker & Mehlinger, 1992,
p. 835). The use, much less the selection, of images is often looked upon as contributing further to this inadequacy, because it is held that their presence alone
uses up space better used for serious instructional content.

Rise in Visuals/Decline in Content

Following Mulcahy and Samuels, researchers, one and all, note the gradual increase and sophistication of visual information of every kind: photographs, illustration, fine art, maps, diagrams, graphs, and so forth, appearing in social studies
textbooks over the decades (see Bliss, 1990; Chall, 1977; Chall & Conrad, 1991;
Fitzgerald, 1979; Tyson-Bernstein & Woodward, 1989). Where they sharply dis-
agree is its purpose for being there. Ideally, researchers have offered conceptual
frameworks to determine the instructional purpose of illustration in text. Duchastel's
(1978) is most often cited. He frames the issue in "functional" terms. Illustrations,
and so forth, may have three types of functional purposes, all of which may occur
in any order or combination. Images can have either an Attentional, Explicative,
and/or Retentional function (p. 37). Though related to the "attentional" function,
Joan Peeck (1987) argues that the "Affective-Motivational domain" should be
added as a category in its own right which warrants serious research (p. 144).
Nevertheless, it has been observed that:

> No one seems to know if bigger books with their numerous illustra-
> tions help the student to learn better, or motivate the student more. But
> everyone seems to be caught in the dilemma of increasing text size and
> number of illustrations. Publishers seem to fear that, if they cut down

on text size and number of illustrations, they will lose competitive edge
in adoptions and sales. . . .We need research on optimal book size,
including optimal number of illustrations. (Chall & Conrad, 1991, pp.
112–113)

The problem with such observations is that the entire issue is framed incor-
rectly. The larger "dilemma" lies less with market anxiety and optimal number,
than with acknowledging that visual information calls for an entirely different
way of approaching the instructional process. Instead, the usual implication is that
visual information has no other purpose than to make the textbook attractive, hence
more marketable. Here, the position of Arthur Woodward is noteworthy because
he spoke with John Ridley, the Houghton Mifflin editor, about the function of
visuals in the Social Studies Program. It also seems to indicate that Woodward
(1989) has only the most superficial grasp of aesthetic issues. In an article co-
authored with Harriet Tyson-Bernstein he stated:

The place of illustrations and other instructional features in the design
of a textbook must be secondary to content as represented by the written word. For it is through the text that the content and concepts of a
discipline are conveyed. (1989, p. 100)

And elsewhere, he asserted that:

Teachers and administrators equate attractive layout and stunning photographs with instructional quality. Unfortunately, there is no necessary connection between bountiful and attractive illustrations and learning. Rather, studies have suggested that many illustrations fail to enhance learning and in fact, may consume a large portion of limited
space that could better be devoted to content. (1993, p. 132)

Woodward, coincidentally, echoed the assertion made by Squire and Morgan (1990)
in the second chapter on the place of visual design. In Woodward's view, aesthetic
criteria appear suspect, because they are always connected to marketing. Word
and image seemed trapped in that "feud for scarce space" which Tufte (1983 p.
180) described. Though Woodward correctly assesses the key problems concerning images and instructional design, he obviously would not grant a parallel track
to images. Such a conservative view is hardly unusual.

John Ridley, the Houghton Mifflin editor, like Woodward is reluctant to give
images the same status as words. Speaking for himself, he said, "I'm not ready to
give parity" to images as content. "The reason I say this is this: I think teachers still
have to have words as their base. They're not going to work with the visual as their
base. I don't think teachers are willing to have a parity per se." For Ridley a visual
"is the anchor." This point is revealing, and perhaps very leading, because it suggestively reverses the functional purpose assigned to words, especially captions,
as we have seen, to name, explain, or describe the image. According to Roland
Barthes (1977) "anchorage" is the function of "the linguistic message

. . . that helps to identify purely and simply" what is being seen, "to fix," or anchor, its meaning (p. 39). In a sense this difference in opinion rests upon the institutional presumption, which holds to more conventional notions of what should properly constitute a *text*book. For those on the other side of this divide, particularly, the Ligature designers profiled here, there seems to be a recognition that a distinct cultural shift from word to image has occurred, presciently theorized by Barthes (1977), and ironic in light of Ridley's comment:

> Formerly, the image illustrated the text (made it clearer); today the text loads the image, burdening it with a culture, a moral, an imagination. Formerly, there was reduction from text to image; today, there is amplification from one to the other. (p. 26)

Joe Godlewski felt that, "you can talk about that battle of text and image forever, but you can never figure it out." Perception of cultural shifts can tend to be generational. Dan Rogers, the senior project editor, acknowledged that "we were pushing the edge [of established convention] in terms of the presentation" with a nonlinear approach. Mimicking the resistance by teachers who look at it solely with a linear "mindset," he said, "I read this text and then I look at the picture. And then I read some more text and look at this picture. And I don't know what to look at first." Whereas, "kids generally respond very positively. This is the kind of presentation they're familiar with and very able to cope with." Such a distinction recalls the Houghton Mifflin editor's empathy with teachers who still teach using a traditional recitation method. "You're dealing with teachers on quite a continuum. [Some] are really into a constructive approach, and [others] are into the old way of read and answer the following question kind of mode." As with Barthes' observation, Mulcahy and Samuels (1987) observe that during the 1940s children's reading primers changed. A number of illustrated books appeared which had a more constructive style of presentation. With these books,

> the child learned that reading is a process in which the reader constructs meaning from information contained on a page, regardless of whether the information is in the form of a picture or a printed word. This new function of illustrations has continued to the present day. (p. 42)

It is clearly this approach that Ligature had taken with its pages. Definitively moving beyond the "read and look, read and look" type of text, Godlewski acknowledged that the "style" of presentation was "different," because their notion of "literacy" was different. "Our premise was that students can and do read visuals. And that literacy is tied to both presentational and discursive processing of information." Although Godlewski understood the criticism over textbooks having "distracting visuals and graphics," and was sympathetic to teachers who had used a more traditional textbook and method, he nevertheless suggested adjusting to present circumstance.

In any case you may want to say to a teacher, or a teacher might want to say to themselves: "Books I've used a long time have been set this way. This is set *another* way." And get on with it. It's not much more than, "It goes *this way.*"

SS21 PROGRAM ARCHITECTURE: THE TOOLBOX

To give definite shape to a program with over 8,000 pages of text (8,168 pages of text to be exact; see Table 3.1), "specific guidelines" are an organizational necessity. Such a structure gives the product a visual identity discernable in each book of the series. In publishing argot this is referred to as "a tight marketing package" (SS21, 1989, p. 12). In the field of graphic design such "guidelines" can be called a "visual program." This is "a system of parameters used to consistently unify a series or sequence of designs" (Meggs, 1989, p. 80).

Interestingly enough, the in-house term reflected an adaptation of computer terminology. Joe Godlewski, the senior art director, referred to it as the "architecture." And, Frank Loose, design manager at the St. Louis office, perhaps reflecting their move to the Macintosh platform during production, called it simply the "Toolbox." Prior to the Thumbnail Process, Stuart Murphy noted a number of elements were "already in place for each of the books in the program: a scope and sequence, a table of contents, scholarly outlines, writing samples, and prototype boards (visual samples) of what the pages would look like." Frank Loose commented that their "visual/verbal strategy was used to justify a lot of exploratory kinds of things" when these boards were made.

Over and above the other things set "in place" these "explorations" during the prototype phase led to developing "a set of procedures" that the teams could rely on once they entered the Thumbnail Process. "You basically had your tools to use. They were all right in the box. You just picked them out and applied them," Loose said. In effect these "procedures" established a set of "uniform" structures for the entire K–8 program. This "architecture" was quite extensive. According to Joe Godlewski, it involved all the major graphical "structures of the Lesson."

The most significant visual design structures are discussed in the following order:

1. Ratios of Text to Art
2. White Space and the Two Column Grid
3. Rules for Typeface and Head Structure
4. Color Palettes

Ratios of Text to Art: The Terms of Apportionment

The Social Studies Program was the first that Ligature "ever used really specific identifiable ratios on," Frank Loose recalled (Table 3.2). "What it really did is to allow us to [have] variety within a structure. Those percentages and numbers existed the same way that a grid and type existed. It was just a given . . . that we were really glad to work within. It gave us a rationale for putting in visuals, more and better visuals." These percentages were the single most important "guideline" that the Thumbnail teams could "go back on" in the act of dividing up the graphic space of a lesson. The percentages acted like a page template so that the "designers and editors . . . could actually count up their text and their visuals," he said. These counts were made on a standard form (Fig. 3.1). The ratios were also used to determine how many photographs, illustrations, diagrams, and maps were to appear in each grade. This total number per grade was broken down even further to a certain number for each unit and chapter, so that every team generally knew beforehand how many visuals were recommended for a unit. However, this total did not include either the Openers for the units and chapters, or the special features like *A Moment in Time* or *A Closer Look*. These and other features were counted separately.

The actual ratios (Table 3.2) were determined on the basis of consulting with "reading experts, talking with teachers in focus groups, and by looking at a lot of other books." By grade level the amount of information presented visually progressively decreases. Each grade generally corresponds to the reading level of the student. Frank Loose stated that with "limited vocabulary" in the early grades, children "can be shown a lot more of the conceptual stuff through pictures." In the upper grades "a lot more verbal information needed to be conveyed." This gave sort of a cognitive visual/verbal symmetry to the grade levels. The first and eighth grades were exactly the reverse: 30/70 to 70/30 text to visuals. The ratios acted then as the foundation in the program's architecture, the primary structure determining the layout of visual/verbal space.

White Space and the "Self-Revealing" Grid

> **Q**: You don't have any reservations about it looking like USA Today?
> **A**: No.

The ratios alone required a different style of page, because a set number of visuals now became integral to the presentation and display. Just as their "explorations" led them to look at technical illustration manuals and mail order catalogues for the special features like *A Moment in Time* and *A Closer Look*, in their desire to recreate the textbook page Ligature designers gave serious attention to the layout style of magazines and newspapers, which they believed was more suitable to the presentation of visual/verbal information. In this move, Rob Wittig noted that, the senior art director's influence was decisive. "Joe picked up and infused throughout the whole design team . . . that the least interesting workaday aspects of newspaper graphics were a subject of serious reflection." Godlewski felt that a journalistic, tabloid kind of "two column format" was the solution. "We didn't want anybody to look at this so much as a book but sort of a quasi-magazine." It provided "a strong structure from which all the images could break out of," but one "that connected the text to image."

TABLE 3.1. Houghton Mifflin Social Studies Specifications.

Houghton Mifflin Social Studies Specifications

	K	1	2	3	CA4	5	6	7	8	Total Actual
Pupil's Editions										
Pages	24	176	208	272	368	624	560	576	800	3,608
Photos	15	159	237	231	307	615	503	656	629	3,352
Illustrations/ Diagrams	45	187	112	103	107	85	102	51	102	894
Maps	0	8	15	27	45	96	110	80	66	447
Teacher's Editions										
Pages	160	272	304	368	464	736	672	672	912	4,560
Illustrations/ Diagrams	96	36	48	42	64	99	79	89	94	647
Photographs	41	27	20	11	16	16	18	17		182

TABLE 3.2. Ratios of Text to Art, SS21, Final Guidelines, 9/19/89, p. 90.

Ratio of Text to Art

The following are goals for the book; individual pages or lessons may not always conform but should not deviate to any extreme—

Kindergarten	0% text to 100% art
Grade 1	30% text to 70% art
Grade 2	40% text to 60% art
Grade 3	55% text to 45% art
Grade 4	65% text to 35% art
Grade 5	65% text to 35% art
Grade 6	65% text to 35% art
Grade 7	70% text to 30% art
Grade 8	70% text to 30% art

Look for opportunities to include large visuals (maps, illustrations, and photos) in the layouts; in general, we need an interesting pacing of layout, which at the higher grade levels may mean an occasional page or spread that is all text.

Behind this thinking was the desire to break out of that textbook convention which typically used the page simply as a ground for a single column which appeared as a "dense grey wall" of text. During the first postpublication revision of the sixth-grade text, *A Message of Ancient Days*, much discussion focused on abandoning the tabloid look and moving back "to just a single column format." Those consulted (mostly teachers using the first edition) disagreed with this option. They "loved the lively magazine qualities" of the two column format. Here, the art director's basic assumption about going to such a format was confirmed.

> We said it over and over: we wanted a magazine quality. People scan magazines and we wanted kids to be able *to scan* this, particularly because this is new content. We wanted teachers to say, "Okay I get it, they're going to cover this." This is the focus. I don't know what this is but they're going to tell me." It's just the kind of presentation that's self-revealing. That's really the key to what we were trying to do here.

Because such a "self-revealing" style of presentation, especially in the earlier grades, tends more to showing, the fixed columnar structure with numerous visual breaks requires an appropriate ground to emphasize that level of contrast. Graphic white space served this aesthetic purpose. Rob Wittig referred to it as an "open structure," a pictorial element that doesn't "fit into the grid." From his perspective "the key to good and pleasing design is white space." He noted that in publishing it is regarded as a sign of aesthetic quality. The pleasing look of expensive "coffee table books" is a good example, he said. These kinds of books use large amounts of white space. Typically textbooks do not. Such notions of cultural purchase applied to a textbook play importantly into the goal of producing a "beautiful book."

But it also acts as another crucial element in the visual design, which suggests a page more like a pictorial frame, than a flat ground for text.

SS21	Text to art ratio

Great form!

Grade 3, Chapter __1__

Lesson (1)	total lines	total text	total image
3.1.1	31	13	18
2	38	25	13
3	38	19	19
4	38	23	15
5	Skills		
6	Skills		
	145	80 (55%)	65 (45%)
(2)			
3.1.7	31	24	7
8	38	19	19
9	v/v 38	17	21
10	v/v 38	17	21
11	38	17	21
12	38	19	19
13	Decision Making		
14	Decision making		
	221	113 (51%)	108 (49%)
Totals	366	193 (53%)	173 (47%)

FIGURE 3.1. Text to Art Ratio form.

Trigger the Depths: Typeface Design and Head Structure

In line with scanning, the "self-revealing" intent of the typographic design was to create a "navigation strategy," in which the appearance of the text could visually orchestrate how the text was to be read. A letter form was just as important as the visible shape given to the main running text. "Our books keep getting more diagraphic, . . . more a kind of guide book approach than a read-about kind of book," Godlewski said. On the basis of "experience and research we purposely chose a *serif*, instead of a *sans serif* typeface, that is a version of Times Roman (called Times 10 by Adobe, the software publisher). It was more legible than a normal Times Roman and we liked its clarity." Frank Loose added that the font was chosen because the "serifs help lead from one character to another" and are easier to read. It was also "more commonly" known to U.S. children. By contrast in Europe use of a sans serif was prevalent in children's books.

For the running text of the lesson, Dan Rogers, the Senior Editor, commented that "the goal" was to "keep [it] in relatively small pieces [by] having a regular *A Head* (lesson title) and *B Head* (subtitle) structure that has to repeat periodically, so we don't end up with pages that look like solid text." Rob Wittig felt that use of such a structure acknowledged that "people read and write in chunks." The arrangement of this Head structure became progressively more complex as the grades advanced. In the first- and second-grade texts there are only *A Heads*, "because the lessons were short and there really wasn't much text." In the third grade they introduced *B Heads*. In grades four through eight there were also *C Heads*, if necessary, when the amount and complexity of the textual content required it. The Head Structure also had a consistent color scheme to make it visually noticeable. *A Heads* were always *blue*, and the *B Heads*, *red*. *C Heads*, if any, were blue.

Instead of parallel columns of fully justified text, the designers chose to justify it on the left. This uneven edge, called "*Flush Left/Ragged Right*" left a slight, but visible variation in the columns. This straight versus irregular edge broke the monotony of completely parallel columns. An irregular edge was also applied to the wrapping of text around objects. This was another difficult procedure which had become easy with the computer. In this case the decision was made to always wrap text around objects on the left side, because "you had an uninterrupted flow of type, so [again] it was easy for kids to read" (Fig. 3.2). Through attention to the aesthetic aspect of graphic effects—the uniquely concrete shape of a particular typeface, the separation of text sections through a color coded structure, and the variation in columns—text elements were intentionally designed to be more readily noticeable when scanned. Organizing text in this visible fashion seemed to go against the standing conventions of how books were meant to be read. There is a definite "mythology about how books are read," Rob Wittig said. And, "it is this: Books are read in sequence, with full attention, and all at the same time." This "traditional literary method" is the norm. "Any other use, like skimming, for instance, is an aberration." But, he said, there are two less accepted "usage patterns:

Preview and Review which are almost entirely cinematic." Though the layout could be read "in sequence," it emphasized the "other." Wittig remarked:

> We built them consciously for those other usage patterns. In those patterns there is a flow that's not the same as just following columns of text. We tried to design those pages so they would *remind* you. The Heads were really written well, the images carefully chosen—so there would be enough on this pure visual and Head level to trigger the depths.

Visual Codes and Color

The design of the Head structure was one of many components in which color was intended to play an important role. Here it was meant to function in an "attentional and retentional" manner (Duchastel, 1978). But this was only one element in a master plan to achieve a "visually compelling" presentation which involved preparatory research and investigation. Color was also essential to creating a realistic 3-D effect, even though as Frank Loose noted, in printing on paper the "range of color" that you see is much "narrower and flatter" than what one sees in the natural world. Still, working on paper with four color print technology, Joe Godlewski believed "you can deliver a higher resolution, a higher quality image, [such] that the reproduction is . . . closer to seeing the object or the place."

Another area where the realism that color provided was also organized in a highly coded fashion, was in establishing color palettes that conformed to the perceptual level of development of their K–8 student audience. On the basis of research they developed two different color palettes for the program. One palette was to work for the first through third grade, and the other for the fourth through eighth grade. Loose thought that "it was really important that you have colors that kids see and understand as: that's green." As children grow their vision changes, "because eyesight is getting more developed, literally from a physiological standpoint." Younger children "see reds and yellows much more intensely." With the color green then they used "more of a lime green" for grades one through three, brighter, and in keeping with that perceptual level. And with the upper grades they tried "a more kelly kind of green," darker and slightly more sophisticated for those age groups.

Along with matching color to age groups, they also applied basic color codes to maps and photographs. With making maps, Loose stated, "there are certain conventions" that should be followed. During their investigations they actually saw some social studies textbooks that adopted odd color schemes for the simplest of things, which he felt confused younger children. "There are certain colors (grass or land are always green, and water is blue), that you don't mess with." When they took photographs of people for a lesson, whether it was a model or real-life subjects, they generally followed a rule requesting that subjects wear clothing made of primary colors when they were photographed. This acted to visually pattern

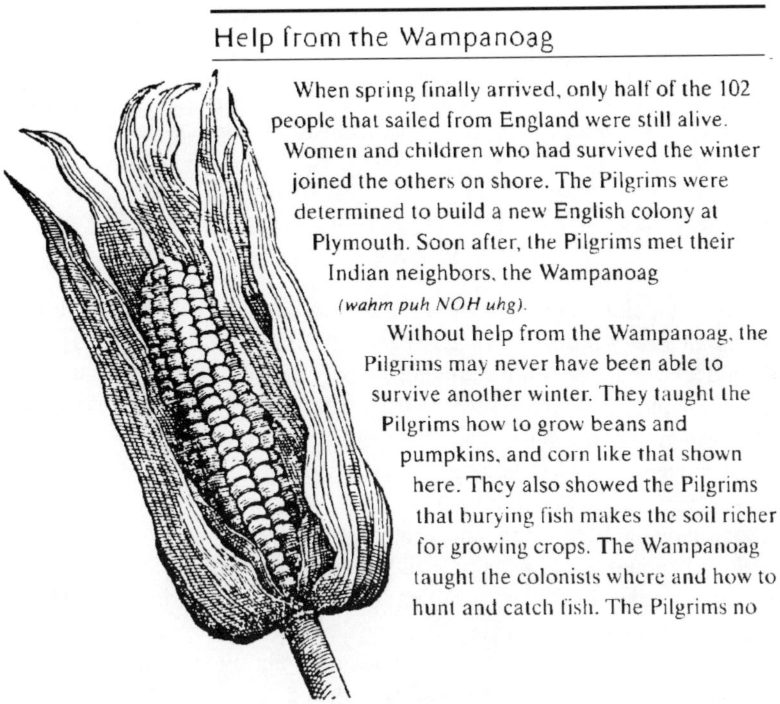

Help from the Wampanoag

When spring finally arrived, only half of the 102 people that sailed from England were still alive. Women and children who had survived the winter joined the others on shore. The Pilgrims were determined to build a new English colony at Plymouth. Soon after, the Pilgrims met their Indian neighbors, the Wampanoag *(wahm puh NOH uhg)*.

Without help from the Wampanoag, the Pilgrims may never have been able to survive another winter. They taught the Pilgrims how to grow beans and pumpkins, and corn like that shown here. They also showed the Pilgrims that burying fish makes the soil richer for growing crops. The Wampanoag taught the colonists where and how to hunt and catch fish. The Pilgrims no

FIGURE 3.2. Text Wrapping, in Life in Plymouth, Lesson 1, Chapter 7, Unit 3, p. 118.

recurring elements in pictures of people, so as to give these images a consistent ongoing similarity.

One lesson following this rule, Loose said, was *People and Peanuts*, found in the second grade text (Fig. 3.3). In this text the entire family wears blue jeans. The son has a red shirt and the father a light white plaid. The mother is wearing a purple shirt, and the daughter a melon colored shirt. Following these color codes also had pedagogical reasons. The viewer, it was hoped, would associate the color of the object (e.g., the red shirt) with the conceptual content of the lesson it appeared in. We wanted to "get recognizable colors, what we call memory colors," Loose said. "These are colors that you use, like green earth and blue sky, so when a teacher has a test question about something a kid can think back to it."

Another area of research that led to a color palette for the entire program was in charts and graphs. They developed color schemes for the presentation of numerical data so that it would be easy to understand, visually clear and obvious. Loose commented on a chart in the third grade text (Fig. 3.4).

> You have a very simple list of year and population. And one column is in a muted brown and the other is in a neutral grey. And those are intersected by red lines. So, it makes the grid obvious, and it shows that you read down, but the red lines also help you read across. . . . So you use color in a way that makes whatever visual information you have *distinct*.

FROM ARCHITECTURE TO OPENERS: SOCIAL STUDIES THAT YOU CAN *STEP* INTO

In the Ratio guidelines the suggestion is made for large visuals. In part, this was assured by the Ratios because the page space was proportionately divided between visuals and text, so that a definite amount of space existed for each element. Frank Loose pointed out a less obvious reason. If you have "a silhouetted photograph the size of a postage stamp you lose the illusion of reality. But . . . a larger visual looks more real and authentic, like you can actually touch it." Although the Openers, as well as special features like *A Moment in Time*, were not included in the percentages covered by the Ratios, the same principle of large visuals was in effect. This was done to heighten the illusion of reality as much as possible, so that the reader could virtually "step into" the visual landscape presented before them. Openers were designed "to help students visualize the themes of history they will be studying." Or, as it states in the *About Your Book* section: "From Unit to Chapter to Lesson each visual step lets you see history in detail" (p. xii, Grade 8). In line with this design objective, Rob Wittig relates that, "our goal was to get the biggest space possible" for the total page. During the prototype phase they experimented with 9 X 12 inch trim sizes and ended up with 8 1/2 X 11 inches. "Most books are 8 X 10 inches," the art director said. With this size, the Openers had a large enough area to create the sense of space necessary for a visual entry into the lessons. The SS21 guidelines specified the format for each of these steps:

1. Unit Openers

> Each unit consists of two to four chapters and begins with a spread that combines a *strong visual* presentation with concise text to create a framework for the content that follows.

2. Chapter Openers

> Each chapter consists of three to four lessons and begins with a chapter opener spread . . . of text and visuals that *vividly* presents some aspect of life today related to the region studied in the chapter; examples should be attention-grabbing and appropriate to the age and experience of the student.

People and Peanuts

THINK

What kinds of work do people do to make peanut butter?

Key Words

crops
harvest
factory

You depend on farmers to grow your food. Josh Wambles's dad is a farmer in Alabama. He grows one of the foods some people like best—peanuts.

Josh is in the second grade. He likes to help his dad on the farm. Josh and his family love to eat the peanuts they grow on their farm. They roast, boil, or fry them. How do you like to eat peanuts?

8

FIGURE 3.3. People and Peanuts, Lesson 2, Unit 1, p. 8.

3. Lesson

> High interest *text/visual hook* should begin each lesson. Elements from
> a visual/verbal menu can include such options as maps, fine art, timelines,
> photos, diagrams, tables, charts, graphs, primary source photos, exposi-
> tory text, and narrative text. (SS21, pp. 118–119)

Following these guidelines during the prototype phase, Godlewski said, "We
continued to refine and explore the idea of these openers, and setting for time and
place." Because the typical social studies curriculum in the early grades is bound
up with inculcating an understanding of this concept of *place* as it relates the concept of society first experienced in the school, then country, and wider world, such
a visual "step" is appropriate. The child can see his or her developing sense of

---

The Silver Runs Out

The boom in Leadville did not last. As the chart on
this page shows, by 1916 Leadville had lost much of its
population. One reason
people left Leadville was
that silver had become less
valuable. Because mine
owners were not making as
much money selling silver
as they had before, they
could not pay their workers
as much. The workers
moved on to better paying
jobs in other places.

Population of Leadville	
Year	**Population**
1877	300
1878	5,000
1879	30,000
1900	12,500
1916	4,500
Present	4,000

▼ *The home of Horace Tabor
still stands in Leadville today.
Visitors can learn about this
man who made a fortune
from silver mines around
Leadville during the 1800s.*

People also left
Leadville because most of the silver there had
been removed from the earth and there were few
new discoveries. People went to other places to
look for minerals or to work in other mines.
Many businesses closed because their customers
were gone.

Leadville did not disappear, but its days as a
boom town were over. It still attracts many
visitors, though. They go to Leadville to enjoy
the mountains and to learn about the interesting
history of western mining towns. ■

■ *What caused Leadville
to go from a boom town to
a quiet mountain town?*

FIGURE 3.4. Color Coded Population Chart, Lesson 4, Chapter 8, Unit 3, p.
163.

social space concretely mirrored by similar images from the actual world. "Strong visual landscapes," with a "huge sweep" vista, where the viewer "could really be made to feel a sense of place," had a double objective: first, to render an aesthetically beautiful image that captured the imagination of the learner, and second, to model the social studies theme in pictorial form.

Like *A Moment in Time*, the Unit Opener was a single image, though it was meant to be panoramic so it always covered two full pages (a double spread). The intention was to create a space the viewer could "step into," suggesting a setting for the lesson. The Opener image could not be looked at so much as a page than as a picture bounded by a frame. This Unit Opener space depicted a setting or an object that was visually concrete and embodied the theme of the unit.

In a Unit Opener on the Southwestern states in the fourth-grade textbook *This is My Country*, the cinematic vista of the Grand Canyon reinforces the unit theme (Fig. 3.5). Here, image complements text by identifying it with a commonly held notion about the Southwest being a place of immense wide open spaces. But over and above this textual link, the visual concretely depicts a deep expansive space that the eye cannot help but "step" into. The "huge sweep" vista draws the reader in to imagine these wide open spaces thus visually participating in the themes. Unlike the Southwest Opener in Grade 4, the visual space created for a Unit Opener in the eighth-grade textbook is not a deep space at all, but instead just a backdrop which foregrounds the object by clearly showing its cast shadow, thus emphasizing its physicality. Here the concrete depiction of an American Eagle is used to present an abstract unit theme on the United States Constitution (Fig. 3.6).

With the artifact of the handcarved American Eagle, the photographic image is reproduced so that its tactile surface qualities are apparent. The shot of the Eagle is strongly silhouetted by the shadow so that it stands in a shallow blue space. The carved surface is visually so well reproduced that it seems as if it can almost be touched. Again the visual complements the unit theme: The eagle in its beak holds the carved ribbon on which *E Pluribus Unum* is emblazoned. Thus the thematic link to the Constitution is embodied in the depicted object. But it should be noted that it is the aesthetically concrete qualities of the object which powerfully lend support to the unit theme.

Other Unit Openers in the program use various kinds of fine art reproduction: paintings, engravings, lithographs, sculpture, weaving, and so forth. Units also begin with archival photographs, reproductions of artifacts, even maps. In Unit Openers the intended effect is to present a visually resonant image for the eye to enter. Included as a graphic element in every Unit Opener are Timelines, which introduce the concept of time as an attribute of space. In the later grades (4–8) all three Openers have Timelines. In the unit and chapter they appear at the bottom of the page, and in the lesson at the top. In either case each visual step is framed chronologically from right to left marking the time period to be covered. Each step specifies a more precise time frame (e.g., in the unit where the Eagle appears it is

FIGURE 3.5. Unit Opener, The Grand Canyon, Grade 4, pp. 202–203.

1775 to 1791; for the chapter: 1775 to 1787, and for the lesson: 1775 to 1781). So the Openers model space visually and diagraphically. Each step visually contextualizes the verbal lesson content to come.

Following the single panoramic image of the unit, the Chapter Opener presents a visual field of several images. The format is similar to *A Closer Look*. The typical Chapter Opener visually layers a combination of three or four images again with a timeline. The intent was generally to "link a primary source or artifact with an illustration, a painting, or photograph that would further contextualize the period about to be covered." In the Chapter 9 Opener, *Farming and Ranching*, which is the next visual step of the Southwest unit in the fourth-grade book, *This Is My Country* (Fig. 3.7), the painting by Frederic Remington, on the right, is juxtaposed with an original illustration of the Sante Fe settlement in New Mexico, on the left. These two pictorial elements are balanced by two artifacts layered over the painting and the illustration. All four elements are unified by a blue timeline at the bottom of the spread. The Zuni pot for storing corn seed seems to rest on it, and the Spanish mission wooden bell ringer overlays it, visually appearing to stand on the trim edge at the bottom of the page, in front of the timeline and the Remington painting.

The effect of "combining viewpoints into one sort of master visual" further sets the scene for the lessons. As a "master" the Chapter Opener functions as a visual preview for the content in the three lessons that follow, forming visual/verbal links. The visual of the Zuni pot links with Lesson 1 on the Zuni Pueblo Indians, which looks at their ability to cultivate corn in the desert. Lesson 2, the theme of the *Spanish Missions and Ranches,* thematically links with the chapter visual of the bell. Lesson 3, *The Cowboys Arrive*, can be visually associated with the Remington painting. Through this "pairing and tripling of imagery, their connection and synthesis, comparison and contrast," the art director hoped that the presentation would leave "an impression that was more than the sum of its parts."

Looking Down Realism

Instead of taking the next step into the visual space of a typical lesson, it is of greater importance to more closely consider the underlying theme of realism which motivates both these Openers and the special visual features which have been looked at so far. In taking this line of sight the visual core of the SS21 program quickly comes into focus. In three-step fashion the theme of realism and how it plays into the spatialization of basic social studies themes is considered:

  1. Realism and Artifacts
  2. Realism and Historical Representation: A Presence of the Past
  3. Looking Down: Planetary Space of *I Know a Place*

FIGURE 3.6. Unit Opener, The American Eagle, Grade 8, pp. 78–79.

Realism and Artifacts

Although the Unit Opener visual of the American Eagle (Fig. 3.6) is shot head on, the eye can still detect a slight shadow in the background beneath the object. In many instances these shadows were added or touched up to heighten spatial depth and the virtual presence of the object depicted. In these shots, Frank Loose remarked, "we tried to hold a shadow [to maintain the] illusion of [it] being on the page." In *A Closer Look* the intent was the same. It would be shot, Loose said, "so that you are looking down and the light is coming from above.... You say looking down, but it's more a *you are there* kind of thing, you're in it! That's really important.... So to a point we tried to keep the telling to a minimum, and the looking at and being a part of, to a maximum."

One notable "design" revealing the potential of this technique, which Rob Wittig characterized as "a very beautiful page," is *A Closer Look: Chinese Writing*, in the sixth-grade textbook (Fig. 3.8). Speaking in terms similar to the principles codified for *A Moment in Time*, Wittig remarked that the heightened realism of the visual was intended to "trigger empathy [by] allowing contact" with the object on the page. "We spent a lot of time thinking about size and relationships." Following the suggestion for "larger visuals" in the ratios, the idea was to get the brushes as close to their actual size as possible, so that the viewer could feel they could almost reach down, pick one up and use it. Audience was also a critical factor. An "interesting... debate" occurred concerning whether the brushes should be positioned for a left or right hand reader. "Demographics" led them to go with the right hand, though the idea "to test" a display for both was considered. As in *A Closer Look*, the page would appear as "a table top," so they "pumped up the shadows so that it really looks like they're there."

An alternate technique with similar intent was to "drop" out the shadow of an object to heighten its tactile surface qualities. This was especially effective for "an object from the times, an artifact, ... a primary source, something that a person used." As with the Zuni pot and the Spanish mission bell ringer from the Southwest Chapter Opener, there were "other things that you just couldn't look down at," Frank Loose said. These objects such as the "Axe," which were too big to show in scale were photographed from a museum collection (Fig. 3.9). Its surface qualities could effectively be displayed by holding "the drop shadow." This heightened the "authenticity" of the artifact. The neutral white ground serves to highlight the surface of the handle and the metal head. The object is linked with another primary source artifact, a 1796 sketch of a log cabin, which adds to the realistic effect by showing the actual effect of the artifact as a tool, tree stumps and log cabin. With historic artifacts these visual combinations were essential to the presentation. As a rule certain guidelines were followed in the presentation of primary source material.

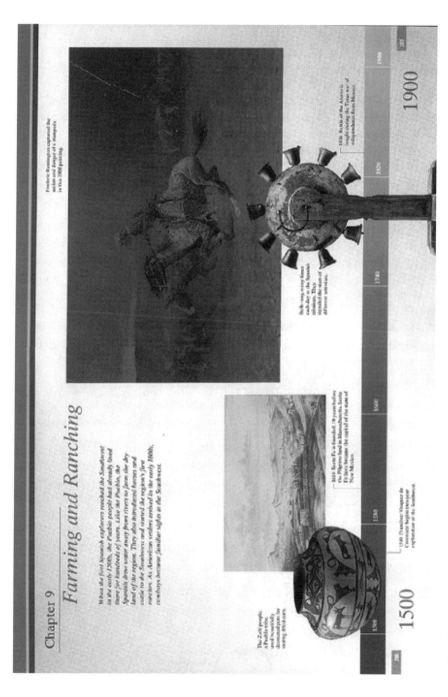

FIGURE 3.7. Chapter Opener, Grade 4, pp. 206–207. *Stampede*, by Frederic Remington, courtesy of Gilcrease Museum, Tulsa, Oklahoma.

Chinese Writing

The brush races across the paper as your Chinese friend draws the word you see below. Can you guess what it means? It's the word for horse! Chinese writing has a long history. Look how the word for horse developed step by step.

Turtle shells were sometimes used to write on in ancient China. The writing on this shell was done around 1200 B.C. Notice that the writing uses mostly straight lines, which are easy to draw.

c. 2000 B.C.
The earliest writers scratched small pictures like this onto bones and shells.

c. 600 B.C.
In this period, writing started to look less like a picture.

c. A.D. 300
When writers began to use brushes, their lines got longer. Where are the horse's feet?

Present
Today the Chinese are trying to simplify their writing by using characters like this one.

Jade brush rest

Signature seal

Take this stick of ink and grind it slowly back and forth on this ink stone. Add water until the ink is just the shade you want it, from the deepest black to the palest gray. Now you are ready to dip your brush and paint the word *horse.*

Is this writing or painting? Chinese people began to write with brushes over 2,000 years ago. For centuries writers in China have worked to make their work as beautiful as possible. So, making a Chinese letter or poem is actually both writing and painting.

267

Ancient China

FIGURE 3.8. A Closer Look: Chinese Writing, Grade 6, p. 267.

◄ *In this 1796 sketch, a settler takes a break from her chores to look at her surroundings.*

▼ *Sometimes settlers used axes to plant seeds if they didn't have proper farming tools.*

After all the hard work of putting up a cabin, settlers enjoyed music, feasting, and storytelling. A finished log cabin might have looked like the one above.

Like the Pilgrims, the Pennsylvania settlers learned many of the skills they needed from their Indian neighbors. In the Pennsylvania forests, these were the Delaware Indians.

Like the Wampanoag, the Delaware knew how to use the natural resources of the land. The Delaware taught the settlers how to grow corn, beans, and squash. The Indians even shared recipes for cooking these foods. The Delaware also showed the settlers which wild herbs made the best medicines. ▪

▪ *How did the settlers adapt to the land?*

FIGURE 3.9. Axe from Lesson Life in the Eastern Forest, Grade 3, p. 125.

Historical Representation: A Presence of the Past

Another guideline, just as closely followed as the visual/verbal ratios, concerned the combinations of textual and visual elements that were linked to a primary source document in order to reconstruct a sense of the past. The combination was simple but quite innovative. It always consisted of a primary source, a photograph, and a map. Frank Loose commented that it "was something that no one in a social studies textbook . . . had done." The primary source document set the scene, creating a textual ground for the images, situating it as a particular place in history. "When we show a picture of where the Appalachian Trail was, we show a picture of: this is what 'The Wilderness Road' looks like today" (Fig. 3.10).

The Wilderness Road

THINKING
F O C U S

Why was the Wilderness Road important for the people who wanted to settle in Kentucky?

Key Terms

- pioneer
- blaze

► *The Cumberland Gap is a natural passageway through the Appalachian Mountains. Thousands of settlers traveled through this gap on their way to Kentucky.*

S atrd April 8th—We all pact up and started crosl Cumberland gap about one oclock this Day We Met a great mancy peopel turned Back for fear of the indians but our Company goes on Still with good courage we come to a very ugly Creek with steep Banks and have it to cross several times....

William Calk, from his journal, 1775

William Calk may not have spelled very well, but he had many adventures along the Wilderness Road. Despite the dangers of travel, Calk was determined to reach Kentucky. It was a beautiful land with lots of open space.

Trail Through the Appalachians

Pennsylvania

APPALACHIAN MOUNTAINS

Virginia

Boonesborough
Harrodsburg
Kentucky
Cumberland
Gap

Wilderness
Road

ATLANTIC
OCEAN

Key
— Wilderness Road
— State borders today

▲ *This is what the Wilderness Road looks like today.*

A Difficult Crossing

William Calk was a **pioneer**, which is a person who leaves a settled place and moves into the wilderness to make a new home. In the late 1700s and early 1800s, thousands of pioneers like Calk moved to Kentucky. Why did they move to Kentucky? For one thing, land cost less there than along the east coast. For another, Kentucky had rich soil for farming. Herds of buffalo and other wild animals roamed there. People said there were so many birds in Kentucky that they could block out the sun.

Kentucky offered much, but getting there was difficult and dangerous. Notice on the map how the Appalachian Mountains blocked all travel west. If people wanted to reach Kentucky, they first had to haul everything they owned over these rugged mountains.

Narrow Indian or buffalo paths crossed some of these mountains. Pioneers had to follow these paths on foot or by horse. The paths were far too narrow for wagons. ■

■ *Why did the Appalachian Mountains present problems to pioneers who wanted to move west?*

FIGURE 3.10. The Wilderness Road, Grade 3, pp. 134–135.

FIGURE 3.11. Vesuvius Victim from Lesson 1, "Understanding History," Grade 6, p. 56.

In *The Wilderness Road*, the primary source was a journal entry by William Calk, dated 1775, describing what it was like to cross the Cumberland Gap. In the layout beneath this entry is a photograph of the Gap. On the opposite page there is another photograph of the road as it looks today, which is layered over a map. In sum there are three different spatial elements which combine to create the representation: the narrative space imagined from the journal entry, the actual space of the road depicted in the photographs, and the flat two-dimensional space of the map. Each element can be taken as a "little clue and shorthand," Loose said. "So where a map can really just kind of tell you [this is] space in a very flat way, we can also show that space by showing a photograph of what that space might have looked like too."

The juxtaposition of spaces, visual, textual, and diagraphic, can be done in an expository fashion making it somewhat understated yet still direct as in *The Wilderness Road*. Or, it can be quite dramatic; a visual/verbal hook to trigger empathy and deeper reflection. Whereas an aerial shot of the Cumberland Gap is juxtaposed with a primary source document to evoke the struggle of settlers long ago, in *Understanding History*, a similar juxtaposition evokes the personal space of human beings in their last moments of consciousness. In this Lesson on how to interpret different types of historical evidence in the sixth-grade textbook *A Message of Ancient Days*, the design links a primary source document with a drop shadow image (Fig 3.11). The document is an excerpt from a letter by Pliny the Younger to the famous Roman historian, Tacitus, about his harrowing escape from death during the eruption of Mt. Vesuvius in 79 A.D. The text of the lesson is wrapped around the visual, a roughly textured plaster cast of a person buried during the eruption. Four visual/verbal spatial layers evoke this dark scenario described by Pliny: the primary source, the concrete weight of the roughly textured plaster cast, the psychological space of the unknown victim covering their eyes in a deaththroe, and the scholarly text commentary of the historian symmetrically wrapped around the visual. The larger intent of the visual design in these image/text combinations is to create not only a sense of virtual space, but to recover the personal dimension of the past through a powerful visual which can trigger empathy and compel the viewer/reader to make connection.

LOOKING DOWN: I KNOW A PLACE OF PLANETARY SPACE

When these *moments in time* become visually real for the learner they can be linked with a particular *place*. What it meant to be an American settler crossing the Appalachian Trail is conveyed not only as an important moment recorded in a diary, but also as a moment that occurred in an actual space which is visually represented. The person past speaks to the student present not just through the text, but from the place where they spoke. Similarly, when such images of the past are plotted on the timelines of these lessons, children learn to situate themselves in the space and time of the present by comparing the spaces in these depictions with the spaces that make up their moment in time: home, school, community.

In this concluding section, a sequence of visuals is presented to show how it can orchestrate a "storyspace" reflecting concepts fundamental to the social studies curriculum. The visual design of *I Know a Place*, the first-grade textbook, depicts space in terms that are unique to American culture. Americans can fly. Through their technology they "look down" at the space of the world. Because of this convention students learn to "construct images and meanings of the social world" by situating America in planetary terms (Armento, 1986, p. 96).

The unit structure of *I Know a Place* consists of four parts. Unit 1: School; Unit 2: Town and Country; Unit 3: City and Suburb; and Unit 4: All Around the Big World. These four units can be simplified thematically to just three: School, Country, and the World, with country basically absorbing units two and three.

Underlying these themes is a basic fact of American life. The SS21 document acknowledges it: "children live in an increasingly complex and highly visual society, . . . [and] spend many hours with visual media such as television, videos, and computers" (SS21, 1989, p. 25). Ligature's product design reflects the status of visual information in U.S. culture as an agent of socialization recognizing its potential as an informal curriculum shaping young American minds. Media provides the normative frame of reference to learn about the world. The visual design of these textbooks works within the naturalized space of this ongoing construction.

Consequently, what this leitmotif sequence reflects is the technological power of a global electronic apparatus which enables the child to construct a planetary view of things. The primary *"Place"* known by the child is the earth. The unit structure can be viewed as a series of windows framing the total planetary space. This series of visual steps serves to totalize the unit themes of school, city and country and world. The sequence consists only of six windows lifted from this series of units in the first-grade textbook:

1. *Title* page
2. *School*, Unit 1
3. *Looking Down*, Think About Maps, Unit 1
4. *Flying High*, Think About Maps, Unit 2
5. *The Earth is Your Home*, Think About the Earth, Unit 2
6. *Our Country, Our World*, Unit 4, Lesson 1

The *Title* page of the book serves as a visual "shorthand" for the three major themes of school, country, and world (Fig. 3.12). The composition has three combinations of visual elements which represent the three themes. From left to right: the two ecology buttons, and the cartoon of students and teacher coupled with the two children hugging each other (who are also in the Unit 1 Opener, represent *School*), and the postage stamp (for country) layered over a photograph of the planet earth (for world). Visually the proximity of the word "Place" directly above the photo of the earth identifies it as the place to be known. The layering of the postage stamp over the earth suggests a *whole in part* relationship. The stamp, an obvious symbol (metonymy) for the U.S.A. is but one part of this whole, while the school classroom is a smaller microcosm (or part) of the country. The two children placed outside the visual frame of the title page are then placed inside the Unit 1 Opener "storyspace" of *School* (Chatman, 1978). On the title page they serve to welcome the reader into the book, and appearing inside they act as a composition device maintaining visual continuity.

The classroom of happy first graders all smile into a camera (Fig. 3.13). Conventionally, the scene reflects something typically American: posing for a picture

FIGURE 3.12. Title pages from I Know a Place, Grade 1.

FIGURE 3.13. School, Unit 1, Grade 1, p. 1.

Looking Down

Imagine that this is your school.

How would the room look?

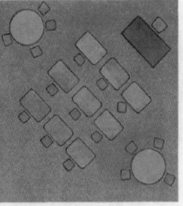

What if you could float up?

Classroom

This is a map of the room.

A map shows how a place looks from above.

Can you tell what these things are?

FIGURE 3.14. Looking Down, Think About Maps, Grade 1, pp. 14–15.

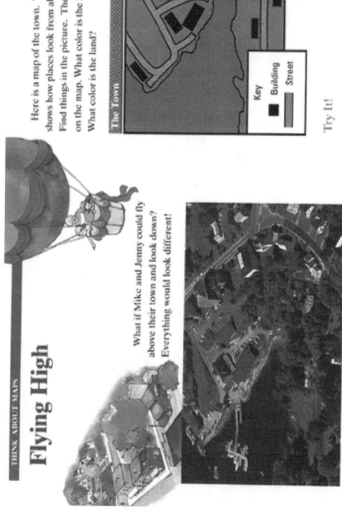

THINK ABOUT MAPS

Flying High

What if Mike and Jenny could fly above their town and look down? Everything would look different!

This picture shows how a town might look from above. Places look smaller from far away.

Here is a map of the town. The map shows how places look from above, too. Find things in the picture. Then find them on the map. What color is the lake on the map? What color is the land?

The Town

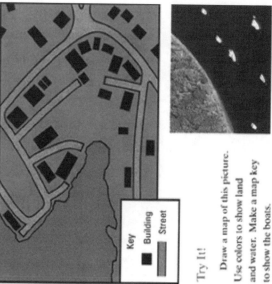

Key
- ■ Building
- ▬ Street

Try It!

Draw a map of this picture. Use colors to show land and water. Make a map key to show the boats.

FIGURE 3.15. Flying High, Think About Maps, Grade 1, pp. 28–29.

to mark a place and moment time. It also functions as sort of an establishing shot, the opening image for the story *School* narrated in the lessons that follow. We cannot look at the children except as spectators looking in. The children in the picture mirror the children reading. In the cartoon *Looking Down* the classroom is seen head on as in the Unit Opener, but it is also seen from above (Fig. 3.14). Like many popular comic superheroes a student magically dons a cape and rises above the class and flies. Beverly Armento commented that there was much discussion in the St. Louis office over the issue of how a child conceptualizes flight. There was some speculation that first-grade children might not be able to engage in the fantasy that magical flying is imaginatively possible, but not humanly possible. It is probably not coincidental that this *Think About Maps* exercise "Looking Down" carries the name of the memo that set the guidelines for the feature *A Closer Look*.

Instead of a scholar's tabletop the flat surface of a classroom map is to be looked down on. Thematically, the notion of "Looking Down" is without question a prominent motif in the program. It recurs again in the next "Think About Maps" exercise *Flying High* (Fig. 3.15). In this exercise two children float above their hometown in a balloon. It culminates in the following unit with *Think About the Earth* (Fig. 3.16), where an astronaut floats in the Space Shuttle cargo bay, with the earth set in deep space above. "Think About the Earth" uses the same image of the earth on the title page set in a deep black space, whereas the earth on the Title page is set in white space. Looking down, looking at, or just looking; we are all viewers and watchers in our visual culture. Just as high technology enables children to see the world whole, it just as easily allows them to visually mediate that larger world in personal terms. The favorite pastime in a Kodak culture is taking pictures. Kids can make snapshots of their friends, but where are they found?

In *Our Country, Our World* (Fig. 3.17), a flat map of the world (with the United States shown in the color green) has callout lines radiating from various points on the globe. Each callout has a flag layered over a snapshot of a child from that country. This simple overlay repeats the USA postage stamp layered over the earth on the title page. The recurring motif visually reinforces the three main themes of school, country, and world. But in this image part and whole merge, classroom becomes planet. Friends not only can be found in the classroom, as in the opening poem of Unit One, but everywhere.

LOOKING AT OURSELVES LOOKING DOWN

Following Tufte's (1990) tenet we might say that in the present all "the interesting worlds" we want to know about in social studies "are multivariate in nature." The visual design provides a platform to look down upon this multivariate world. With present day Imaging technology we need not rely on description, at least initially. The social studies theme of "Place" is captured and rendered in all its complexity by *image* alone. With, for instance, the satellite image of the earth (Fig 3.18) found in the Chapter 2 Opener, *This Land of Ours*, of the fifth-grade textbook, the sheer

FIGURE 3.16. The Earth Is Your Home, Grade 1, pp. 58–59.

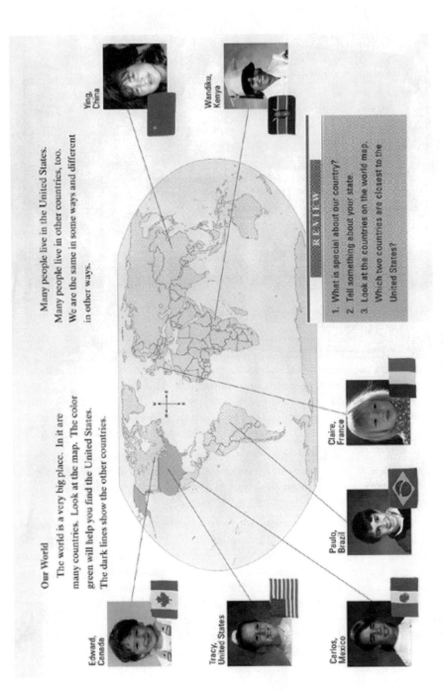

FIGURE 3.17. Our Country, Our World, Grade 1, pp. 120–121.

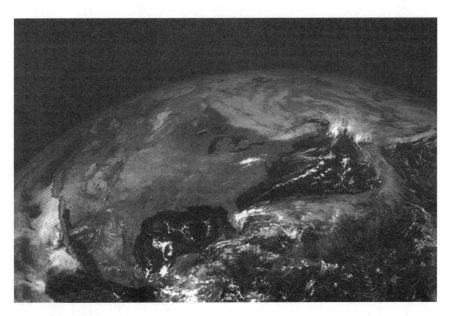

FIGURE. 3.18. Satellite Photograph, Grade 5, p. 29.

presence of the photograph is so data rich with information (compressed within a 4 x 6 inch frame), that to speak of graphic space being wasted as Woodward does, is to entirely miss how visual images communicate content. In treating aesthetics lightly (nothing more than a marketing gimmick), Woodward misses how the processes of seeing and thinking are profoundly recursive in nature. David Perkins (1994) observes that the practiced eye exercises its own intelligence. Wide vistas of planetary space can lead, he suggests, to "wide spectrum cognition."

> Although we tend to think of art as primarily a visual phenomenon, looking at art thoughtfully recruits many kinds and styles of cognition—visual processing, analytical thinking, posing questions, testing hypotheses, verbal reasoning and more. (p. 5)

This "more" as Tufte might suggest is a "wide spectrum" response to the "multivariate" world before us. One is reflexive of the other. And though it points beyond *text* because it is of a "multivariate" order, it is nevertheless multitextual. This is the level of complexity and dimensionality which visual information introduces. It is fundamentally recursive. The visual turn is also linguistic.

In this chapter, the visual design of the Program was shown to contribute to one of the more important themes of the social studies curriculum. The "beautiful book" means having multidimensional presentations so students begin to construct their first meanings of the social world. Space is created on the page to draw them into the aesthetic richness and complexity of that world. In the next chapter the focus shifts from visual to instructional design. Ideally, the textbook unit is considered as a sequence of textually coherent lessons. Composed in visual/verbal terms, it becomes a series of integrated graphical units. Yet when text is spatialized creating a layered visual/verbal "storyspace," it impacts conventional text structure. This alteration and its implication for instructional design is considered next.

A Beautiful Book or Considerate Text

A distinction is now made. The total design of the program can be said to consist of two components: visual and instructional. The intent of the previous chapter was to provide a fairly comprehensive review of the major diagraphic and visual presentation features conceived for the program, which contributed to spatializing the text. This aesthetic dimension prompts serious reconsideration of standard page conventions. The neutral white space is no longer simply a ground for print. Multiple forms of representation, textual, diagraphic, and visual, share space. This multilayered and windowed text basically follows a linear format, but at the same time creates sequences which shape readerly perception differently. The eye moves through visually represented space and across text lines. Ideally, seeing and reading are performed simultaneously. Yet it should be recalled that the lesson in the Thumbnail Process was scripted to a visual storyline. The role of the author became more like that of an "architect." Whatever text was written had to be considerate of the visuals. This subtle if not marked alteration draws into question a number of fundamental assumptions about the structure of *text*. This chapter explores some of the more important issues arising from this re-structuring of the page to accommodate the visual design.

At one level the guidelines established for ratios of visuals to text are simple percentages which divide the page into adjacent areas—one for lines, the other a space occupied by visuals. Yet at the structural level two systems of representation are at work which organize that space according to different rules and principles: syntax and semantics for text, and the principles of pictorial composition followed by graphic designers that are concerned with line, shape, color and form.

A major concern of instructional design is the organization of content into units of instruction. To be teachable these units have to readable. Content has to have a structure suitable for comprehension and learning. This chapter examines how visual design complements its textual counterpart. The instructional design consisted of three basic components: the Pupil and Teacher's Edition, and the Ancillary materials. Chapter 5 will deal with the design of the Teacher Edition. This chapter will focus more or less exclusively on the text structure of the Pupil Edition (P.E.).

Instructional design research indicates three major trends, only one of which is concerned with the questions posed here. Two of the more mainline trends have been concerned with "studying how instruction should be designed, . . . and specifying how it should be used" (Chall, 1977, pp. 129–130). A less visible trend, but central to the focus of this chapter, is the attempt "to create guidelines for effective text" design (p. 130).

Some of these more notable and influential studies provide a theoretical context in which the problems that arose during the design of the instructional component can be considered. A large part of this problem consisted in the competing and often conflicting views of instructional design held by various members of the author and design teams who were involved in the development process.

Finding a middle ground between these respective positions is the larger purpose of this chapter. Ligature's goal of designing a visual/verbal textbook was somewhat at odds with what instructional design research has dubbed the "considerate text." Although there is a well-defined position as to what constitutes a verbally considerate text, there is as yet no generally accepted definition of what a visually considerate text might look like, much less a visual/verbal one. The first part of this chapter considers this design issue from the vantage point of the instructional design and reading specialist who was part of the Author Team. In particular it focuses on her role in the program development and her evaluation of the Pupil Edition. The latter part of this chapter attempts to reconcile the "considerate" text to aspects of the visual component which support and complement the design of these structures.

INSTRUCTIONAL DESIGN IN THE SS21 PROGRAM

In the account of the development process the focus was on Ligature's innovative procedures. In that review the role of the Author Team was minimized. With the exception of Karen Wixson, an instructional design and reading specialist, all the subject specialists who were later designated as authors had greater or lesser involvement in the earlier stages. Those who were active participated in the preparation of subject area outlines. A few even observed or took part in the Thumbnail Process. Gary Nash and Beverly Armento were heavily involved in all stages of program development. Early on, Christopher Salter, the geography specialist, consulted with scholarly outlines. But he had only peripheral involvement in the Thumbnail Process through the St. Louis office. Whereas these individuals had some degree of involvement in the earlier stages, Karen Wixson was brought into the project by Houghton Mifflin only after the Thumbnail Process had ended.

Karen Wixson entered the project late and in a sense by default, replacing another instructional design expert when other commitments prevented that person from participating. Already an author for Houghton Mifflin's flagship product reading series, Dr. Wixson was brought into the project by Houghton Mifflin in order to consult on the design of Teacher Edition instructional aides and assessment instruments. But the publisher also felt that her name recognition with the reading series might be attractive to teachers.

According to Wixson her major input was in three areas. First, she contributed to the design of the prototypes for Unit Openers which are located in gray side margins of the Teacher's Edition. Unit Openers were meant to provide an overview of key concepts and their connection to any visual images and timelines to be found throughout that unit. The emphasis was on arranging that information in these side margins to help teachers focus on and make explicit the connections between verbal and visual content. She also worked on the design and writing of the Graphic Overviews. These are graphic organizers that are found in the bottom margin on the opening page of each lesson, also in the Teacher Edition. And lastly she contributed to the Review section assessments at the end of lessons and chapters. But all of this activity took place just prior to the first Edits; the major part of program design and development, discussed in the opening chapters, had already been completed.

On Making Instruction Considerate

One important record of Karen Wixson's view about a properly designed textbook is found in the Teacher Edition Professional Handbook. Preceding the actual text as found in the Pupil Edition it serves as an introduction to the various instructional components making up the Social Studies Program. Like the Openers it is also an introduction one can "step into." Each page is an artful reconstruction of typical scenes lifted out of the development process. In the *Program Overview* section the reader looks down at the Author team at work with the Ligature designers. On the following pages you meet the individual authors. From page to page they each sit on a stool facing their audience along with an introductory statement describing how their subject area expertise is realized in the program. These tableau photographs immediately personalize the abstract notion of a textbook author making them appear very collegial and accessible. The photographic presence of the authors effectively reinforces their statements, and takes on added impact because we see the person behind the words of the text. According to the Professional Handbook the goal of the Houghton Mifflin program is to "develop literate citizens." A Social Studies Program of "depth rather than breadth," its components are designed to be powerful classroom tools. The Program is intended to "captivate, develop, question, and stretch" students' awareness of their place in society and the world. It will prepare them to become "active and reflective participants in the world of the twenty-first century" (p. T6). Karen Wixson's appearance and accompanying statement on what constitutes a "considerate text" appears in the Third through Eighth grade Teacher Edition book (Fig. 4.1). A similar but slightly different statement for "younger students" appears in earlier grades. The photograph is from the third-grade text, *From Sea to Shining Sea* (p. T18). As stated, she identifies four major characteristics that a textbook should possess to be instructionally effective. First, a "considerate text" is designed to "help the

Karen Wixson on
Making Instruction Considerate

"Instructional design really is a model of the thinking process that most of us learn to engage in through experience. Considerate instructional design makes the thinking process explicit. It helps the students become conscious of the thinking process."

B eing considerate of the student means working out an instructional design that helps the student learn. The text, for example, must have a logical flow of information, and the lessons, chapters, and units must be woven together by meaningful transitions. There must also be unity in the focus of the text so that the student stays with the big ideas. Instructional supports in the text, such as headings, graphics, and charts, have to relate to important information in a way that guides the learner through the text. Finally, the material has to be appropriate to the audience."

T18

Karen K. Wixson
Associate Professor of Education
University of Michigan, Ann Arbor

FIGURE 4.1. On Making Instruction Considerate, from the Teacher Edition Professional Handbook.

student learn." Second, such a text helps the student when its lesson, chapter, and unit content structures have a "logic and flow" that is "woven together by meaningful transitions." Third, this overall textual quality is aided by its "instructional supports" such as "headings, graphics, and charts," which should reinforce that logic and flow to "guide the learner through the text." Finally, a "considerate text" is appropriate to the reading level of its audience.

Her second point about the logic of the text is particularly noteworthy because it closely follows the current standard held in her field. In the Handbook statement Wixson basically reiterates that dominant view. That view has been most successfully articulated in a series of co-authored articles written by Thomas Anderson and Bonnie Armbruster (1984, 1985; see also Armbruster, 1981, 1986). Synthesizing the accumulated research of recent decades they have constructed a conceptual framework that focuses on the major characteristics of textbooks which affect comprehension and learning. Two of the most prominent are "textual coherence and unity" (Anderson & Armbruster, 1985, pp. 167–171). To be *considerate* a text structure must possess both characteristics. Anderson and Armbruster define *coherence* as a relatively high degree of "logical . . . flow of meaning in the transition from one idea to the next." This "smoothly woven [pattern of ideas] makes it easier for the reader to perceive the message as an integrated unit" (pp. 167–171).

Similarly, *textual unity* "refers to the degree to which the text addresses a single purpose. The . . . unified text [tends to avoid the inclusion of] irrelevant and distracting information" which may not reinforce that larger overall theme and purpose. In their conceptual framework textual "coherence [should] operate at both the global and local levels; that is at the level of the whole text as well as at the level of individual sentences" (p. 167). "Global and local" coherence are more or less equivalent to the unit and lesson level of a textbook. In the statement found in the *Professional Handbook* Wixson's view tends to closely follow the dominant view of the field represented by Anderson and Armbruster.

The Missing Piece

Brought into the development process to consult on the Teacher Edition after the Thumbnail Process was over, Wixson's lasting impression of her entry into the project was that she (or someone with her expertise) should have been involved before the process started. This late arrival was an indication that she felt Ligature had regarded instructional design in terms far different than her own. "They wanted input on the elements of the Student Edition that would make it considerate to the reader and appropriate. But their view related entirely to what I call adjunct aids. . . . Where my view of what makes a text considerate encompasses a lot more. It encompasses really the coherence and unity of the text itself. And that's where we ran into difficulty."

This point is elaborated further in her rating of the Author team according to those who seemed to share her view and those who did not. "Beverly Armento was one of the other three who maybe had equal concerns for the way information was presented with the content of the thing" while the other views did not reflect an understanding of "considerate text" issues. "Frankly," she said, "they didn't understand the principles of simplicity and depth. . . . They don't really think of content in that way; . . . thinking in terms of what are the overarching concepts here, and how do we keep hitting them from multiple perspectives."

Lack of textual coherence was first noticeable when she attempted to devise Unit Openers and Chapter Reviews. "Oftentimes," Wixson noted, she had difficulty "identifying the big ideas that were the thrust of the whole unit." It was also evident when she tried to design graphic organizers for the bottom instructional margin of the Teacher Edition. In her mind graphic organizers were integral to the content structure of a text. Consequently, they needed to be conceived at the beginning, not at the end, as she was attempting to do. "The problems," she said, "with doing these graphic organizers after the fact were great. What you discovered was that you didn't have a very coherent text." Had these graphic organizers been "made part of the Outlining and Thumbnail Process, then their text would have been a lot more coherent." Overall, she attributed this absence of textual coherence to Ligature's development process.

The First Edition, she said, only "appears [to have] this unit, chapter, and lesson organization." She continues, "the fact is, if you read them the lesson is really the primary unit. And this is no surprise because that's the way they were developed, lesson by lesson." The key point in her criticism was to "rethink the way they went from Outlines to Thumbnails." To Wixson this reorientation was the "missing piece." It meant "that the whole process of developing outlines, Thumbnails, and the first edits" would focus on basic considerate text questions such as: "what are the key concepts, what are the linkages, how are we going to pull them through, and how do they recur from unit to chapter to lesson levels." In her opinion, doing this would have produced a more coherent and unified text. And, she said, it was these essential characteristics "that really set apart newer from older materials." With newer materials, she remarked, "the unit isn't just like a loosely related bunch of information, but really is going for depth of understanding about some very big powerful ideas."

Contra Considerate Text

Meeting with the Author team and the Ligature project directors for the first minor revision of the K–8 program, which took place during the summer of 1993, Wixson "made a very strong plea that the [development] process be altered" along the lines she had recommended before the final edits and production. Needless to say she met with a great deal of resistance when she first made these recommendations, because at that point it would have meant in some cases "ripping apart the whole structure of the lesson. And, they weren't prepared to do that," she said.

During the revision meeting everyone seemed to listen, but as she remarked, "who knows what they did with" her suggestions.

The differences over "considerate" text issues, which seemed to inspire passionate disagreement between what might be simplistically called the visual and verbal camps of the textbook project, clearly prompt a call for deeper probing into the critical points at issue. Going deeper will serve to adequately represent the larger implications of what is involved with what might be called two competing models of instructional design. It is fair to say that we might begin simply by asking, "What, if any, were the missing pieces in Karen Wixson's evaluation of the process and product of the instructional design?"

Wixson was essentially correct in homing in on how critical the thematic alignment between unit and lesson levels of the text is. By referencing a commonly held principle from the instructional design literature this point is easily supported. Venezky and Osin (1991) stated that "the most critical distinction [necessary to consider is] between the overall instructional design for a course and the specific instructional design for lessons" (p. 97). Employing the analogy "of a series of concentric circles," they describe a threefold process. It consists of a hierarchy where the outermost level, designated as the curriculum, determines the following linkages at the course and lesson levels. Here, the "curriculum" can be taken as analogous to Wixson's outline and organizer.

Wixson's point about making sure the content specified at the lesson level was linked to larger unit themes, and didn't just appear as a series of interesting but "loosely related bunch of information," was something of a nonstarter for the Ligature project directors. They felt such content problems had already been taken care of during predevelopment with the in-house writing of the Scope and Sequence. Based on the new California History-Social Science Framework (1988), Ligature developed a Scope and Sequence for the entire K–8 program. Such a master plan gave the visual/verbal teams a blueprint for each lesson. As Frank Loose, art director for Grades 1–3, pointed out, the Scope was developed the same time as the "Toolbox" specifications. It was considered to be a master plan which resolved form and content issues before the Thumbnail began.

Though Wixson never witnessed a Thumbnail session, and relied on "their description" to understand it, her criticism of the process also extended to its product: the visual/verbal lesson format. Commenting that "most" students have trouble reading "traditional textbooks," she thought the addition of a "visual aspect," only made reading more difficult. "I think that reading texts like that is not easy, because you have to bounce around, and I think that if it's not easy for skilled readers it may be even more difficult for novices. And all the data that we have suggests that kids' ability to read and comprehend textbooks is pretty dismal." While such an opinion indicates where her priorities lie, it also indicates that she views content in verbal terms. This distinction should not be overlooked, because it fundamentally contradicts Ligature's design principle of visual/verbal integration.

Though largely unstated, Wixson indicated that the visuals were also a significant factor contributing to the lack of textual coherence. Certainly, Wixson did not consider visuals as equal to verbal content. This is indicated in her comments regarding visual information as "adjunct aids." Standard to instructional design, adjunct aids are "pedagogic devices" such as "advance organizers, behavioral objectives, and summaries . . . [which are] commonly used to enhance the accessibility of a text by explicitly declaring its conceptual framework, goals, and structure (Waller, 1982)." Wixson's position on adjunct aids can be found in her published articles.

In *"Comprehension Assessment,"* Wixson places in the category of adjunct aids: "charts, and illustrations, inserted questions, and headings . . . " (Wixson & Peters, 1987 p. 351). This group includes some of the major visual elements found in Ligature's visual/verbal layouts, (i.e., charts, illustrations, etc.). In this article, she states that adjunct aids, "are part of the context of a particular text and the discipline it represents, and, therefore must be interpreted within that context and not independent from it" (pp. 351–352). By stating that these aids "are part of its context," Wixson is making a fine but crucial distinction between the verbal "core" (de Beaugrande, 1984, p. 153) and its adjuncts. Visuals are subordinate to verbal text. This reversal of Ligature's standing principle is suggestively reinforced by the "concept map" she presents in this same article. Adjunct aids are numerically listed at the very end as the eighth and ninth items. The principle items in descending numerical order are all textually based, concerning "the central purpose, major idea, and supporting ideas" of the verbal content (p. 349). Such mapping recalls her plea to rethink the process of going from Outline to Thumbnail, just as it may reveal the logical preeminence of the word over image in her thinking. But it also poses another question: To what extent are "considerate text" criteria appropriate to evaluate a visual/verbal text structure?

THE POSTLINEAR TEXT

Some people were not comfortable with that as far as presentation because it's very recursive and not linear. And so there was fear that the students would be distracted and that there was too much for the student to put together.

—Joe Godlewski (1992)

Because linearity is intrinsic to the problem of textual coherence, it is also, one might say, the theoretical point of departure for Ligature. In practice it meant viewing the graphic space of the page in recursive terms; a ground for integrating text and visuals. In design and appearance Ligature's "goal" was not a "traditional textbook." As Godlewski remarked, "We didn't want anyone to look at this so much as a book, but sort of a quasi-magazine." Jay Bolter (1991) observes that "magazines, newspapers, advertising, tabloids and billboards all tend to subvert the primacy of linear verbal text in our culture. They work against the ideal established by the printed book. [And, this] ideal was and is a sequence of pages containing ordered lines of alphabetic text" (pp. 73–74).

Such style is the antithesis of *text*. Resistance to it, coming from the field of reading pedagogy, seems natural. "I think that the fact Joe and his crew have degrees in visual semiotics is sort of very telling in terms of where they were coming from in trying to integrate the visual and the verbal," says Wixson. In thinking beyond conventional book forms those standards didn't necessarily apply. "You just can't apply the traditions of the study of reading to this. . . . It's a different study altogether," Rob Wittig claimed. Reinforcing this point, he also stated that "there's a highly developed culture within the education world of talking about reading and what goes on. And compared to that, a very minimally developed language about how visuals work." The Social Studies Program can perhaps be seen as a prototype in the development of that language.

Robert Waller and Visual Informativeness

Textual coherence depends on having the "core structure" of the text apparent to the reader. The overarching theme (or topic) of the unit is developed and elaborated upon in the sequences of lessons. As it is read, the unfolding sequence reveals the "core." Linkages are clear and obvious in a "considerate" text structure. Can only text, if it is well designed, be "considerate?" Is a visual/verbal text structure a contradiction in terms? If the problem of "coherence" is crucial to the design of text, how is it handled with the introduction of visual information. Can "coherence" be redefined in visual/verbal terms? As the Web becomes more localized in the classroom, and digital space becomes synonymous with actual place, and event with content, understanding the fundamental basis of this redefinition becomes crucial. To consider this problem it is necessary to understand the theoretical points at which Ligature and Wixson diverge. The difference may not be as great as it seems. Even a "good read" is essentially visual. While Wixson stressed the semantic dimension of text structure, Ligature more than emphasized, indeed creatively exploited, the visible (graphemic) aspects of the same structure.

To illustrate the graphic dimension of structure and its relevance for "considerate" text issues we can rely on the work of the British typographic design theorist, Robert Waller. Like Edward Tufte, his research studies the traditions, institutions, and industrial practices of print culture, though perhaps his work is more directly relevant because it has long been focused on how this culture impacts the design of instructional materials. In "Typography and Discourse" (1991), Waller reviews major trends in typographic research and the design of instructional materials in terms of a principle he calls "visual informativeness" (p. 357). Following the visual/verbal intent implicit in this title he states that a textbook consists of a "topic structure and access structure" (p. 357). The goal of the designer is to enhance the "informativeness" of these structures. Waller (1991) indicates that a well designed "access structure" in turn makes the meaning of the text apparent. Like Landow and Tufte, he shares a position which holds "that graphic design must figure prominently in the analysis of patterns [which make for] cohesive structuring" (p. 349).

"Topic structure" may be seen as a representation of a subject organized as a series of connected arguments. Waller acknowledges that graphic organizers are essential to mapping this structure. "Access structure," he says, is concerned with giving *visible form* to the "communicative goal" of this topic through pictures and typographic layout. In contemporary graphic design development processes Waller (1991) notes that, "many educational . . . texts are . . . designed as doublespreads, integrating words and pictures in a series of self-contained graphic arguments" (p. 354). Given the issue of "newer" versus "older" materials, it is somewhat ironic to hear that when texts are developed this way, "the topic frame of the school lesson is most suited to designing by spreads" (pp. 371–372).

Look Back: Access Through Architecture

Wixson stated that "unity and coherence" are the defining characteristics of "newer materials." The trend in "educational literature," she noted is to "deal with fewer bits of information." Ideally, four questions should motivate each stage of development: "What are the key concepts? What are the linkages? How are we going to pull them through? How do they recur from unit to chapter to lesson levels?" A product reflecting this process, she said, would be "a unit [which is] is not just a loosely related bunch of information."

In contrast to this semantic orientation, Waller (1991) suggested that a well designed *access structure* can give visible form to a topic making it coherent in visual terms. "Text features that are graphic" allow the reader to "perceptually apprehend . . . [what typically] must be cognitively apprehended. . . . Text features that are solely verbal . . . [are now made] explicit in graphic form" (p. 356). The Openers and the Program "architecture" detailed in the last chapter are quite obviously access structures. But together can they make "a loosely related bunch of information" coherent? They may, but only if the same "bunch of information" is looked at again in graphic terms. Several features suggest that the Program architecture is intentionally designed to emphasize the structural components of the running text. Two of the more "explicit" are the *Head* structure, and the *Scholar's Margin*.

The visible effect of such access structures should properly be viewed in progressive terms: as 8,000 pages of visible regularity; a uniform set of structures that appear on every page. In one sense this may be no different than imagining the same number of pages as simple text on white paper. Yet there is a distinct difference. On every page these features create regular perceivable patterns that conform to the topic structure of the text.

In a way it is almost inappropriate to take the *Head* structure out of context. Visually it is set with other layout elements: the double columns of the grid, the timelines of the page layout, the captions. Two complementary colors switch for

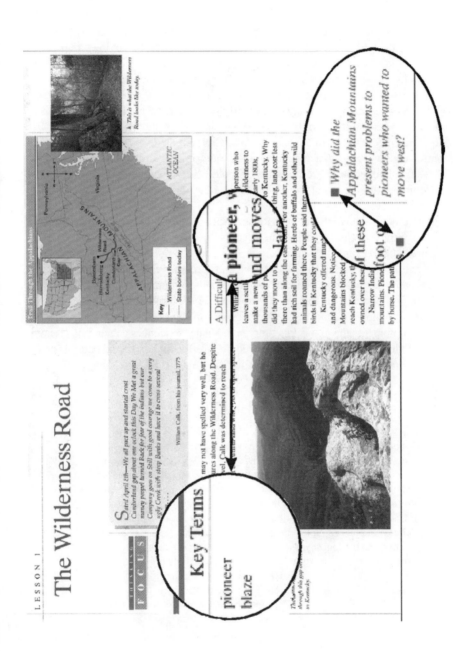

FIGURE 4.2. Scholar's Margin, Head Structure, The Wilderness Road, Grade 3. (See Figure 3.10)

chapter and lesson. Chapter *Heads* are in *red*, the Lesson *blue*. Paragraph titles in the Lessons are red. This color coded structure was another "navigation strategy" designed so the reader could locate his position in the text. Waller calls this graphic function "Look Back" (p. 356). Dan Rogers said, "We didn't want to end up with pages that look like solid text." The *Heads* kept "the text in relatively small pieces." Such chunking, as noted, was intended for "cinematic preview and review."

In the Scholar's Margin of the Lesson *Wilderness Road* there are two types of typographic "signaling" that are particularly relevant (Meyer, 1985, p. 76). The *Thinking Focus* question (in blue type) that appears at the top of the Scholar's Margin introduces the lesson. It acts as a "preview statement" focusing the reader's attention on *Key Terms* that appear below the question highlighted by blue bullets, and then embedded in the running text in bold black typeface (p. 77). There are also "pointer" questions that are linked to the Margin and the text by red squares (p. 77).

These diagraphic features provide an explicit perceptual structure (a sort of ongoing graphic organizer) which in effect is the more visible aspect of the Unit structure. The principle of "visual informativeness" can be examined further in the Openers. Considering the Openers is appropriate in light of Wixson's criticism, because textual links between each level in her estimation were weak. If the "architecture" serves as a "look back" structure for the topic, can the images in the Openers act as topical links also? The question of a possible visual "coherence" which complements the text is taken up next. Visual sequences can and do create their own kind of stable patterns. The structuring effect of perceptual patterns can best be explained by their theoretical affiliation with Gestalt psychology.

THE VISUAL PATTERN OF MEANING
AND THE PRINCIPLES OF GESTALT

> Gestalt theory was the first theory of perception which systematically opposed the 'bucket theory' of a passive registration of stimuli. It denied the possibility of an 'innocent eye.' . . . We cannot see any configuration neat as it were, because the tablet on which the senses write their messages has certain in-built properties. Far from leaving the arriving stimuli intact, it puts them into pre-arranged slots. There is observable bias in our perception for simple configurations, straight lines, circles and other simple orders and we will tend to see such regularities rather than random shapes in our encounter with the chaotic world outside. Just as scattered iron filings in a magnetic field order themselves into a *pattern* (my emphasis), so the nervous impulses reaching the visual cortex are subject to forces of attraction and repulsion.
> —E. H. Gombrich, *The Sense of Order* (1979)

How does one read a graphic argument? In the previous chapter Mulcahy and Samuels (1987) spoke of how children reading storybooks can construct meaning out of visual/verbal information layered on the page. Visuals like text create patterns of coherence that are discernable, yet the traceable structure is not of a semantic order as exemplified in a "considerate" text. In the concluding section of this chapter a sample of visuals from a unit is examined for the presence of this kind of structuration.

Graphic Argument as 3-D Lesson

Whereas Karen Wixson entered the project as the Thumbnail Process was concluding, Beverly Armento, the social studies specialist "was intimately involved" right from the start with the program's development, especially for Grades 1 to 3 working with the St. Louis office. Though Armento tended to agree with Wixson's criticism about the shortcomings of the development process, she viewed the product more from her subject area comparing it to social studies programs already in use. In that regard she saw the books as a special achievement. Despite her "frustration" with the process, she said, "we've come out . . . remarkably strong on many lessons." Whereas Wixson felt Armento shared "her concerns for the way information was presented with content," Armento herself viewed its presentation in terms that didn't necessarily correspond with the readerly ones Wixson used. Besides regarding the First Edition instructional design as "masterful," she held that these textbooks couldn't be judged as a standard "linear text," to which terms like textual "coherence" and "unity" readily apply. In her estimation this product was "real different." Instead of the basic hierarchical outline where exposition was set up as definition and example, and social studies content was cast in "straight narration," more often than not, a great many of the designed lessons achieved, she said, a "3-D" effect.

To illustrate this point she commented on a lesson found in the third grade book, *An Early Prairie Town*, which describes the growth of Abilene, Kansas as a westward link for the railroads and the Chisholm Trail. The presentation, she said, "blends together . . . different kinds of (visual) data along with the text . . . to illustrate the major points . . . and builds almost a 3-D lesson." In addition, the text is also a "nice blend of poetry and analysis." The lesson opens with the song, "The Old Chisholm Trail," and concludes with a graph plotting the rise and decline of the town by the number of cattle driven from Texas to Abilene. Such a "blend between formal and metaphoric" (or visual/verbal) text segments was characteristic of "almost every lesson."

The movement from two to three dimensions reflects a profound shift in instructional design strategy. It is a move away from the "semantic structures" ordering a "considerate" *text*book. This clearly linked hierarchy of propositional units and lessons which Wixson advocated is replaced by a series of "heterarchical units" (i.e., graphic arguments) which are structured more like an "electronic text" (Reinking, 1992, p. 18). Duchastel (1986) characterizes this different type of organization as a "format structure." In principle it is analogous to Waller's "access structure." The explicit difference in these two types is that the structural principles of the latter are of a pictorial orientation. Simply put, it is that change from two to three dimensions described by Armento. What may be less apparent is how a "format structure" creates its own type of coherence. In this shift in emphasis from the semantic form of meaning to the visual pattern of meaning, a typical textbook lesson also becomes a series of visual fields which can be read pictorially. This visual turn can be understood in terms of basic gestalt principles.

Putting Together the 3-D Lesson

Joe Godlewski was emphatic in his insistence that the "key" to viewing any series of spreads forming a lesson meant that "all elements were relational to others." Implicit in Godlewski's words are the principles of perceptual organization derived from Gestalt psychology. Consideration of some of the more essential gestalt principles can contribute in part to an understanding of how the visual and verbal elements in a typical lesson were meant to "blend" together forming configurations and patterns contributing to a coherent text. Selections from the Unit in which the Lesson on Abilene, Kansas and the Chisholm Trail appears can demonstrate how visual/verbal structures create gestaltic patterns perceptually associated with the unit theme. A review of basic gestalt terminology as it applies to the selections taken from Unit 3, Grade 3, provides the necessary context to begin discussion of these examples.

On Gestalt

As an art historian, Ernst Gombrich properly situates gestalt theory in context of the constructive process of perception which discerns in visible form patterns of meaning. Adding to Gombrich's historical passage opening this section, Stephen Palmer (1992) noted that the founders of the movement, "Max Wertheimer, Kurt Koffka, and Wolfgang Kohler succeeded in overturning" the ruling assumptions of the day. "In place of atomism ["the bucket theory"] they advocated *holism*: the idea that a perceptual whole is different from—and not reducible to—the sum of its parts. [And], in place of associationism, they offered the concept of *organization*: the notion that visual experience is inherently structured by the nature of the stimulus as it interacts with the visual nervous system" (p. 40).

According to Edwin Boring (1957), the term "gestalt" loosely translated into colloquial English "means . . . good form" (p. 588). Gestalt psychology can be mainly characterized by its investigation of the perceptual processes which structure visual forms (gestalten). "Gestalt psychology," Boring states, "deals with wholes . . . and the emergent . . . properties of those parts which constitute that whole" (p. 588). The relationship of part to whole is a basic characteristic of pictures. Pictures are typically regarded as "perceptual fields" (pp. 591–611). Gestalt principles may be useful for re-conceptualizing textual coherence in visual/verbal terms.

Gestalt and Analytic Seeing

In principle, Karen Wixson's critical evaluation of the Unit design of the Program rests on the well articulated position concerning a "considerate" text. However, Ligature's visual/verbal structures can only be understood by considering how text is organized as a "format structure." One type of informational text designed with a "format structure" that has direct connection to visual/verbal structures is a training manual with diagrams, illustrations, and callouts; an influence noted in the previous chapter (Kerr, 1986a, p. 373). Duchastel (1986) argues that textbooks can be structured either way: semantically or formally (pp. 403–409). The design of a "format" structure embeds the text in a visible structure. Wittig noted this emphasis when characterizing the function of the *Heads* for a "cinematic preview and review." In similar terms Fredette (1994) states that the act of reading involves the analysis of a visual/verbal text surface to "perceive its essential structure" (p. 252). To make sense of this "structure" requires that the reader perceive "the interrelatedness of parts and wholes" (p. 253). This analytic process "of perceptually organizing and reorganizing the given information," Fredette says, is the means "to find the key to its coherence" (p. 253). Citing Howard Gardner (1982), she describes a skill that involves being able to

> look beyond the dominant figure or gestalt, to pay attention, instead, to the fine details or microstructure which cut across figure and ground. The development of this skill builds upon the natural tendency to organize what we look at into patterns by perceptually grouping parts "to make sense" of what we see. This pattern-seeking effort is the perceptual tension which craves resolution. Resolution comes when meaning can be assigned to what is seen. (p. 253)

In the act of reading a visual/verbal text, Joe Godlewski talked about students being able to "scan" the magazine style format. This type of scanning is quite similar to the process of "analytic seeing," which Fredette describes. Picture reading is informed by a number of basic gestalt principles that may be useful in this re-conceptualization of textual coherence. Sterns and Robinson (1994) state that, gestalt "psychologists have identified several principles which are used in organizing stimuli. These include simplicity and pattern, proximity and similarity, figure and ground, closure and good form, and perceptual constancy [or continuity]" (p. 39). Of these, four are relevant for this analysis of the perceptual patterns structuring the Openers:

> *Figure/Ground* is the perceptual ability to distinguish between a foreground object and its background.
>
> *Proximity* is the perceptual tendency to group together those things that are located close to one another.

Similarity is the perceptual tendency to group elements because they seem to be alike in shape, color, size, sound, and so forth.

Continuity (or Perceptual Constancy) is the tendency to extend any suggested continuing pattern along the direction previously established, or to persist in perceiving something after the . . . event has changed.

(Adapted from Sterns & Robinson, 1994, pp. 40–41 and Solso, 1994, pp. 87–99)

Patterns of Visual Coherence

The selection of examples from Unit 3, *Settling the Land*, in the third-grade text is also where the lesson on the Chisholm Trail appears, which Armento described as a 3-D lesson. The main topic of the third-grade text mixes geography with history in an overview of the North American continent which considers its past and present inhabitants. The topic is derived from the California Framework which states, "third graders . . . can begin to think about continuity and change in their locality and nation . . . by exploring . . . [and making] contact with times past, and with people whose activities have left their mark on the land" (California State Department of Education, 1988, p. 40). The opening Unit, *Listen to the Land*, sets the stage, considering the geography of North America. This nicely segues to a unit on *The Land and the First Americans*. After considering the original inhabitants, it is followed by the Unit *Settling the Land*. The book concludes with a unit on the United States, *The Land Today*.

The analysis (or analytic seeing) of the two "perceptual groups" of visuals from Unit 3 is outlined in Fig. 4.3. The first set is a series of Openers and the second a sequence of Maps. Both can be viewed as an "access structure" that visually informs the reader/viewer about the theme (or topic structure) of the Unit. In the sequences of Openers and Maps that follow, the "pictorial constituents" that make up these visuals can be said to form a series of visual patterns (perceptual groups) that can be viewed as creating "strong associations" with the topic (Bower, 1972, p. 86). These "constituents" form patterns according to the four gestalt principles of figure/ground, spatial proximity, similarity, and continuity.

Gestalt Pattern and Strong Association

Bower (1972) argues that the "spatial relations" of such gestaltic patterns can be viewed as "the basic relational predicates of a picture grammar" (p. 86). Well-designed pictures and other forms of visual information inherently tend to "good form" and are perceived as coherent. According to Bower, a "strong" pattern is evident when "the figural component is *a constituent of* the other, or is *a continuation of* the other, or is *an integral surface of* the other, or is *as part-to-whole* with the other" (p. 86).

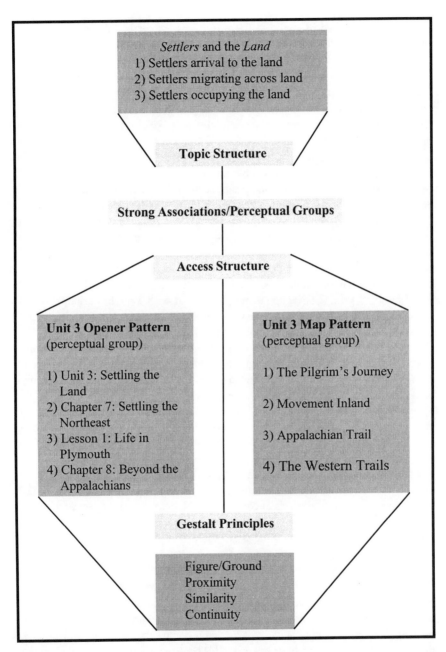

FIGURE 4.3. The Visual/Verbal Pattern of Association in Unit 3 Openers and Maps.

Though couched in slightly different terms, Bower is only referring to the four gestalt principles already outlined. Expressions like, "a constituent of, . . . or is a continuation of" refer to proximity, similarity, and more obviously good continuity. Expressions like, "an integral surface of," or "as part to whole" refer to the principle of figure/ground. Basically, all of this terminology emphasizes that shapes can only be seen in relation to each other. In gestalt terms the tendency to "good form" creates "strong associations," or relationships of close correspondence that are perceptible. If these relationships recur from picture to picture a visible pattern is established. When such patterns are perceiveable in a sequence of pictures, the relationships strengthen not only the internal composition of the separate picture but the entire group. If these contiguous visual relationships are also in a sense contiguous with the topic, then a type of coherence can be said to occur.

That seems to be the case with the first "perceptual group" of Openers. It should be stressed that the strength of these patterns is evident when viewed in sequence. Though this is a selective sample of only four Openers from Unit 3, which has a total of nine (one for the Unit, two for the Chapters, and six Lessons), it nevertheless represents the basic gestalt tendency of all the visuals in this Unit. The following group shows the same pattern but with a slight variation. When analyzed together the total sequence with variations forms a visual rhythm. These variations strengthen the association by their slight difference.

In the first and last examples of the Openers (Fig. 4.4), the "figural components" of the primary source photographs can be said to be "strongly associated." Their figure/ground elements can be analyzed into similar shapes that are proximately composed. *Settling the Land*, the Unit Opener, shows the Speese family of Nebraska posed in front of their sod house with a horse in the background. *Beyond the Appalachians*, the Chapter Opener, shows settler teachers and pupils standing in front of their schoolhouse in Kansas, also with a horse in the background. The "constituent" elements of the photographs are nearly identical and form a "continuous integral surface." In outline the shapes of both Openers are nearly isomorphic, similar in their basic shape pattern (Fig. 4.5). Both depict settlers (standing and sitting), the land (the plains of Nebraska and Kansas), their houses and horses.

In the second and third examples of the sequence (Fig. 4.6) similar figure/ground elements form strong visual associations. In the Chapter 7 Opener, *Settling the Northeast*, the painting, *Thanksgiving with the Indians*, is "strongly associated" with elements in Lesson 1, *Life in Plymouth*. The painting *Thanksgiving with the Indians* consists of figure/ground elements similar to *Life in Plymouth*: groups of Indians and groups of Pilgrims. In figure/ground terms, the elements can be read as positive shapes on a negative ground. These shapes are: Pilgrim settlers under trees looking at native Americans being served by Pilgrim women at the first Thanksgiving sitting on the ground. The visual field can be broken up into three areas: foreground, middle ground (land), and background (sky). Although the figural constituents are not exact, similar elements of land, sky, Pilgrims, and Indians appear in each picture. In *Life in Plymouth*, the painting depicts the Pil-

FIGURE 4.4. Unit 3 Openers, Settling the Land, and Beyond the Appalachians, Grade 3.

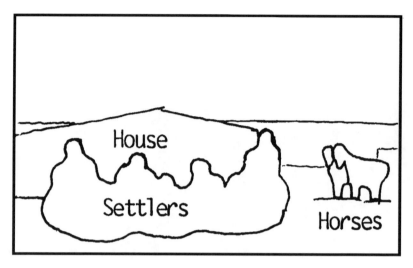

Settlers, House, Horses: Figure(s)

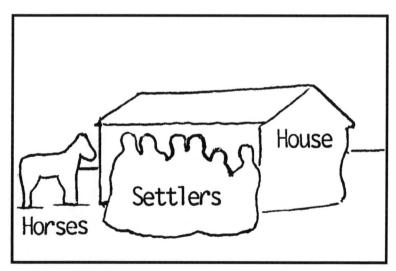

Settlers, House, Horses: Figure(s)

FIGURE 4.5. Figure/Ground Outline of Settling the Land and Beyond the Appa-lachians, Unit 3, Grade 3.

FIGURE 4.6. Unit 3 Openers, Settling the Northeast and Life in Plymouth, Grade 3. *Corne's Landing*, courtesy of the Pilgrim Society, Plymouth, Massachusetts.

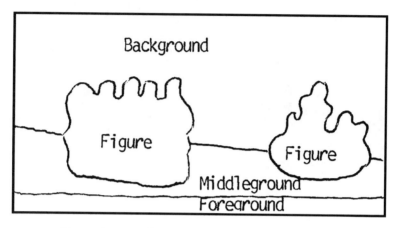

Settlers & Indians: Figure
Land & Sky: Ground

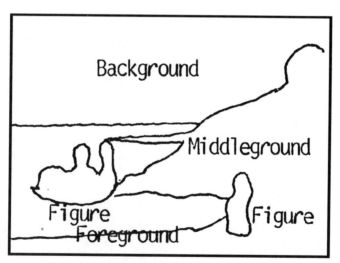

Settlers & Indians: Figure
Land & Sky: Ground

FIGURE 4.7. Figure/Ground Outline of Settling the Northeast and Life in Plymouth, Unit 3, Grade 3.

grims' first landing. Again, similar elements of land, sky, settlers, and Indians can be seen, but with a variation: the fore and middle ground is land and water.

Continuity in postlinear terms is this principle of visual coherence. It poses the question whether it can be considered equivalent to its textual counterpart. According to Rob Wittig, the Openers were designed to appear like a sequence of "establishing shots" in a film. The analogy is important. Unit 3 can be viewed in cinematic terms. The sequence of Openers can be looked at as a "static movie" (Trachtenberg, 1989, p. 259). These visual frames have the same "basic relational predicates." Together they form a "strong" structural pattern which complements the topic structure at each frame in the sequence. Just as a sequence of shots in a film visually constructs the verbal narrative in a scene, from unit to chapter to lesson the pattern of coherence visible in these Openers supports the topic structure of the text.

As the eye moves from the 3-D space of photographs and illustration to the two-dimensional plane of locator maps, patterns of similarity become easier to trace because the amount of information is reduced from the more complex relationships of form and content found in pictures, to the simpler formal conventions of line, shape, color, and pattern. "Land" does not have the spatial depth of a picture, but instead is represented by the flat surface of a map. The early United States appears simply as a larger shape broken up into adjacent smaller shapes representing the early eastern colonies and states, with the Atlantic Ocean as a border. In the Map sequence shown (Fig 4.8) four maps form a consistent visual pattern which supports the subtopic of settlers moving across the land. This westward progression in time and space is represented as a directional line, a **Y** shaped vector.

The Pilgrims' Journey	(p. 117)	
		(4 pages)
Movement Inland	(p. 122)	
		(12 pages)
Trail Through the Appalachians	(p. 135)	
		(13 pages)
The Western Trails	(p. 149)	

Because all these maps have the same directional line they not only form a visual pattern, but can also be conceived of as a loosely structured mnemonic device. In the *Pilgrims' Journey* this directional line moves across the Atlantic Ocean. In the maps that follow the same **Y** shaped path of settler movement progresses west to California and Oregon (*The Western Trails*). In gestalt terms this repetition reflects continuity and similarity. The perceptual group forms a consistent visual pattern from lesson to lesson of the unit, which reflected a visual structure consistent with the sequence of the verbal text. Thematically the **Y** can symbolically represent the settlers' movement of westward expansion. This pattern orchestrates the unit theme through this visual motif.

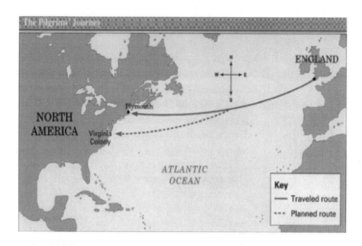

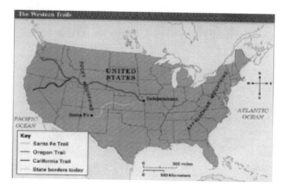

FIGURE 4.8. Underlying **Y** Schema of Unit 3 Maps (reflect gestalt principles of similarity and continuity).

Such a visual pattern could be used as a cognitive "scaffold," but the question for a designer is whether a reader/viewer will notice it. I have noted the number of pages between each map in the sequence. Is the repetition "strong" enough if it only appears 5 times in 39 pages? How many times must this **Y** shaped line repeat before it becomes memorable (a visual schema), such that it links cognitively to the unit theme of settler movement? These are basic design questions that should be considered when visual forms are used to structure verbal content. Such questions are of even greater importance in the design of hypertext structures where overall visual patterns need to be conceptualized across a series, array, or configuration of links, and between and within, multiple screens of windowed and layered information. These design questions are considered in Chapter 7. Repetition of similarly shaped elements is a standard composition device used to organize graphic space. As "format" or "access" structures the architecture and the Openers regularly employ it. Such repetition reflects the perceptual principles of *proximity, similarity,* and *continuity* and contributes to visual coherence. Potentially such "strong associations" may affect learning and comprehension.

ON THE MYTH OF COHERENCE AND THE CONSIDERATE TEXT

In determining considerate text structures Robert Calfee and Marilyn Chambliss (1987) note that Anderson and Armbruster have a simple test. They ask that we begin with "the text as written . . . and apply a single criterion: Can the text be read and understood with a minimum of effort?" If the answer is "yes," then the text is a considerate one. Inconsiderate texts, they say, "cause comprehension problems for readers primarily because of organizational deficiencies" (p. 358).

Ligature's goal of a "beautiful book," according to Joe Godlewksi, would hopefully produce a visual presentation that would "make children be able to, through the association of images, walk away with an impression or understanding that is larger than the sum of the parts of the presentation." Implicit in this statement is the notion that visual images can be ordered into structures, which in turn form their own kind of cohesive patterns that cognitively function by much different rules than those required for verbal texts.

Yet Godlewski was the first to admit that the visual structuring of material was largely by rules that were untested. In grappling with the design problems encountered with the "modeling" of the Scholar's Margins, he said

> There's just so little on how people perceive and respond to these things.
> . . . Ultimately, there was nothing scientific to it. It became just a case
> of preference and inclination. But we had people of all different inter-
> ests and perspectives saying, "Well, I think this architecture works."
> Based on what we're trying to do the consensus was: This is a pretty
> considerate way to structure the material.

On this point Waller and Godlewski seem to be in agreement. The "issue," Waller (1991) stated,

> is how the appearance of printed material affects not just how much is understood, or how fast, but what is understood from it. . . . Whereas psychologists can experiment with sentence comprehension secure in the knowledge that the concepts such as "sentence" and "verb" will generally be understood (if not agreed upon by all linguistic scientists), no such agreement exists about variations in page layouts. (p. 346)

For Karen Wixson the "issue" was a question of having the same sense of certainty over the way visual/verbal page layouts were supposed to work, which meant for her "evidence on the effect." As Waller suggested earlier (quite in agreement with Wixson), such questions are a matter for future research, though he also notes, they are again of serious interest because electronic screen display is becoming as common as the printed textbook.

The only answer then to Anderson and Armbruster's question is *who* can answer *yes*. In that sense, "coherence," like the "beautiful book," is in the eye of the beholder; or in Wixson's, the reader. Beverly Armento commented that in sampling student reactions to the visual/verbal presentation she found that proficient readers had no trouble with it, but poor readers did. It was critical, she said, that they have more hard data on this. Apart from the question of how such studies could proceed, the purpose of this chapter is to consider the theoretical issues, with which future studies of visual/verbal display, electronic or otherwise, will have to grapple. Though Wixson felt such questions needed to be addressed simultaneously, to do so requires a definite shift in theoretical focus away from the textual to the perceptual. A framework of analysis for considerate visual/verbal text structure requires a dual but integrated focus. Attention must be paid to those perceptible aspects of the page which are visually coherent, yet also complement and enhance the coherence of verbal text.

A larger point, made by Waller (1991) in his study of typographic research, is the basic opposition to such research by the field of "mainstream linguistics" (p. 346). In noting this "exclusion" by language specialists, he is also pointing to their presumption that language "is cognitively ideal" for learning (p. 354). In Chapter 5 the visual thinking behind the development of the Visual Learning strand is examined, especially the alternate learning styles that are "cognitively ideal" for a visual frame of mind. In the program Scope and Sequence this strand involves the acquisition of skills to critically view, interpret, and evaluate various types of visual information. The visualization of social studies instruction is considered next.

CHAPTER
5

A Different Model of Reading

Children live in an increasingly complex and highly visual society. With little or no formal instruction they learn to interpret traffic signals, brand logo-types, directional arrows, and other signs and symbols of our modern world. Some children spend many hours with visual media such as television, videos, and computers. The SS21 program recognizes that some children are more receptive to information presented in a visual format and that all students need training in visual learning skills so that they can process visual information critically. The SS21 visual learning program is both explicit and implicit. Selected visual learning skills are explicitly taught along with learning skills at every grade level, and are integrated into the overall comprehensive scope and sequence program.

—SS21 (1989, p. 25)

Kids live in a very fast world with all kinds of layering of images. . . . Things are very complex. But the whole experience of Nintendo and those kind of things show that kids can handle it. People in general can handle a lot more complexity than you ever give them credit for.

—Rob Wittig (1992)

Inevitably, the construction of a "beautiful book" requires more than just a native aesthetic sense to enter and comprehend its 3-D lessons. When visual information is placed on a "parallel track" with verbal text, and is considered like this text as content, then the question becomes how is this visual information taught? The design of the Teacher Edition Margins was meant to provide a set of instructional tools at the disposal of the teacher. With the wealth of visual information set in a purposeful frame they could then carry out instruction through this visual mode. The question engaged throughout this chapter is: "Just how successful was Ligature in designing for Visual Learning as it is called in the program Scope and Sequence?

A large part of Chapter 4 was taken up with considering whether the design of the highly visible graphic "access structures" (or in the art director's words: "architecture") of the Pupil Edition text exemplified a different kind of "coherence" than that found in the traditional linear format textbook. Suggesting, as was the case, that "coherence" might be reconceived in terms of the visual and graphical patterns structuring the verbal text, entails serious rethinking of what constitutes the act of reading. A visual/verbal text structure perhaps requires a more holistic kind of reading, one that combines looking at the page in pictorial as well as textual terms. If theoretically there may be much at stake (the respective views of the participants seem to indicate that), instructionally there is perhaps far more.

As was previously shown, the structural features of textual coherence, self-evident in a "considerate" text, are strongly supported by research in the field of reading instruction. Wittig points to this fact: "There is a highly developed culture within the education world of talking about reading and how it [the act of reading] goes on. And compared to that a very minimally developed language about how visuals work." Karen Wixson, coming from this "culture," was hardly versed in this other "language." One consequence was her resistance to the imposition visual/verbal design places upon textual coherence. Considering the limitations of this view, an attempt was made not so much to re-conceive the terms of textual coherence, but to show how the "language of visuals" can possibly work in gestalt terms to form structural patterns which act in correspondence with the textual content. The terms that were sketched would seem to closely correspond to the views of the Ligature designers.

However, these patterns are not necessarily evident, nor can it be said whether they actually support in any degree the structures of a "considerate" text. Depending on the resonance of the images and the strength and coherence of the pattern, they may serve to shape and act as a "cognitive structure" which might enhance reader retention. This is a question that remains speculative, a matter that can be tested under narrowly defined circumstances in a classroom setting (Jonassen & Grabowski, 1987; Shavelson, 1985; Tharp & Gallimore, 1988). The visuals were certainly meant to be so "compelling" that they would engage the reader and hold their attention, acting as a visual "step" into the text. Yet, this in itself is another hypothetical area largely untouched by research, which looks into the affective dimension of reader response, whose attention to the text is motivated by visuals (Peeck, 1987, p. 144). It is evident too, this chapter shows, that the Ligature designers had certain types of readers in mind. They assumed that "kids can handle it." They designed page spreads which, although readable in a straight linear fashion, were "consciously built" for a type of "cinematic viewing" (as described by Wittig), or a kind of "scanning," which Godlewski said was the way the magazine-like format should be approached.

In fact the entire Visual Learning strand seems to rest on the presumption that Visual culture is so pervasive that children informally pick up these skills. As the introductory quote from the SS21 document states, the strand was meant to formalize an ability, which was normally acquired simply by being a visual consumer. Acculturation by watching, it seemed to suggest, is the normal course of spectatorship. Given this observation, the major question engaged in this chapter is: Just how does the Visual Learning strand formalize these skills through the instructional support found in the Margins? Do the Teacher Edition Margins provide the kind of instructional tools to read and decipher (scan) this sophisticated visual/verbal design, so that the student comes away with an "impression greater than the sum of its parts?"

The T.E. *Margins* are intended to link with these "access structures" through a series of instructional scripts and guidelines which the teacher can choose to follow or not. They serve as a kind of instructional metatext bordering the Pupil Edition. There are a number of instructional features provided for the teacher in these Margins, reflecting different skill strands of the Scope and Sequence (e.g., Critical Thinking, Study Skills, Map and Globe Skills). However, the main focus in this chapter is on the Visual Learning Strategies, though the connection between it and other features is drawn to the extent that they complement the objectives of these strategies.

In a sense the "dialogue" of the Thumbnail Process is carried on in the Visual Learning strand of the program. Instructionally the dialogue of the team is analogous to the dialogue of teacher and student engaged with the visual/verbal text. But to what extent is it a dialogue? What kind of instruction is the design of the Margins suited for? Is the Visual Learning component more geared for typical "direct instruction" (a recitation tool), or for a more opened-ended "constructive" type of inquiry? Another question is whether the instructional support is neutral enough so that it can easily be adapted to fit the style of the teacher? Finally, if visuals are *content* to be learned, how is it to be assessed? This series of questions forms the topical agenda explored in this chapter.

In the opening section, Ligature's formative thinking behind the design approach taken with the Visual Learning strand is discussed. In the following section, the design of the instructional sequence is analyzed step by step, with discussion of how the Visual Learning strategies follow these steps and are linked with the Openers and the Lesson. The paramount question concerning these steps is with the kind of instruction these strategies tend to support. In the concluding section the question of assessment and the Visual Learning strand is considered by evaluating the design of the Chapter Review sections in relation to the material covered in the Visual Learning exercises appearing in the instructional sequence.

FORMATIVE THINKING IN THE DEVELOPMENT OF THE VISUAL LEARNING STRAND

Even early in the development process there seems to be a realization that the inclusion of a Visual Learning strand calls for a "different model of reading." This is evident in the running notes of Dan Rogers, Senior Editor, which were taken at an early meeting where the agenda concerned conceptualization of the strand (see

Fig. 5.1). Helen Chandra, an in-house editor who had the responsibility of writing the program Scope and Sequence in which all the skill strands appear, recalls that "there was genuine staff interest in doing it. . . . What we have now didn't suddenly come about. It was a slow process." During the early stages of the Social Studies project, she said, "we used to have informal voluntary lunch meetings for staff members," which were used as consciousness raising sessions "to discuss social studies issues." At one of these lunches the "subject was visual learning." Both Rob Wittig and Frank Loose were present. "We just had a very productive meeting that turned us all on, and none of the hierarchy was present. And, we decided [since] we're hearing about this Visual Learning, let's do it!"

According to Frank Loose, the "development" of the SS21 program was really about advancing the cause of "visual learning." Stuart Murphy remarked that in the "evolutionary process" of development, "visual literacy" always figured prominently. "We were very concerned about it. Basically in our decision making what we wanted to do was to help teachers create a more literate citizenry using the Program. That means that there was a high degree of responsibility for kids learning how to get better at gaining information from visual presentations."

He further noted that social studies programs always have "all sorts of skills strands." Although the use and understanding of maps, charts, diagrams, and graphs in social studies textbooks implicitly suggests the necessity of basic visual learning skills, he felt that the approach to it in existing programs has usually been "superficial." Because it was his goal to set a "new standard," he "believed there is a great deal of responsibility on the part of publishers to provide materials [which] . . . emphasize this skill strand, and [similarly for] teachers to teach those visual learning skills."

But whereas, "some of these things like graphs and charts would always be in textbooks," others "had never been attempted before," Helen Chandra said. Using the California Framework as a "model" was only so helpful. Chandra notes, "Although observation was stressed in the Framework," as it is in the actual strand, it did not have skills that required "understanding and using symbols." Nor did it have, she said, "interpreting and responding to different kinds of illustrative materials," which are among the five skills included in the strand. Echoing Murphy's sentiment, Chandra said, "We thought that if we wanted to teach content through illustrations, fine art, and photographs, then we needed to give students (and teachers) the skills to do that."

Though all children should learn such skills, two special groups of students figured predominently in their plans. Following Howard Gardner's theory of multiple intelligences, Murphy observed that children with "different learning styles," particularly "visual learners," are faced with "materials" in the classroom which are "created more for people who receive information in a verbal fashion." Of those multiple "frames of intelligence," he noted, "our public school system really only rewards three or four." He believed "the Social Studies Program is an exem-

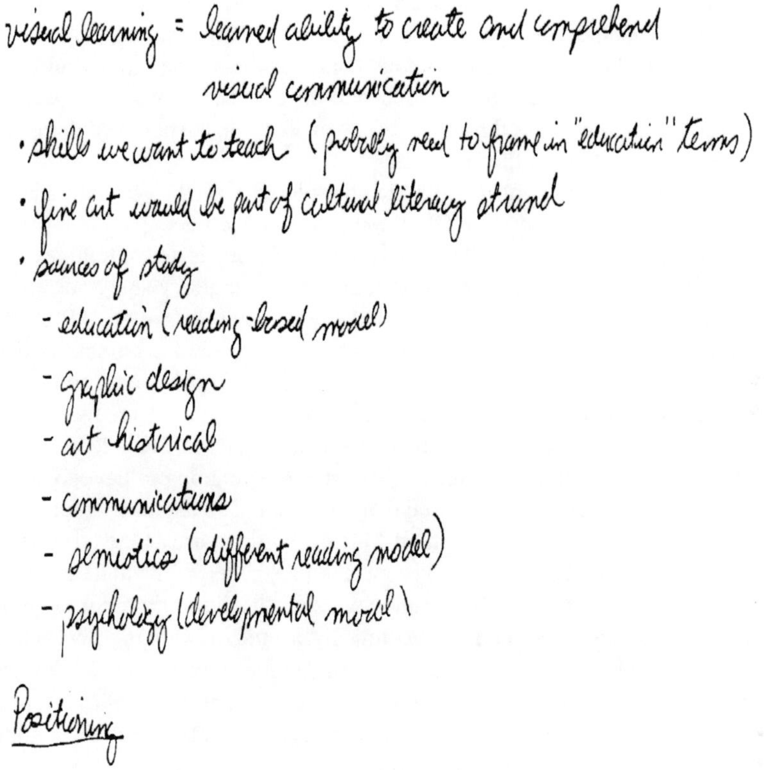

visual learning = learned ability to create and comprehend
visual communication
- skills we want to teach (probably need to frame in "education" terms)
- fine art would be part of cultural literacy strand
- sources of study
  - education (reading-based model)
  - graphic design
  - art historical
  - communications
  - semiotics (different reading model)
  - psychology (developmental model)

Positioning

FIGURE 5.1. Meeting Notes, Dan Rogers, Senior Editor.

plar in addressing that kind of thing." In this respect, though the program was intentionally designed to acknowledge the visual learner, Murphy still believed the presentation was more inclusive. "One kid gets it one way. One kid gets it another. Some kids get it even more so, because they're in both."

The design of visual/verbal access structures also had a more strategic group in mind. In assessing the need for a new social studies program nationally, especially for the state of California, children of limited English proficiency (LEP) were viewed as another group that might benefit. Murphy assumed that the visual component of the textbook could provide "a back way" into reading English words and understanding concepts. "There has always been this equity of access concern," he said. Consequently, "how can we give those kids . . . the same information that kids who speak English get, and at the same time help them [both] become more proficient in English." He believed visual information held the key. "It's very typical . . . for them to learn the words that are associated with [the visual], to understand the caption." So, he felt basic language acquisition could occur in reverse: "instead of reading about it, understanding the concept and [then] seeing the visual," one could be introduced to the concept through the visual and begin to articulate the words through subsequent caption. He believed there was a "great deal of potential" in this approach.

Advancing a textbook program which premiered Visual Learning meant expanding the scope of literacy. Joe Godlewski stated unequivocally: "Our premise was that students can and do read visuals, and that literacy is tied to both presentational and discursive processing of information." The parallel visual track added a more "concrete" level of representation to the text (Levin & Mayer, 1993, p. 98). More importantly, the visual stimulus was meant to "engage and attract" students, not "distract" them, Godlewski said. "The more that text represents context and [shows them a] time and place giving them a [visual] reference, the more we felt they would be able to process what the text was telling them," he added.

Rob Wittig felt that "terms like Visual Literacy are going to have to be considered transitional terms." He stressed that it was not at all useful to "pretend that it's just another kind of reading." Stuart Murphy avoided use of the term for different reasons. Acknowledging that he chose to use the term Visual Learning (instead of visual literacy) for the Scope and Sequence, he did so more for pragmatic reasons. By so doing he avoided the theoretical "argument" with those who found the combination of the mere words "visual with literacy objectionable." Ultimately he felt it was not important. "I purposely vacillate back and forth [between use of the two terms], because frankly I don't care." His "issue" was simply that children "learn how to . . . observe [visual] information more effectively."

MULTIPLE INTELLIGENCES AND VISUAL LEARNING

In the discussion so far the question of what constitutes "literacy" already calls for clarification because it bears upon how Ligature's thinking determined the final form of the instructional Margins. If "visual literacy" is a "transitional term" does the Visual Learning strand in its actual conception and design move beyond more conventional instructional modes to innovatively teach "another kind of reading?" Or does it serve to complement more basic literacy skills, like text comprehension and learner feedback in the form of question/answer recitation? These questions take on crucial importance as the chapter progresses.

First of all, the comments by Godlewski on "literacy" and Murphy's on Gardner are related. When Godlewksi states that "literacy is tied to both *presentational* and *discursive* processing of information," he is making a not so obvious reference to Suzanne Langer (1957), whose work is a precursor to Nelson Goodman's theory of symbol systems (pp. 93–96). Howard Gardner's (1993) research on multiple intelligence is based on Goodman's theory (p. 135). This is an important connection to make. Langer and Goodman's philosophical work has "challenged the widespread notion that linguistic and logical symbol systems had priority over other expressive and communicative systems" (Gardner, 1993, p. 135). In a profound sense the multiple perspective seems to level the cognitive playing field, because it does not privilege one mode over another, a perspective that quite naturally aligns with the notion of different learning styles. Indirectly then, Godlewski's comment provides the fundamental cue directing us to the theoretical basis on which visual/verbal design rests. How secure is this ground?

Robert Sternberg (1990), another cognitive psychologist of importance, views Gardner's theory of "multiple intelligences" as less a theory and more a critique of "Western culture," which traditionally has not looked upon these "abilities" as "intelligences" at all, but instead as "talents." However, such a critique would certainly have its appeal to artists and graphic designers, simply because it "places on equal footing" abilities like spatial and bodily-kinesthetic intelligence (domains usually in the province of the artistically talented), which are not "conventionally viewed as intelligence" (p. 266). For example, Stuart Murphy's comment about the lack of any real priority in the curriculum to teach to or reward the visual learner, almost shares word for word a common critical view held by visual artists, notably Betty Edwards (1979), who espouses instructional techniques for right-brain, or visual learners. Edwards reenters this discussion at another level in Chapter 7.

Sternberg's (1990) criticism goes further. There is nothing "specific" about Gardner's theory. He equivocates on the number of intelligences there are. Usually he "lists" seven, other times he has "suggested" there may be more. Though each is named and listed, it is never made "clear what exactly is involved in them or what their boundaries are" (pp. 266–267). Because these "underlying processes" remain unclear and are not "specified," the kind of "intelligences" Gardner is talking about are difficult to assess (Sternberg, 1988, pp. 41–42; 1990, pp. 267 & 289).

However, although Sternberg (1990) regards "Gardner's theory as overinclusive and too vague," he still believes that it "represent[s] a new contribution in terms of synthesizing metaphors for understanding the mind" (p. 268). Such "metaphors" are useful because they "generate a series of questions about intelligence, which the theories and research seek to address" (p. 4). Because this is a textbook designed by highly artistic people, the idea of "multiple intelligences" can be looked upon as providing a powerful metaphor which connects with their background and experience. Indirectly it may have provided a justification for the necessity of visual learning, as well as another theoretical basis for considering images as content. Yet, it perhaps offers only that: a metaphor, nothing systemic or theoretically precise which might have allowed them to construct a conceptual framework to articulate the terms of a "transitional" literacy.

Rob Wittig emphasized the eclectic "approach" which guided their research in conceptualizing the strand. Stressing that because "the culture of visual study in the education world [is] tiny [compared to reading], a lot of writing and criticism needs to be done. People have to invent some terms. What we found when we were studying visual literacy for our Scope and Sequence, is that you have to look for fragments of those studies in different realms, . . . in education, art history. But the tough thing is you can't just apply the study of reading to this. It's a different study altogether."

Whereas the theory for "multiple intelligences" reflects an emergent discipline that seems to have provided an inspirational metaphor that rationalizes the need for visual learning, Murphy's comments on "learning styles" for visual or LEP learners are based on more firmly established precedence. Research supporting different cognitive styles has been underway for several decades. This area of study that distinguishes visual and verbal learners is called "field dependence/ independence." According to Grabowski and Schroeder (1994), "FD/I describes the degree to which a learner's perception or comprehension of information is affected by the surrounding perceptual or contextual field. . . . When field dependents interact with stimuli, they find it difficult to locate information they are seeking because other information tends to mask what they are looking for. Field independents, on the other hand, find it easier to . . . recognize and select the important information from its surrounding field" (p. 3). The connection of FD/I to the perceptual processes involved in viewing and comprehending pictures suggested here should be fairly apparent, especially after the discussion in the last chapter concerning the sequence of "gestaltic" patterns noted in the Unit and Chapter Openers.

On the basis of FD/I research Kirby, Moore, and Schofield (1988) developed an instrument to test for typical characteristics of visual and verbal learners. Their findings demonstrate that, "visual learners" tend to be "field independent." Therefore, they process information in a "simultaneous, . . . holistic" manner. Visual learning is "gestaltic" in orientation. In contrast, verbal learners tend to be more "analytic," processing information "successively" in a linear and logical fashion (p. 182). Generally the average learner has some skill in both. Grabowski and Schroeder (1994) view the style difference in "simpler" terms, one of "preference to learn via words and pictures." Like Stuart Murphy they note that "some students are equally comfortable using either visual or verbal information for learning" (p. 10). Kirby et al.'s (1988) distinction between "simultaneous" and "successive" processing is important because it underscores Wittig's point about the fundamental difference between "reading" words and looking at pictures. Whatever visual learning is, it is not about "literacy" per se. Yet this becomes something of a paradox, considering Murphy's position to assist limited English students through visuals.

The Professional Handbook in the Teacher's Edition should bear cursory examination as there is a section on LEP instructional strategies. In it the Visual

Learning strategies are highlighted as a "unique" instructional bridge for the limited English student. Unlike words, images of things are more universally recognizable. The Handbook states that:

> No matter what their spoken language, all students have basically the same visual language. Thus the unique Visual Learning strand and prominent instructional visuals throughout the program provide a channel of access for LEP students. . . . Every unit and lesson has many LEP-appropriate features built in. . . . These features include the following: LEP Unit Activities, Access Strategies, Access Activities, Graphic Overviews, Visual Learning Strategies. (p. T32)

These LEP unit activities together with the other instructional features, including the visual learning strategy, direct the student to the verbal meaning of the text. Here, Visual Learning strategies can be adapted to support basic language acquisition. The use of visuals in such a manner generally follows accepted LEP instructional practices (Finocchiaro, 1989; Sinatra, 1981). For example, the *Key Words* of each lesson in the first- and second-grade textbook are repeated in a visual/verbal Glossary found in the back pages (Fig. 5.2). Every key word has a visual counterpart, so that the concept identifies the picture, and the image mirrors the concept. The Glossary format can be looked at as a simpler version of the picture/caption structure specified for features like *A Moment in Time*.

This matching of word with picture is a helpful strategy, especially if it is an abstract concept and not a concrete object. This "backdoor" visual/verbal strategy helps the student to make connections between the words and what they see.

THE DBAE CONNECTION TO VISUAL LEARNING

Q: There is a lot of DBAE (Discipline Based Art Education) in your
Visual Learning strand . . .
A: Exactly.

Because Ligature designers were intensely involved in researching the topic of visual literacy/learning for the program, they are aware of trends in allied fields that were applicable to the strand. Wittig was correct in assessing the possible scope of such research. Art education and art history were two disciplines in their own right with direct connection to articulating a conceptual framework for Visual Learning. In fact, during development several of Ligature's senior people had approached the J. Paul Getty Trust in an attempt to interest them with their plans for the Social Studies Program. The Getty personnel declined to meet. For over a decade the Getty Center for Education and the Arts developed, and continues to disseminate on a national basis, a unique art education curriculum program known as *Discipline Based Art Education* (DBAE). Helen Chandra, who wrote the Scope and Sequence, mentioned that she had "seen DBAE materials. Some of it is relevant, and we tried to do some of that in the Social Studies Program."

The similarity is instructive to note because DBAE, like the Visual Learning strand, is basically visual/verbal in approach. The goal of the DBAE program is to make children highly articulate about art. Though the content areas are obviously different in orientation, depth, and breadth, like the strand the larger goals are nearly the same: to enable children to develop various skills that involve learning how to approach and use visual information. Though DBAE has a more complex and sophisticated theoretical framework the basic dual emphasis is identical. In DBAE there are four modes of inquiry which generally correspond to the skills found in the Visual Learning strand.

DISCIPLINE CONCEPTS FOR DBAE

Information and modes of inquiry are drawn from four disciplines:

1. Aesthetics—the nature and values of art
2. Art Criticism—judgments about art
3. Art History—cultural and historical context
4. Art Production—techniques for expression
    (The John Paul Getty Trust, 1993, p. 23)

Visual Learning Skills

1. Develop careful and directed observation of images, objects, and the environment
2. Understand, use, and create graphic information (timelines, charts, tables, other graphic organizers, graphs, diagrams)
3. Interpret and respond to photographs, paintings, cartoons, and other illustrative materials
4. Understand and use symbols
5. Express meaning through sensory forms of representation
    (Scope and Sequence, Professional Handbook, Teacher's Edition, p. T-42)

Such a comparison is not meant to suggest that Ligature relied on DBAE to develop their strand. All skill frameworks concerning visual learning, regardless of the subject matter, are quite similar in makeup (Debes, 1970; Dondis, 1973). In fact, visual learning skills typically tend to be advocated as essential to the social studies curriculum (Banks, 1990; Jarolimek, 1990; Naylor & Diem, 1987). But the point of difference, as Stuart Murphy noted, is they are not usually "built right into the Scope and Sequence" of a program, as he felt they should be, so as to insure that it would be taught.

One other parallel with DBAE is noteworthy. A great deal of emphasis has been placed on how visual learning involves a "different kind of reading." In the *Looking Down* memo discussed in Chapter 2, guidelines for the "order of reading" to view the special visual features were suggested. In Chapter 3 Wittig noted how the spreads were designed for "cinematic . . . preview and review." And most

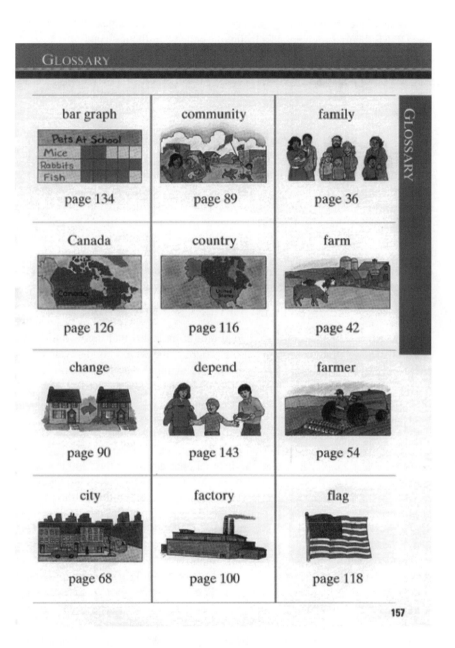

FIGURE 5.2. Visual/Verbal Glossary, Grade 1, p. 157.

importantly, the art director spoke about "scanning" the magazine-type layout. The DBAE theorists developed a technique called "aesthetic scanning."

> It is essentially a perceptual activity that directs the viewer's attention to what is in the work of art: visual elements such as color, space, and texture; how these elements are unified, balanced, and contrasted. Scanning is an "entry" strategy. It is a perceptual rather than a critical activity.
>
> —(Final Report, 1993, p. 51)

It should be noted that "scanning" as a learner activity is commonly researched in many fields, particularly cognitive psychology and reading research (Grabowski & Schroeder, 1994). What is of importance for this discussion is whether the Visual Learning strategies teach such skills. This is a question that is considered in the next part of this chapter. In the review so far some of the more important formative influences involved with conceptualizing the strand have been discussed. Of these, the theory of "multiple intelligences" and DBAE are particularly relevant to the discussion in the concluding section on assessment. In the next section, the instructional design of the Teaching Margins is examined.

A DIFFERENT KIND OF GUIDED INSTRUCTION

Stuart Murphy and Joe Godlewski "had the [initial] idea that there would be a Visual Learning strategy throughout the program that would build developmentally from the lowest . . . to the higher grades." After much research, Helen Chandra with the assistance of in-house staff wrote the Scope and Sequence. There are five skill components in the Scope. Including Visual Learning there are: Study Skills, Map and Globe Skills, Critical Thinking, and Social Participation. Following the basic Ligature principle of visual/verbal integration, the "visual strand" was intended to "reinforce" the other "thinking skills strands" of the program.

As the last chapter indicated the instructional design of the Margins began after the Thumbnail Process was finished. A number of people including designated authors like Beverly Armento and Karen Wixson "modeled" the instructional strategies found in the Margins. From this modeling "we set guidelines" for the writing of the Visual Learning strategies, Godlewski said. According to Dan Rogers, the actual writing was mostly done by contracting "out of house." Still, the writers hired for these "special assignments" had to closely coordinate their activity with the "editors and designers who worked on the Teacher Edition." Rogers noted that because these teams "were for the most part the same people who had worked on the Pupil material," they were the ones most familiar with the specifications set for visuals. This meant they were coordinating the research and selection of images. All the Visual Learning strategies (as written copy) had to conform precisely to the images that were finally selected, especially all the factual and historical background information.

Visualizing Instruction

As an instructional tool, the Teacher Edition text is distinguished by its Margins (Fig. 5.3). As shown in the Teacher Edition Professional Handbook, "the design of the teacher's Margins" consists of "two distinct channels of information." In the Opener "*gray side* Margins offer suggestions for previewing the chapter . . . and discussing the images on the opener pages." For the Lesson both side and bottom margins provide information to organize the instructional sequence. "The *gray side* Margins present the three-part lesson plan: *Introduce, Develop, Close.*" And "the *bronze bottom* Margins" provide "additional context information . . . including lesson objectives." The unit, chapter and lesson sequence consists of six steps and a corresponding Visual Learning Strategy:

Unit	Visual Learning Strategy
1. Overview	1. Understanding the Photograph
Chapter	
2. Preview	2. Understanding the Visuals
Lesson	**Visual Learning Strategy**
3. Introduce	3. Graphic Overview, Access Strategies & Activities
4. Develop	4. Visual Learning
5. Close	5. Close
6. Review	6. Assessment

If the analogy of a "dialogue" is extended to an instructional sequence, then the design of the Margins can be viewed as a script to initiate a series of conversational exchanges between teacher and student. Within the context of a typical classroom lesson, each exercise may then be viewed, according to Cazden (1986), as a series of "speech acts" within a larger "discourse structure" (p. 436). The design of this instructional sequence (Overview through Review) generally conforms to "the three-part sequence of teacher initiation, student response and teacher evaluation (IRE)" found in the research on classroom discourse (p. 436). Though the focus here is not on the "event" but on the scripts available to the teacher to initiate instruction, the Margins as designed can still suggest the kind of "participation structure" provided for teacher and student (p. 437). Concerning this "structure," Cazden (1986) remarks that students "learn to speak within the structure [the teacher] describes" (p. 437).

The Margins then, are a like a metastructure preparing the ground for the actual "speech event" of a lesson, but here the object of the lesson is not just text but visuals. Given this, what kind of visual learning is possible through the instructional support found in the Margins, and what kind of "discourse structure" (teacher/student talk) do the strategies encourage? Given the visual/verbal access structure any answer is perhaps twofold. First, the instructional purpose of each Visual Learning strategy in the sequence is described, using as an example the first Unit, Chapter, and Lesson of the eighth-grade textbook *A More Perfect Union*. Following this, the different kinds of instructional scripts for Visual Learning found in each of these steps are analyzed from three textbooks in the program. The dialogue of this "speech event" structured by the Visual Learning strategies in the Margins is broken down into two basic parts referred to as: Teacher *Talk* and Student *Task*. The analysis details the type of *Talk* found in these Visual Learning strategies. From this, it can be determined what kind of instruction the strategies tend to favor or suggest. Analysis of *Task* looks at the kind of visual learning asked or required of the student. In order to see if any "developmental" change is reflected in the sophistication of scripts or type of task from "lowest to higher grade," the analysis will rely on a broad sample of Visual Learning strategies taken from the Margins of Grades 1, 5, and 8 in the program.

Instruction That Helps You See . . .

The art director commented that the Openers were structured as a "visual navigation strategy." The Margins are designed to complement this access structure. In the *Unit Overview* the Visual Learning strategy is called *Understanding the Photograph*. Karen Wixson related that "we designed prototypes for Unit Openers." In this scripting they "attempted to focus on key concepts reflected in the [Opener] image and timeline, [which they] thought [should be] addressed throughout the unit." Beverly Armento who was also involved felt "that concrete representations [like the Unit Opener photograph] are easier for kids to access because they draw on prior knowledge. Kids identify with images and understand them more than they do text. I think the literature supports the idea that images are easier for kids than verbal ability and that they can stimulate verbal generation."

This is generally correct. Use of "concrete objects and pictures" for the presentation of social studies material, particularly for prereading activities, is a widely accepted practice (see Martorella, 1985, p. 33; Naylor & Diem, 1987, pp. 321–323). In fact, looking at a typical Unit Overview indicates just that. The script for the Unit Overview and Understanding the Photograph is organized first as a prereading activity and then as a visual learning exercise. The Overview opening line usually states: "After students have read the title of the unit and the narrative underneath it, ask them . . . how they might feel upon encountering this view . . ." So as not to entirely strip the context from this Overview the full text is provided below from Unit 1 of Grade 8. This suggests a larger, more nuanced scope of inquiry the Overview is attempting to make.

> Ask them to imagine that they are explorers or settlers from a small, densely populated European town. How might they feel on encountering this view of the American landscape? (Excited; maybe frightened or overwhelmed.) In what ways are the Rocky Mountains representa-

Student Text with Teaching Notes

The Houghton Mifflin Social Studies Teacher's Edition provides reduced Student Text pages with accompanying teacher's notes. Two pages of additional teacher information precede each chapter.

Openers

On unit and chapter openers, the teacher's margins present strategies where they are most useful—at the point of use.

The gray side margins offer suggestions for previewing the chapter to come and for discussing the images on the opener pages.

The bronze bottom margins contain a unit bibliography and chapter background information.

Chapter Interleafs

Two pages immediately preceding each chapter provide a Chapter Organizer Chart, a Chapter Rationale, and chapter Activities and Projects.

Lesson Pages

The design of the teacher's margins of all lesson pages continues the two distinct channels of information that were established on the opener pages.

The gray side margins present the three-part lesson plan: Introduce, Develop, Close. Again, critical teaching notes are located at point of use.

The bronze bottom margins offer long-range support, including lesson Objectives and additional Context information, plus a wealth of activities and extensions.

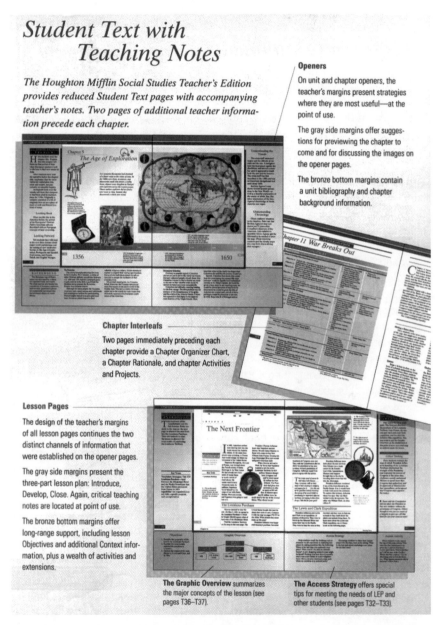

The Graphic Overview summarizes the major concepts of the lesson (see pages T36–T37).

The Access Strategy offers special tips for meeting the needs of LEP and other students (see pages T32–T33).

FIGURE 5.3. Student Text with Teaching Notes, from the Teacher Edition Professional Handbook, p. T3.

tive of the New World? How does the photograph reflect the spirit of
the unit title? (*A More Perfect Union*, 1991)

In the right Margin, Understanding the Photograph provides factual and historical background information on the image. In this Unit students are asked to place the photograph of the Rocky Mountains into a geographic context by referring to maps in the Time/Space Databank in the back pages. The *Chapter Preview* and *Understanding the Visuals* generally have the same purpose as the Overview. *Preview* suggests that students read the title and opening narrative and then determine how the visuals reflect the chapter theme. Answers for the student are generally found embedded in the text of the captions which accompany the visuals. Like Understanding the Photograph, Understanding the Visuals provides further historical background information for each of the four visual items in the Opener. In these initial steps of the instructional sequence the major emphasis is acquainting the student with the content of the lesson to come through the visuals. The student prereads the title, opening narrative paragraph, and captions in order to get that preview. Questions that the teacher can ask about the photograph in the Unit Overview and the Chapter Preview tend to focus on the major themes of the Unit and Key Concepts that are developed in the lesson text.

The Opener strategies provide background factual and historical information. Teacher prompts in the Margins ask the student *to look* at the picture, but no instructional support found in the Margins tells them *how to look*, except insofar as looking at the picture and identifying it by the caption. Not to be found in these Openers is any mention of *scanning* as an observation technique. The instructional emphasis is to content not form, or more precisely accessing content through form. Given this absence, if children were expected to "scan" the visual/verbal design of these pages, then perhaps, like the SS21 statement on Visual Learning (quoted in the chapter opening) it is considered something children typically learn "with little or no formal instruction" simply by living in a "visual society" (p. 25).

What the Margins Openers *are* organized for, tends to be a more conventional prereading exercise, which uses the visuals as concrete examples to engage and hold the attention of the reader so that they maintain their focus on the *text*. This is, one might say, a *verbal/visual* strategy. The reversal is only meant to suggest that the textual focus is the dominant instructional objective. Such a cognitive structuring technique, presently, has a well-established precedence. Visuals, Peeck (1987) suggested, which support and complement a text, especially those which "depict spatial–structural relationships," facilitate verbal comprehension (p. 142). Overall, a substantial body of research has found that the "combined . . . representation" of visual/verbal elements, depending on the reader, can potentially support retention of the text portion (see Levin & Mayer, 1993). What may be problematic with this is the issue raised in the last chapter. What is it in the image which facilitates comprehension? As indicated previously, a sequence of images sets up its own internal patterns. The issue for instructional design is whether such patterns can support cognitive structuring. The Visual Learning strategies as designed seem to suggest a more conventional prereading exercise rather than the kind of aesthetic scanning advocated by DBAE experts.

From Visual to Verbal Maps

> As any photographer knows, the frame of the viewfinder organizes the image within it, creating a visual statement where, without the frame, one might see only clutter. And, as any builder knows, the frame of a building supports its totality. Both metaphors highlight a crucial feature of thinking frames: they support and organize thought, but they do not do the thinking. They are guides, not recipes.
> —David N. Perkins (1988)

Though visuals occupy a greater part of the graphic space in the first two steps of the Openers, the principal focus is still to the text: a visual entry for verbal access. However, entry to the Lesson takes a diagraphic turn with the *Graphic Overview*. In the Handbook, a teacher is told that the "Graphic Overviews summarize the major concepts of the lessons." They "help you show your students [how to make] connections among key ideas." Later in the Handbook in a section titled: "Developing Concepts and Vocabulary," there is a more formal definition and a three-step instructional strategy for their use in the lessons (Fig. 5.4). This strategy generally appears in every Lesson in a form that can easily be adapted to preview, present, or review the material. In the *Develop* step which opens the first Lesson of Unit 1, Grade 8, the Margin makes the suggestion to "copy the Graphic Overview on the board," and then have the students "make an organization chart for each area described in the lesson" (p. 5).

Just as Unit and Chapter Openers make visually concrete the theme of the unit evoking space, time, and place, the actual text of the lesson becomes a diagraphic space through the Graphic Overview when the teacher draws it on the board. Text is again spatialized, but in a fundamentally different way. In the Unit and Chapter Opener instruction consists of making the student focus on a series of visual frames, an activity done in the service of prereading. With the Graphic Overview the conceptual or thematic space is actively constructed (drawn out) by teacher and student. The teacher can use the Overview to conceptually frame each of the linked concepts key to the Lesson, which are also found in the Scholar's Margin. The Margin usually suggests that the Overview be drawn on the board, so that the content structure of the lesson can become visually apparent to the student. The instructional sequence moves step by step then from a series of visual spaces framed in the Unit and Chapter Opener to a series of conceptual or cognitive spaces that organize the Lesson. One is a representation of reality as seen, the other a mental map.

The issue of space came up in a different way during prototype development of Lesson Openers with the Graphic Overviews. Joe Godlewski recalls that, "the original concept" was to have "two books," a main text and "a study guide that would be a separate metacognitive and learning strategies," which included Overviews for the student. In the final version they only appear in the bronze Teacher Margin below the first page of the lesson. The design of these earlier Openers with an Overview "had this rather clinical look, which seemed to be fighting [the idea of] engaging the beautiful book," Dan Rogers said. Ultimately, it became a space issue and they were removed. There was too much graphic information to pack onto the page. In Beverly Armento's mind this was a good thing. She "liked keeping it in the Teacher's book." The more appropriate instructional strategy is to have the teacher model the organizer for the student. She stated:

> In my view the graphic organizer should not present content to be learned. It should be a pedagogical technique. The way I like for teachers to think about graphically representing ideas . . . is to get children after they have studied the lesson to generate their own outlines. That's the most powerful use of the graphic. [One that is] owned by and actually constructed by the kids.

She stressed that there are many "different ways" it could be used throughout the lesson, always emphasizing its constructive aspect. "The graphic ought to be a dynamic tool for helping kids see the big ideas."

In addition to the Opener strategies Visual Learning is accomplished through the *Access Strategy* and *Access Activity* found in the bronze Margin opposite the Graphic Overview. These sometimes have a Visual Learning focus. For example, in the *Access Activity* for Lesson 1 in Grade 8, the script suggests to "Have students describe the landscapes (photos) on pages 6, 7, 9, 11, and 12." Then it proceeds to ask them to use the captions to find the location of each landscape . . . . on the map on page 5. This simple strategy is an excellent example of visual/verbal integration which builds upon the conceptual framework of the Overview. The photographs are an additional visual framework complementing the key concepts of the Graphic Overview. In turn, each visual is plotted on the map. Here, the access activity is an indicator of how the different skill strands of the Scope and Sequence can be "integrated." Similarly, the Visual Learning strategies in the Margins can fulfill objectives of other skill strands. In the Teacher Margin for Lesson 1, Grade 8, there are three Visual Learning Strategies. Of these, one is explicitly titled as *Geography: Visual Learning*. It "asks [for] students to study the picture of the Pacific Coast . . . and compare and contrast it to the Atlantic coast" (p. 12). In addition to the Access features in the bronze Margins the *Art Connection* strategy is also oriented to some type of visual learning, usually an art making activity.

Learning to See What Is Described

Having reviewed the major instructional steps of the Openers and the Lesson and their purpose relative to Visual Learning, the next issue considered is what kind of

---

Graphic Overview

Graphic overviews like the ones provided in the Teacher's Edition for each lesson are visual representations of relationships among sets of ideas or events. You can use graphic overviews effectively in a wide variety of ways in the classroom:

1. **Present the Graphic Overview before the lesson to provide an advance organizer for students.**
2. **Have students start a graphic overview for the lesson based on their prior knowledge and their preview of the lesson. As they read the lesson, students can add to, change, and refine their graphic overviews.**
3. **Have students complete a graphic overview to review and summarize a lesson or chapter.**

FIGURE 5.4. Instructional Strategies for the Graphic Overviews from the Teacher Edition Professional Handbook, p. T37.

"discourse structure" is *described* by Visual Learning strategies in the Margins? What kind of instructional scripts are available to the teacher? And more importantly, what do the Margins generally reveal about how the Visual Learning strand can be realized? To answer this question three books in the program are sampled: Grades 1, 5, and 8. The total number of Visual Learning Strategies (VLS) in the Teacher Edition Margins for these textbooks in the program are summarized in Table 5.1.

Though not looking at the actual "event" of instruction the scripted Visual Learning strategy can nevertheless reveal what kind of suggested instructional strategy (*Teacher Talk*) predominates. Similarly, enumerating the recurring forms

TABLE 5.1. Visual Learning Strategy Totals.

Grade 1: **34** *VLS* (4 Units, 16 lessons, 150 pages)

Grade 5: **101** *VLS* (7 Units, 20 Chapters, 68 lessons, 526 pages)

Grade 8: **137** *VLS* (7 Units, 20 Chapters, 69 Lessons, 620 pages)

---

of *Student Task* can indicate what kind of Visual Learning experience and activities are suggested. Also, looking at the beginning, middle, and end of the program may indicate whether the type of tasks reflect any cognitive developmental trajectory from lower to higher grades. Although the inclusion of a Visual Learning strand, as well as the visual/verbal style of presentation, is definitely innovative for a Social Studies textbook program, perhaps a larger, more important question is whether the instructional design for the strand is equally innovative.

The sample indicates that the "predominant form" of instruction generally reflects the conventional "recitational pattern" for social studies (Wilen & White, 1991, p. 483). In this regard, Wilen and White state that "the two major forms of discourse in the social studies classroom are recitation and discussion" (p. 483). Overall, variations on a question and answer format is the most frequently scripted instruction (Table 5.2). Of the *Ask* scripts for Grade one, 7 were Q/A requests; Grade five: 19 Q/A; and Grade eight: 20 Q/A. For the *Have* script the most frequent request in all three grades was to either *identify, look at,* or *create* some kind of visual. Again, for all three grades, some form of question/answer interaction was scripted. And, in Grade 8 this script predominates, where 78 out of 123 *Ask* and *Have* scripts were modeled for a Q/A type recitation. To a lesser extent the script requests that the student compare, describe, or discuss a visual in some way.

The predominance of this script follows accepted social studies instructional practice. Jarolimek (1990) recommends that "in teaching children how to use pictures and illustrations" posing a series of directed questions about the visual is the most "appropriate" strategy (p. 237). This correspondence notwithstanding, the question strategy Jarolimek recommends is of further interest because it is similar in intent to the Thumbnail dialogue. Though he lists 16 possible questions the first is of principal importance. It simply asks: "Exactly what is being shown in the picture?" (p. 237). Recall Wittig's remark to the same effect: "Why is that image there? What is it doing, or what is being shown?" But the script in the Margin is less a dialogue like the Thumbnail Process and more a recitation, where the teacher requires an answer. Although some scripts found in the Margins suggest that the teacher "brainstorm" or "work with" the students, the preponderant script suggests a more directive approach, especially if the term "Have" is taken literally

TABLE 5.2. Teacher Talk/Student Task Totals (see summary, Appendix 2).

Teacher Talk Script			Student Task	
Grade 1:	Ask students to...	7	Answer Question	7
	Have students...	28	Answer Question	1
		35		8
Grade 5:	Ask students to......	61	Answer Question	19
	Have students...	61	Answer Question	18
		122		37
Grade 8:	Ask students to......	61	Answer Question	20
	Have students...	62	Answer Question	58
		123		78

(i.e., to cause to be, or please do this at once). What minimal guide the Professional Handbook may offer in this regard seems to indicate that the recommended model for the program is "direct instruction," though "collaborative learning" is also suggested (p. T34).

Still, as Karen Wixson noted, in the final product there was no concerted effort to convey a definite instructional model. Far too much that went into the Margins, she thought, was very "general," its reason for being there only to fulfill "political concerns." Overall, "there's not a lot of specific stuff about instruction in this Manual." Not enough that "might be really directly usable." The design, she felt, reflected current trends in teaching. "The spirit of the times [dictates] that Teacher Manuals shouldn't be quite as directive as they once were."

Because the sophistication of the visual design for this program must be considered innovative, one obvious question is whether it requires an equally innovative instructional design. If the analysis is any indicator, the visual design appears joined to a solid but standard form of instructional practice. Because of its conventionality it might not allow the inherent richness and sophistication of the visual information to be accessed at a similar level. Ultimately perhaps the instructional design depended on the sophistication of the teacher, not the visual.

Yet if the instructional design is conservative, perhaps it is appropriately so, because social studies content in the program does determine the scope and purpose of the Visual Learning strand. As the SS21 statement indicates (quoted at length in the introduction to this chapter), "Visual Learning skills are explicitly taught along with learning skills [from the other strands], and are integrated into the overall scope and sequence" (p. 25). This intention is most evident in the eighth-grade text where of the 137 Visual Learning strategies in the T.E. Margins only 2 are directly linked to skills in the Visual Learning strand (*A More Perfect Union*, 1991, pp. 184 & 520).

The remainder are integrated with other skill strands. Visual Learning is in support of history, geography, or economics for example. Given the interdisciplinary nature of social studies content, such Visual Learning skills though having a definite formal (or aesthetic aspect) inevitably tend to work in service of the content orientation, just as the prereading strategy in the Unit and Chapter Openers do. For this reason a Q/A recitation strategy which relies on "careful observation" of visuals, and a response which entails basic identification, description, and explanation of what is looked at, is perhaps the most appropriate mode of instruction given the age groups (K–8) covered by the program. Such basic "labeling" and "interpretation" is a common social studies questioning strategy (Martorella, 1985, pp. 261–262), though observation of visuals is also fundamental to higher level thinking skills. Naylor and Diem (1987) state:

> Pictures and photographs are not only useful for developing observation skills. They are also useful for building concepts and generalizations, drawing inferences, initiating inquiry, formulating hypotheses, and testing hypotheses. A series of pictures and photographs may also be used to show patterns, variations, and change over time. (p. 280)

Such comments reinforce David Perkins' (1994) assertion made in Chapter 3, that looking at art involves a "wide spectrum" of cognitive styles (p. 5). Nevertheless, if the predominance of questions in the Visual Learning strategies is appropriately designed for instructional assistance, how are other Visual Learning question strategies linked to the Chapter Reviews assessed?

ON THE QUESTION OF ASSESSMENT

Preceding every Unit Opener in Grades 1 and 2, and every Chapter Opener in Grades 3 through 8 of the Teacher Edition, are the *Organizer* and *Rationale* pages which have a *Planning Chart* that lists the learner objectives in each Lesson for the Pupil Edition. The objectives appearing in these charts are linked to both the strands in the Scope and Sequence and the instructional steps of the T.E. Margins. For example, in the Chapter 13 Organizer of the fifth-grade textbook (Fig. 5.5), the Objective in Lesson 4 to "Make and use cluster diagrams" is linked to the second skill in the Visual Learning strand (p. T42) and the *VL* strategy in the bronze T.E. Margin (p. 335). This strategy accompanies the special feature of the objective titled: *Understanding Graphic Organizers: Using Cluster Diagrams* (pp. 334–335). Yet overall this is one of the few Visual Learning activities which is linked in all the Chapter Organizers in the fifth grade textbook. Very few of these objectives are actually linked from the Visual Learning Strand in the Scope and Sequence to the Chapter Organizer and then to the Chapter Review.

More often than not, the instructional function of the Visual Learning strategy found in the Margin is to "assist" with instruction (Tharp & Gallimore, 1988, p.

TABLE 5.3. Assist/Assess Instructional Function.

Grade	VLS	Assist	Assess
Grade 1:	34	32	2
Grade 5:	101	93	8
Grade 8:	137	131	6

59). Taking Grades 1, 5, and 8 again as a sample the breakdown indicates the predominance of this function (Table 5.3). Armbruster and Ostertag (1993) state that such *assistance* can have manifold purposes. It can "promote learning [by] motivating students, set purposes for reading, focus attention, promote and assess comprehension, and foster skill development" (p. 69). The review of the instructional sequence already taken indicates that the Visual Learning strategies in the Margins are designed more specifically to do just that: "promote learning" by providing assistance to the teacher in the ways just noted.

If the Visual Learning Margin strategies are largely designed to assist students during instruction, how are the remainder assessed? In a typical Chapter Review where Visual Learning assessment is carried over as an objective from the Scope and linked to material covered in the lessons, the emphasis is less on reviewing skills and more on art-making activities, which concern the fifth skill in the strand. This is perhaps the most interesting aspect of the Review sections, because it ties in with Stuart Murphy's concerns to provide learning activities for different cognitive styles. An example of this approach is already noted concerning the use of Cluster Diagrams (see Fig. 5.5). Following the constructivist approach taken in the lesson modeling Graphic Overviews, students in this exercise first receive a demonstration and then are asked to try it by making one.

This demonstration style self-tutorial format is used in all these special *Understanding Skill* features. There are four basic steps: *Here's Why, Here's How, Try It, and Apply it*. Both process and product combine to have a student learn by doing. Another example from the seventh-grade textbook is *Reading Mughal Paintings* (Fig. 5.6a–c). Helen Chandra thought this particular feature reflected how innovative the Visual Learning strand was for a typical social studies program. From the fifth through the eighth grade these Special Features and the Visual Learning strategies repeat basic social study skills like using and making timelines, charts, and graphs. As the grades progress there is a slightly higher level of sophistication and complexity. For example, in both the fifth- and eighth-grade textbooks there are *Understanding Skills* that have the students analyze and make political cartoons which are related to the American history strand. The fifth-grade feature is concerned with interpretation and the eighth with analysis. Both are accompanied

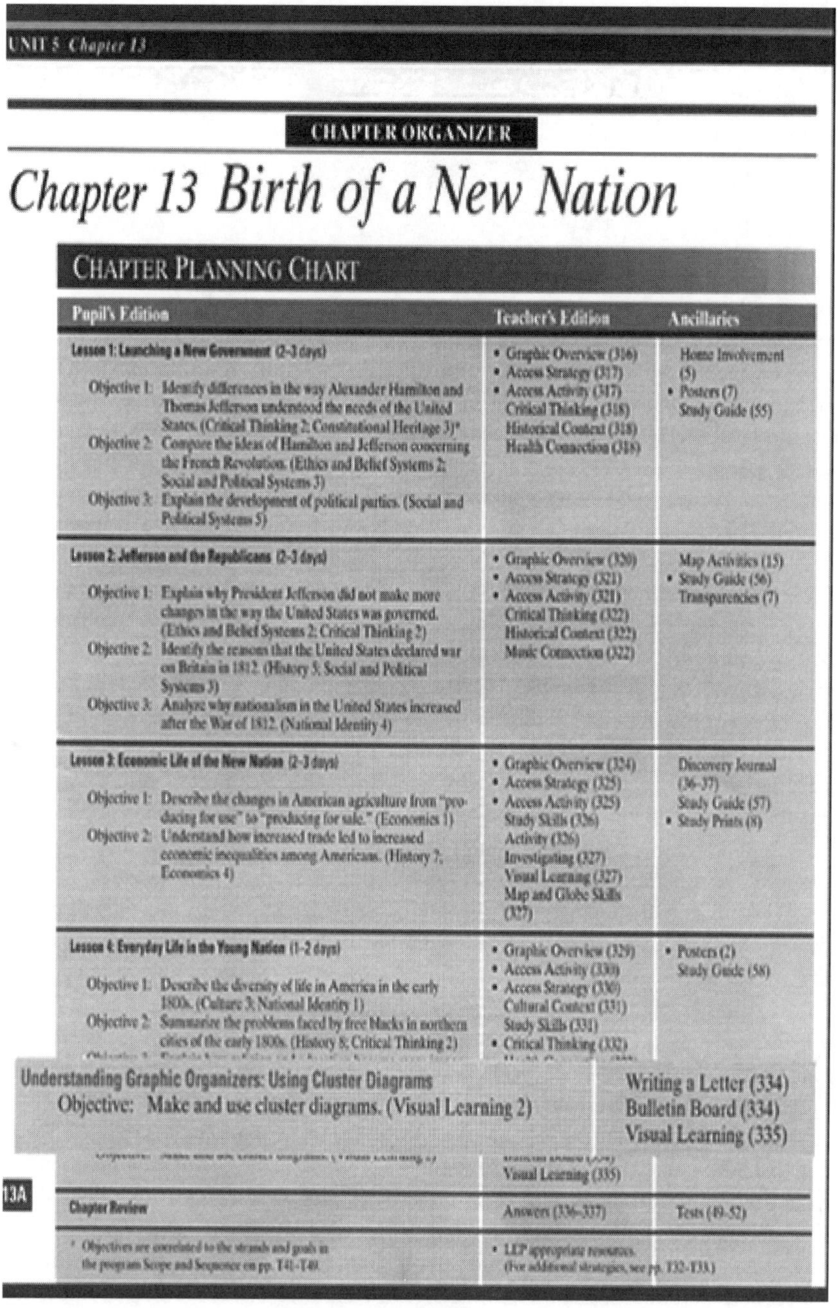

CHAPTER ORGANIZER

Chapter 13 Birth of a New Nation

CHAPTER PLANNING CHART

Pupil's Edition	Teacher's Edition	Ancillaries
Lesson 1: Launching a New Government (2-3 days) Objective 1: Identify differences in the way Alexander Hamilton and Thomas Jefferson understood the needs of the United States. (Critical Thinking 2; Constitutional Heritage 3)* Objective 2: Compare the ideas of Hamilton and Jefferson concerning the French Revolution. (Ethics and Belief Systems 2; Social and Political Systems 3) Objective 3: Explain the development of political parties. (Social and Political Systems 5)	• Graphic Overview (316) • Access Strategy (317) • Access Activity (317) Critical Thinking (318) Historical Context (318) Health Connection (318)	Home Involvement (5) • Posters (7) Study Guide (55)
Lesson 2: Jefferson and the Republicans (2-3 days) Objective 1: Explain why President Jefferson did not make more changes in the way the United States was governed. (Ethics and Belief Systems 2; Critical Thinking 2) Objective 2: Identify the reasons that the United States declared war on Britain in 1812. (History 5; Social and Political Systems 3) Objective 3: Analyze why nationalism in the United States increased after the War of 1812. (National Identity 4)	• Graphic Overview (320) • Access Strategy (321) • Access Activity (321) Critical Thinking (322) Historical Context (322) Music Connection (322)	Map Activities (15) • Study Guide (56) Transparencies (7)
Lesson 3: Economic Life of the New Nation (2-3 days) Objective 1: Describe the changes in American agriculture from "producing for use" to "producing for sale." (Economics 1) Objective 2: Understand how increased trade led to increased economic inequalities among Americans. (History 7; Economics 4)	• Graphic Overview (324) • Access Strategy (325) • Access Activity (325) Study Skills (326) Activity (326) Investigating (327) Visual Learning (327) Map and Globe Skills (327)	Discovery Journal (36-37) Study Guide (57) • Study Prints (8)
Lesson 4: Everyday Life in the Young Nation (1-2 days) Objective 1: Describe the diversity of life in America in the early 1800s. (Culture 3; National Identity 1) Objective 2: Summarize the problems faced by free blacks in northern cities of the early 1800s. (History 8; Critical Thinking 2)	• Graphic Overview (329) • Access Activity (330) • Access Strategy (330) Cultural Context (331) Study Skills (331) • Critical Thinking (332)	• Posters (2) Study Guide (58)
Understanding Graphic Organizers: Using Cluster Diagrams Objective: Make and use cluster diagrams. (Visual Learning 2)	Visual Learning (335)	Writing a Letter (334) Bulletin Board (334) Visual Learning (335)
Chapter Review	Answers (336-337)	Tests (49-52)

13A

* Objectives are correlated to the strands and goals in the program Scope and Sequence on pp. T41-T40.

• LEP appropriate resources.
(For additional strategies, see pp. T32-T33.)

FIGURE 5.5. Chapter Organizer and Planning Chart, Grade 5, p. 313A.

Reading Mughal Paintings

Here's Why

By studying art from the past, you can learn about the beliefs, actions, values and customs of people who lived long ago. Art flourished under the patronage of the Mughal emperors. Mughal paintings are rich in information. But first, you must learn how to "read" paintings.

Here's How

Like books, paintings often tell a story. When you study a painting, look for the main idea and identify the major characters. Examine how the painter sets the scene and determine what action is taking place. Then look for cultural details and clues to the emotions of the characters.

Study the painting on the opposite page. This scene by Nar Singh was painted to illustrate Abul Fazl's *Akbarnama*, or history of Akbar.

Akbar's religious and cultural tolerance is the main theme of the painting. The central figure is Akbar, who sits enthroned under a bright red canopy. You may recognize him: on page 182, you saw a painting of his return to Fatehpur Sikri. The key on this page identifies Akbar with the numeral one (1).

The figures who form a circle in front of Akbar are all religious scholars. Find the figures labeled in the key by the numeral two (2). These men are two of the three Jesuit priests whom Akbar had invited to teach about Christianity in 1580. One is Rudolpho Aquaviva, the head of the mission. The other is either the translator Francisco Henriques or the Jesuit priest Antonio Monserrate. The rest of the figures in the circle are thought to be Muslims and Hindus.

Outside the courtyard, in the painting's second level (3), The bottom level shows horses and passersby (4).

The painting's setting is the Ibadat-Khanah, or House of Worship, located within Akbar's palace at Fatehpur Sikri. Akbar encouraged scholars of diverse faiths to engage in religious discussions at the Ibadat-Khanah. Muslims, Hindus, Christians, Parsees, Zoroastrians, and Jews were all made welcome by Akbar.

This scene shows an evening session at the House of Worship. A heated debate is underway, with participants vigorously discussing the merits and flaws of Christianity and Islam.

In the *Akbar-nama*, Abul Fazl gives a version of what took place that evening. Fazl claims that Father Aquaviva challenged a Muslim religious scholar to a trial by fire. Fazl says Aquaviva offered to enter a fire holding the Bible if a Muslim scholar would do the same, holding the Koran. Other accounts say that it was actually Akbar or the Muslims who challenged the Jesuits. Although the versions differ, it seems clear that a trial by fire was discussed but rejected.

Now look for important details in the painting. Notice that many of the men hold books, and that books lie scattered on the floor. In this respect, the scene is typical: Akbar enjoyed religious and philosophical debate, and he surrounded himself with learned men.

The fact that Akbar sits above the others symbolizes the power of the emperor. The architecture, decorations, and beautiful floor coverings show the splendor of the royal court. The absence of women in the painting is significant. Women were excluded from the business of the Mughal court, except as entertainers.

Note how the painter conveys the emotions of the religious scholars and the vigor of the debate. You can see that many of the men are gesturing. This suggests that the scholars were speaking emphatically, and that several conversations were taking place at once.

You have seen how to "read" paintings. Now try to use what you have learned and interpret a painting on your own.

Try It

Look again at the painting of Akbar being welcomed to Fatehpur Sikri, on page 182. What is the painting's main idea, or theme? Who are the major characters? Where does the scene take place, and what is happening in this scene? What cultural information can you gain from examining the painting's details? How does the painter suggest the characters' emotions?

Apply It

Find books that include paintings by American artists of the 1900s, such as Grant Wood, Andrew Wyeth, or John Sloan. Choose a painting that shows an aspect of life in the United States. "Read" the painting, using the approach taught in Here's How.

FIGURE 5.6a. Reading Mughal Paintings, Understanding Skills for Art, Grade 7, pp. 186–187

Reading Mughal Paintings

Here's Why

By studying art from the past, you can learn about the beliefs, actions, values and customs of people who lived long ago. Art flourished under the patronage of the Mughal emperors. Mughal paintings are rich in information. But first, you must learn how to "read" paintings.

Here's How

Like books, paintings often tell a story. When you study a painting, look for the main idea and identify the major characters. Examine how the painter sets the scene and determine what action is taking place. Then look for cultural details and clues to the emotions of the characters.

Study the painting on the opposite page. This scene by Nar Singh was painted to il-illustrate Abul Fazl's *Akbar-nama*, or history of Akbar.

Akbar's religious and cultural tolerance is the main theme of the painting. The central figure is Akbar, who sits enthroned under a bright red canopy. You may recognize him: on page 182, you saw a painting of his return to Fatehpur Sikri. The key on this page identifies Akbar with the numeral one (1).

The figures who form a circle in front of Akbar are all religious scholars. Find

the figures labeled in the key by the numeral two (2). These men are two of the three Jesuit priests whom Akbar had invited to teach about Christianity in 1580. One is Rudolpho Aquaviva, the head of the mission. The other is either the translator Francisco Henriques or the Jesuit priest Antonio Monserrate. The rest of the figures in the circle are thought to be Muslims and Hindus. Outside the courtyard, in the painting's second level, two guards stand watch (3). The bottom level shows horses and passersby (4).

The painting's setting is the Ibadat-Khanah, or House of Worship, located within Akbar's palace at Fatehpur Sikri. Akbar encouraged scholars of diverse faiths to engage in religious discussions at the Ibadat-Khanah. Muslims, Hindus, Christians, Parsees, Zoroastrians, and Jews were all made welcome by Akbar.

This scene shows an evening session at the House of Worship. A heated debate is underway, with participants vigorously discussing the merits and flaws of Christianity and Islam.

In the *Akbar-nama*, Abul Fazl gives a version of what took place that evening. Fazl claims that Father Aquaviva challenged a Muslim

religious scholar to a trial by fire. Fazl says Aquaviva offered to enter a fire holding the Bible if a Muslim scholar would do the same, holding the Koran. Other accounts say that it was actually Akbar or the Muslims who challenged the Jesuits. Although the versions differ, it seems clear that a trial by fire was discussed but rejected.

Now look for important details in the painting. Notice that many of the men hold books, and that books lie scattered on the floor. In this respect, the scene is typical: Akbar enjoyed religious and philosophical debate, and he surrounded himself with learned men.

FIGURE 5.6b. Reading Mughal Paintings, Understanding Skills for Art, Grade 7, p. 186.

Note how the painter conveys the emotions of the religious scholars and the vigor of the debate. You can see that many of the men are gesturing. This suggests that the scholars were speaking emphatically, and that several conversations were taking place at once.

You have seen how to "read" paintings. Now try to use what you have learned and interpret a painting on your own.

Try It

Look again at the painting of Akbar being welcomed to Fatehpur Sikri, on page 182. What is the painting's main idea, or theme? Who are the major characters? Where does the scene take place, and what is happening in this scene? What cultural information can you gain from examining the painting's details? How does the painter suggest the characters' emotions?

Apply It

Find books that include paintings by American artists of the 1900s, such as Grant Wood, Andrew Wyeth, or John Sloan. Choose a painting that shows an aspect of life in the United States. "Read" the painting, using the approach taught in Here's How.

187

The fact that Akbar sits above the others symbolizes the power of the emperor. The architecture, decorations, and beautiful floor coverings show the splendor of the royal court. The absence of women in the painting is significant. Women were excluded from the business of the Mughal court, except as entertainers.

FIGURE 5.6c. Reading Mughal Paintings, Understanding Skills for Art, Grade 7, p. 187.

by Visual Learning strategies in the Margins which suggest discussion and/or draw-ing activities to make political cartoons.

Such project oriented hands-on activities encourage children to approach learn-ing in ways that cannot be easily tested or assessed. Whereas some of these art-making activities obviously appeal to the visual learner, others use art as a basis to write a report on a painter or write a description based on analysis of a chosen painting, cartoon, or historic artifact (e.g., Writing a Description, Grade 8, p. 11). In so doing they suggest Howard Gardner's influence on the strand. Fundamental to the theory of multiple intelligences is the recognition of different learning styles. Children should be encouraged to represent the same content in ways that suit the mix of their intelligences whether linguistic, spatial, or quantitative (Bruer, 1993, p. 265). Given Stuart Murphy's comments about Gardner, the place of art-making activities, usually regarded as a frill activity in the curriculum, becomes essential to learning in other subject disciplines. This insight stresses that learning can and does occur through representing content in symbolic modes other than language and number. It is these two paradigmatic symbol systems upon which are based not only all present standards of assessment, but also up until recently, the domi-nant models of cognitive development. That being the case it should be noted that assessment tools for Gardner's theory have yet to be fully developed, though some informal performance-based evaluations of student portfolios have been devised (see Bruer, 1993 p. 268: Gardner, 1993, pp. 86–99). Similarly, development of DBAE curriculum materials has been weakest in the area of assessment (see Hamblen, 1987, p. 74).

In keeping with this underdevelopment, assessment appears to be the weakest aspect of the Visual Learning strand. There are no criteria in the Margins of the Chapter Reviews to evaluate these activities. They are simply suggested projects. Because "assessment drives instruction" the question comes to mind whether the Visual Learning instructional design for the program will be taken seriously (Gardner, 1993, p. 79). Given the extensive use of *VL* questions in the Margins perhaps the balance should have been shifted so that assistance type questions were followed up with more assessment questions in the reviews.

There is an important curricular reason, relative to the nature of social studies content and how it is approached through visuals, which makes the problem of assessment doubly important. Stuart Murphy makes the crucial point about the reciprocal "integrity of the visual presentation [which had to] parallel the integrity of the text. We placed, [he said], a high degree of importance on why it is there, what it is doing, [and] what it is conveying to the student." But this "integrity" can only be maintained by the teacher. S/he must know precisely what is being conveyed to the student by the instructional assistance given in the Mar-gin and linked to the presentation. This ties in with Armento's (1986) comment that the social studies teacher must somehow influence the student so that they can "construct images and meanings of the social world" (p. 946). In the *About Your Book* section in the first-grade textbook "images and meaning" are described in terms of real and unreal with the distinction made between a cartoon of a talking ear of corn and a photograph of corn being harvested. In later grades a similar question is posed again in terms of the truthfulness and credibility of historical evidence (e.g., *Evaluating Historical Evidence*, Grade 5, p. 419; *Understanding Fact, Judgment, and Opinion*, Grade 6, p. 62). Such an instructional responsibility places an added burden on the designer to meet that standard of integrity.

One intrinsic purpose of social studies content, especially in terms of the kind of constructive "meaning" Armento speaks about, is that it must adhere to the historiographic standards applied before. It follows that one test of this credibility is ascertaining what is actually conveyed to the student. Only then can the "integrity" of each mode be maintained, because seeing is verified in the verbal complement (and vice versa). In metacognitive terms it is somewhat circular: this truth is verified by a correct answer to a question about what is seen. How then may the "realness" of history be assessed, if not through linking assistance questions in the Margins to review? Of course, this is easier said than done. Gary Nash felt that as the number and quality of images increased in a textbook, so did the necessity of helpful textual support to teach with such information. Hypothetically, this places a greater burden on the instructional designer working with the Thumbnail team and visuals researcher to devise assessment tools.

Visual images, especially historical ones, have in slightly different terms a potential depth and breadth all their own. This basic recognition can be seen in the instructional design of the titles, callouts, and captions that direct the viewing and attention of the student in highly sophisticated ways to read the image in accordance with the text. If the role of Visual Learning in the overall plan of the Scope and Sequence is to be "integrated" with the core social studies content, then a larger role for assessment would seem critical to the success of the Visual Learning strand.

Research on this problem tends to concur. The perennial question is "how [do] teachers and students [actually] use questions provided by textbooks" (Allington & Weber, 1993, p. 51). A number of studies have indicated that when questions are not directly assessed in textbooks teachers often tend to overlook them entirely (pp. 51–52). Instructional design that does not link lesson objectives to assessment can potentially be ineffective. "Accountability," according to Allington and Weber is what makes the difference (p. 52). On this point Karen Wixson was in basic agreement. Speaking about this issue from the teacher point of view she commented

> Teachers are not quite sure how to deal with the visual aspect of the text in the first place. I know from experience that some of them do not ever look at it. Others think the material is not relevant [because] they are not going to test on it, so they can just treat it casually. And others recognize that there is new information in this material.

The sophistication of this "new information" appearing in the visual design requires an instructional design equal in kind. The implications are numerous. Two of the more important are that the objectives of the Visual Learning strategies are more tightly linked with some form of assessment in a progressive and sequential fashion. Another, is that the skills in the strand have further documentation for both teacher and student, instructional support which explains and elaborates upon the formal aspects of each skill. As in the special features: more information stating *Here's How* to accompany the *Why*. Here Wixson's observations were to the point.

> Rather than have a strand in the Teacher's Edition that is either just attending to the verbal or just attending to the visual, . . . there probably needs to be all the way through [the text] more direct questions that ask kids explicitly to make links between the two with the information that is carried [equally] by the two [T.E. and P.E.]. And they [Ligature designers] probably could enhance a student's ability to do this on their own by modeling this type of thing through the directions of the teacher or through the questions that they ask the students and [by] the activities they ask the student to engage in. I think that calls for a different way of approaching guided instruction.

The architecture and Openers are definitely one key aspect of "guided instruction" which was handled in an exceptionally original way in the design of the Pupil Edition. They provide a "discourse structure" in which the student can learn to talk about images, but also a parallel visual structure designed as a sequence of visual windows, which help the student to see what they are talking about. This is a unique instructional platform for teacher/student "discourse." Given the instructional design issue raised in the previous chapter concerning the potential to "cognitively structure" visual information (i.e., architecture and Openers) for patterns of visual (gestaltic) coherence, the issue of *how to link* visual/verbal content takes on added importance. It should be noted that the importance of such "patterns" is acknowledged in the overall design of the Visual Learning strand, but only at the kindergarten level. In the back pages of *The World I See* there is a series of 11 black on white cut-out patterns depicting basic recognizable shapes seen in the world at large by any child (e.g., a clock face, a traffic light, a stop sign, and so on).

Because "building" a Visual Learning strand "right into the scope and sequence" for an instructional program is relatively innovative for social studies, no existent guidelines or models were available to rely on. At the same time it is a promising area for research and study because the issue involved, designing for "visual informativeness," will increasingly become, as Waller noted, a factor to be weighed and considered as text-based instruction is pulled in the direction of the computer.

The "standard" that was set is a definite marker not only for the field of Social Studies but educational publishing as well because it introduces the fundamental issues that will concern curriculum theorists and instructional designers in the next decade: how to return learning and instruction to cultivate the "concrete" (Papert, 1993, p. 155). Ironically, Rob Wittig's remark that the language of visuals is only minimally developed is nevertheless indicative of how far they were able to take the strand. Similarly, the whole notion of Visual Learning for instruction is not so much new as just relatively undeveloped. Yet embedded in the strand are issues germane to the future of "guided instruction" as it pertains to an emergent language of visualization driven now by the computer.

However, before we proceed to Chapter 7, *A Window in the Text*, which deals specifically with these visualization issues, we must reconsider the Visual Learning strand by looking at its pedagogical limitations in light of the California adoption controversy surrounding these textbooks. Not only do we live in a highly complex visual culture largely orchestrated by the mass media, but the larger social environment in which the media operates is a multicultural space marked by extraordinary ethnic, racial, and religious diversity. The California adoption controversy can be critically sited at the intersection of our visual media culture and American multiculturalism. For this reason, it is important to review this textbook adoption process as it came to bear upon some of the innovative visual/verbal features in the K–8 program. In Chapter 6, we take a closer look at some of the more controversial images that were drawn into critical focus during the adoption process; we may consider what a Visual Learning curriculum strand that critically addresses the complex visual realities of America's multicultural society should be.

CHAPTER

6

History as Our Best Guess

The careful study of the of the development of the school curriculum makes very clear that one of the outstanding reasons for the conservatism of the curriculum is the entrenchment of private interests of both publishers and authors. The curriculum can advance not much more rapidly than the great publishing houses of America and a small group of authors who dictate its major outlines can be persuaded to permit it. The forward looking curriculum-maker is persuaded at the outset, therefore to undertake the education of these agencies. . . . It is [their] *task* to bring constantly before the authors and publishers of schoolbooks the need for continuous reconstruction of their materials and especially for the inclusion of up- to-date materials.

—Harold Rugg (1926, p. 32)

The push for stronger curriculum standards and quality textbooks and instructional materials is one of the most crucial challenges facing California's sweeping educational reform movement. Because too many textbooks are not well written and fall short of the quality we want for our students, our state has taken a strong stand on providing textbooks that reflect curriculum integrity. Publishers will produce better textbooks when their customers insist on higher standards.

—Bill Honig (1989, p. 125)

Although stated in the 1920s, Harold Rugg's comments on textbook reform are markedly similar to the more recent views of Bill Honig, the former Superintendent of Instruction who backed the adoption of the K–8 Social Studies series. In his formal pronouncements Honig speaks about California's "Textbook Adoption Process" in the same "forward looking" terms as Rugg. Honig (1989) describes this reform process as "the primary avenue for providing quality instructional materials" (P. 126). One of the recurring rituals of profound democratic importance in the political economy of textbooks is the forum for review provided by the adoption process. Although it has become highly institutionalized over time, it is nevertheless the one point in the entire process of textbook production where the form and content of the book under consideration for adoption is open to public review.

Honig (1989) describes this reform in typically bureaucratic and rational terms. "The lengthy, complex process," he says "has three major levels of review: social content, educational content, and public comment" (p. 126). However, when the actual reviews got underway in the summer of 1990, especially the public school board adoption meetings held statewide, this rational process turned out to be anything but. Instead, California's reform of its Social Studies curriculum became one of the most important fronts in the nation's culture wars during the late 1980s and early 1990s. The level of review referred to as "public comment" became a public battleground over the contested nature of the "multicultural curriculum." Comment became heated criticism. Spoken words became salvos and volleys in a divisive struggle over the nature of history and representation in a multicultural perspective.

In the first major section of this chapter, the multicultural connection between the Framework and the textbooks is discussed. This will serve as an appropriate background to examine several of the most heavily criticized *Closer Looks* and *Moments in Time* visual/verbal features. These were described as "hot spots" by Gary Nash. The "hot spots" included:

- *A Closer Look: The Grand Canyon*, Grade 3
- *A Moment in Time: A Cro-Magnon Toolmaker*, Grade 6
- *A Moment in Time: Escaping Slave*, Grade 5
- *A Moment in Time: A Caravan Camel*, Grade 7

However, although I frame some of the most important issues in the adoption controversy as a whole, my primary aim in this chapter is to shift the focus away from the problems found with the *text* content to look at several examples of visual imagery in the series which were equally controversial. Such a focus builds on the issue of visual literacy discussed in the previous chapter. It also provides an opportunity to explore the complex couplings of political and cultural power embedded in the content of visual images, which can tend to support dominant political and social ideologies.

Up to this point the design of these books has been considered largely in formal terms. In Chapter 3 aesthetic criteria were employed to show how images add a spatial dimension to content. In Chapter 4 the principles of Gestalt psychology were introduced to discuss how visual images have a perceptual structure that seems contrary to the structural characteristics of text. In the earlier chapters we considered the design process and the theory motivating it. From various formal perspectives the material form of the textbook has been closely examined.

In the Visual Learning strand described in Chapter 5, the Ligature designers conceived a set of skills with which to look at their books. One might say that the skills represent the way the makers of these books would like to have their work evaluated visually. Yet it is fairly evident that the instructional design of the Visual Learning strand speaks only in the most general of terms. Though the Visual Learning skills emphasize that students should learn to "interpret and respond to [various visual media and] understand and use symbols," such skills are couched in a neutral aesthetic pedagogy (p. T42). Visual content is evaluated by a type of formal criteria perhaps more suggestive of those embodied by the phrase "a beautiful book," the expression often used by designers to describe the textbook program. Such a tendency perhaps elevates surface over substance. Indeed, a primary focus of my discussion up to this point has been the wonderfully refined and almost obsessive care given to the graphic construction of the total page.

Yet such a design strategy does not move beyond the circle of producers. If design is truly an iterative process, then production of these textbooks is not complete until that circle is closed by reception, not just the showy presentations pitched to target audiences for market testing, but the deeper meaning embedded in these visual images which is perceived by the eye of the beholder.

It then is the "task" of the adoption audience to complete the visual/verbal message. How this task unfolded during the state adoption process is examined here for the insight it may provide in adding a critical dimension to the Visual Learning component of the series. For if Visual Learning is about how children learn to see, analyze, and interpret visual material, it is also about what is overlooked by the designer and editor yet is nevertheless latent in the frame of the picture.

The criticisms brought "before the authors and publishers" were taken very seriously by the Ligature designers. Rob Wittig, who conceived the visual/verbal feature *A Moment in Time,* several of which were noted earlier as "hot spots," was stunned by the negative reaction. Such features, he suggested, represented their "*best guess*" at what [might be] a common ground for all cultures to meet on." At the same time he emphasized that these images were just representations, and in every sense of the word: constructed. "One shouldn't pretend," Wittig said, "that it [the image in *A Moment*] appeared of itself and [was] some sort of natural phenomena." Rather, he said, "You can try to let kids in on the fact [that] it's *our best guess*. We chose this stuff. Some of it is arbitrary. [But], it's our best guess." Yet as the adoption process revealed, in some instances their "best guess" was not good enough.

The so-called "hot spots" will be looked at from a semiotic perspective. Semiotics is the study and analysis of signs and symbols produced by culture. One might say that semiotics is the study of communication in its widest sense. It investigates the symbolic products of culture. It does not distinguish between high or low culture, that is mass media and the fine arts. All signs and symbols are invested with meaning. Semiotics studies the process whereby society attributes meaning to symbolic forms, in this case "public imagery," an expression Todd Gitlin (1995) used to describe the visual images in the adopted textbooks.

The introduction of a semiotic perspective is important in coming to understand the California adoption controversy, since one of the central elements of the controversy was related to the way in which different multicultural audiences interpreted the visual messages in the *Moments*, from within their own personal and cultural milieu, and not that of the designers. Today, our media saturated visual culture demands that we look at its products critically. The introduction of some basic semiotic terms will serve to frame the pedagogical issues discussed in the concluding section of the chapter. Here, the question of whether some type of critical visual pedagogy is necessary to the Social Studies curriculum is explored.

Rugg's observation that the "curriculum" reflects the "entrenchment of private interests of both publishers and authors" is no less true today. What was at stake in California's adoption controversy is still at issue today: Who will define the multicultural imaginary and represent those who *now* only want to represent themselves?

A CONTEST OF IDENTITIES: CALIFORNIA ADOPTION POLITIK

> To understand this nation's identity, students must: Recognize that American society is now and has always been pluralistic and multicultural. . . . Understand the special role of the United States in world history as a nation of immigrants. . . . [And] realize that true patriotism celebrates the moral force of the American idea as a nation that unites as one people the descendants of many cultures, races, religions, and ethnic groups.
> —*California History-Social Science Framework* (1988, pp. 20–21)

> Before we can agree on what American identity is made of, we have to concede that as an immigrant settler society superimposed on the ruins of a considerable native presence, American identity is too varied to be a unitary and homogenous thing; indeed the battle within it is between advocates of a unitary identity and those who see the whole as a complex but not reductively unified one.
> —Edward Said (1993, p. xxv)

> It's important for youngsters to see themselves. How do we balance what they see on TV, lots of violence and crime. Their self-esteem is way down. They are portrayed as Willie Horton's. Oakland's challenge is how to truly have a multicultural curriculum.
> —Toni R. Cook, Oakland, California School Board (Reinhold, 1991, p. 52)

The timeline of the California Social Studies curriculum reform begins much before the "Adoption Process" that Bill Honig describes. Submission by Houghton Mifflin of the Ligature designed Social Studies program began in the spring of 1990. But renewal of the state's social studies curriculum had been underway since 1985. After 3 years of deliberation by an appointed committee, the State

Board of Education approved the new Framework in July of 1987. It was just one in a series of wide ranging subject area reforms brought about Bill Honig. Perhaps no state during the 1980s responded to the educational crisis depicted in the "Nation at Risk" as if it were a call to arms more than California under his dynamic stewardship (Ravitch & Vinovskis, 1995, p. 180). Viewed in hindsight, the Honig era might best be characterized as one of last great movements of state sponsored curriculum renewal, a virtual "Manhattan Project for curriculum," which reflected the activist spirit of big government and a deeply held political liberalism (Ravitch, 1995).

The high points of controversy during the California adoption process that took place during the summer and fall of 1990, were driven according to Todd Gitlin by an obsession with "identity politics." Gitlin observed that in a zero-sum society the most marginalized groups have lately been compelled to reject the society at large. If they could not genuinely participate as equals in American society they could at least control their own identity by creating a cultural space counter to the dominant one which already largely excludes them. Movements such as Afrocentrism may be understood in this light.

But the more adamant adoption critics saw themselves not as obsessed with their own particular identities, but as legitimately concerned about the fact that their identities were ill defined by the new state Framework and poorly represented in the adopted textbooks. One key criticism of the Framework was that its notion of a "National Identity" seemed to subsume all other identities, in the sense that we are all Americans first and only then African, Arab, Asian, Hispanic, and so forth. The deliberate emphasis is on Unity, not diversity, though it acknowledges the fundamental plural and multicultural nature of American society.

The other serious problem was related to assumptions about how this diversity came to be. America, the Framework exclaims, is a nation of immigrants, an assumption that reflects classic liberal motifs. History is conceived as a grand unfolding narrative, in its words, "As a story well told." In this "story" American ideals of "equality and freedom" are progressively realized. Critics thought this "National Identity" motif reflected a Eurocentric perspective. African American critics did not see themselves as immigrants at all, but as free human beings who were brutally enslaved and forced to come to this country against their will. The most prominent of these critics, Joyce King, a member of the Curriculum Commission to develop the new Framework, argued that the Framework should espouse a "Multicultural Identity" rather than a *National* one (Cornbleth & Waugh 1995, p. 65). This symbolic reversal of *pluribus* over *Unum* was rejected by state education officials who approved the final version of the Framework. Unfortunately, this ideal posturing did not connect with the real politik of a basically conservative state power structure. Charlotte Crabtree, another member of the Curriculum Commission, noted that King and her supporters failed to recognize that their own preferences won little support. In fact, they were vigorously rejected not only by their ideological opponents in the battle, but by large majorities of those who were looking for a common ground.

Nevertheless, King made an important point which played itself out again and again as various ethnic and religious groups lodged their complaints about the ways in which they were represented in the soon to be adopted textbooks. This overarching symbol, the "National Identity," which was central to the new Framework was also the dominant trope structuring the narrative of the textbooks. In his efforts to produce a version of American history that reflected the spirit of the Framework, as well as meeting the depth and breadth constraints for a conventional length textbook, Gary Nash resorted to a two-track narrative strategy which, in effect, told "two contradictory stories" (Gitlin, 1995). There was a grand Eurocentric narrative which was a hegemonic history told from above, recording the actions of those who held the power. And interspersed with this "master narrative" are "snippets of social history . . . from below" (p. 20). It was largely through these "snippets" that a mosaic of multicultural voices and images was orchestrated to complement the more traditional story.

Just as the National Identity subordinated America's diversity in the Framework, this master narrative could, likewise, only subordinate these *other* narratives. Though content-wise these textbooks were far ahead of anything that had been done before, "the most pluralist textbooks ever brought before the state of California," as Gitlin had noted (p. 28), once a multicultural narrative line was introduced, so too was the desire not only for a place in that story but for a determining voice in how that story would be constructed. Though Nash was often in agreement with the identified shortcomings of minority representation in textbooks, the issue of ceding authorial control to those minorities was not a negotiable one. Pragmatically, the best a political middle ground would allow was inclusion. Still, being a seasoned textbook author he believed that "you can't produce a book which is all-inclusive. . . . You can't write the history of every ethnic group in California." And, "you certainly can't do it for the entire country" (Gitlin, 1995). To do so, he said on another occasion, would require that "you carry it around in a wheelbarrow." We return to his interesting remark at the conclusion of this chapter.

In the traditional social studies curriculum the teaching of "history, especially national history, has been linked explicitly to the cultivation of good citizenship" (Fullinwider, 1996). The teaching of history in the California Framework was part of a larger national curriculum reform advocating the study of history as central to this "cultivation" (see Gagnon, 1989; Ravitch & Finn, 1987). But Michael Kammen (1989), a member of the Bradley Commission that led this reform, observed that although the study of history served to enhance the goals of civic education it also had another more important purpose, and that was "to enrich the understanding of identity. . . ." (p. 149)

On this point the Commission wholly concurred. Besides being an important factor in enabling students to become better citizens, the study of history would "satisfy young people's longing for a sense of identity, and of their time and place in the human story" (Gagnon, 1989, p. 22).

Yet with the articulation of this identity in the narrative of the textbooks, which attempted to blend a *national* with a *multicultural* storyline, no one group could be fully satisfied. Echoing Toni Cook's (1991) remark that "it is important for kids to *see* themselves" represented positively in a multicultural curriculum, Todd Gitlin remarked that "minority parents" believe that "their children . . . need to find [visual] exemplars who look like them in history books." They need, he said, to have a place in that "public imagery" of the dominant culture which has excluded them (Gitlin, 1995). The question of how such a "public imagery" might be re-imagined in multicultural terms may be important in coming to understand the criticism directed at the "hot spots." It may be that these controversial images arose from the same "public" source.

AT THE VISUAL/VERBAL CENTER OF THE ADOPTION STORM

> Since all political struggle in the postmodern era necessarily passes through the simulacral realm of a mass culture, the media are absolutely central to any discussion of multiculturalism. The contemporary media shape identity; indeed many argue that they now exist close to the very core of identity production. In a transnational world typified by the global circulation of images and sounds, goods and people, media spectatorship impacts complexly on national identity and communal belonging.
> —Ella Shohat and Robert Stam (1994, pp. 6–7)

> When you're reading a book your supposed to be ignoring everything that's outside it. It's just here, [you and the book]. But with TV it's that kind of total picture we're so used to, not just what's on screen but what's outside it. What a real multicultural world is like, is [that] you can't draw those lines anymore.
> —Rob Wittig (1992)

Embedded in the text of the *Cultural Literacy* strand of the California Framework there is a prescriptive statement which encourages students to "develop a multicultural perspective that respects the dignity and worth of all people." One way such a "perspective" can be shaped, it states, is for students to learn about "what visual images portray their idea of themselves as a people." It is, however, essential that we as educators realize that this learning largely takes place outside the classroom, and address the implications of this fact. Today children learn about themselves and others largely from the media. From an African American standpoint, Toni Cook suggested that a "multicultural curriculum" was necessary to counteract the negative stereotypes coming from the dominant public culture which is largely maintained by the mass media. While Gitlin seems to be arguing that minority children need to see themselves positively represented in textbooks by visual "exemplars," need to see themselves included in this "public imagery," we would have to admit that such "imagery" doesn't exist solely within the context of a textbook. Rather, it is also, as Cook notes, already out there in the mediascape which has redefined traditional democratic notions of a "public sphere" to which Gitlin seems to be alluding (see Calhoun, 1992, and Robbins, 1993). This Image industry that is now synonymous with most major publishing houses, rarely represents minorities as part of this "public imagery," but tends, as Cook (1991) observed, to serve up, either deliberately or unconsciously, dehumanizing images which reflect the darker side of a "public" imaginary.

In terms of the visual/verbal features that became "hot spots" in the adoption controversy, it should be noted first that it is quite remarkable, given the actual number of images used throughout the K–8 series, that only a handful were controversial (see Table 3.1, Chap. 3, Houghton Mifflin Social Studies Specifications for totals). Nevertheless it is instructive to examine various adoption audience reaction to these "hot spots," because in their analysis may lie the fundamental path of approach to give the Visual Learning strand a critical edge. As noted earlier, in order to evaluate some of the more controversial visual/verbal features a number of basic concepts from semiotics will be introduced which are incidentally part of a vernacular common to the field of graphic design, especially advertising, as well as to the academic disciplines of cultural and media communication studies.

To be fair, there is really nothing inherently offensive about the four examples at which we will look. The first is technically nothing more than an editorial oversight of the photo researchers and caption writers. Visually, the others indicate that the artists tried to render the most neutral, inoffensive images possible. Yet from a semiotic perspective what seems to have been overlooked was not the image itself, but the viewpoint of their interpreters; how these images would be looked at by the minority audiences who were being represented. According to Charles Peirce a sign is "something that stands for someone or something in some respect"(Nöth, 1990, p. 42). All signs, or in this case visual/verbal re-presentations (literally *to present again*), as Wittig observed, are "arbitrary." Every sign is the product of a three-way relation between what Peirce would call the "representamen, the sign's object, and the interpretant." In this case the concrete visual image of *A Moment in Time* would be the "representamen" often referred to in semiotics as the signifier (Nöth, 1990, pp. 42–43). The "sign's object" would be what the image refers to (what is signified), and the "interpretant" would be the discerning mind that views the image and gives it a particular meaning. Though signs are "arbitrary," they nevertheless function within a cultural system. Within this system they have a conventional meaning, but the correspondence between meaning and sign is never wholly exact. Meaning still depends on the relative position the "interpretant" has within that culture. For example, the school children from Oakland, California whom Toni Cook refers to, who might tend to be at the socioeconomic margins of American society, would more than likely not have a conventional mainstream interpretation of these visual images.

This type of discontinuity in interpretation was the basic issue with the four "hot spots." Signs have two communicative functions: denotation and connotation. "Denotation is the direct meaning of a word, sign, or image. Connotation, a second level of meaning, is conveyed or suggested in addition to the denotation" (Meggs, 1989, p. 14). One can say that in their two-way thumbnail dialogues, the Ligature designers overlooked connotation. They interrogated the image and what it signified, but they did not, it seems, ask how an audience might respond to it connotatively. The four features looked at here are:

1. *A Closer Look: The Grand Canyon*, in *From Sea to Shining Sea*, Grade 3, pp. 20–21, in which the photograph inset of the explorer John Wesley Powell and Tau-Gu, Chief of the Paiutes, appears.

2. Lesson 2: The Development of Culture in *A Message of Ancient Days*, Grade 6, pp. 97–100, in which *A Moment in Time: A Cro-Magnon Toolmaker* appears.

3. *A Moment in Time: Escaping Slave* which appears in *America Will Be*, Grade 5, p. 454

4. *A Moment in Time: A Caravan Camel*, in *Across the Centuries*, Grade 7, p. 56

Some of the more general semiotic terms introduced here, including those already mentioned, are:

- a *sign* is a physical perceptible form used by people to refer to something other than itself, for example, the word *camel* is an accepted English graphic term used to refer to the desert animal.
- *signifier/signified* are the dual components which make up a sign. The *signifier* refers to the physical form and the *signified* is the associated mental concept which generally refers to an object in external reality.
- *denotation and connotation* describe relationships between signs, external reality, and viewers. Denotation is the simple and direct relationship between a sign and what it refers to, for example, a photograph of a camel denotes a camel. Connotation refers to the interpretation by the viewer of a sign, giving it a metaphorical meaning which is not denoted by the sign itself. For example, the connotated meaning given by viewers to *A Moment in Time: Caravan Camel*.
- *anchorage* describes the function of words used as captions for images. The words literally anchor the image to a specific meaning by naming, defining, or explaining its content.
- *polysemy,* literally: "many meanings." The tendency of images to connote, to exceed the intended meaning, even when they are anchored, that is, named and defined.
- *icon/index/symbol* are three categories or ways signs can convey meaning. An *icon* resembles its object, it looks or sounds like it. In an *index* there is a direct link between a sign and its object, for

example, smoke is an index for fire. In a *symbol* there is no direct connection, except the one conventionally agreed upon, for example, the eagle is an American national symbol.

• *encoding and decoding* is basically the process of communicating meaning through signs in which the sender *encodes* a particular meaning in a sign which is communicated or transmitted in some fashion and then *decoded* or interpreted by the receiver.

• *preferred/negotiated/oppositional reading* are different meanings attributed to signs by senders and receivers. The *preferred* reading (denoted) is the one acceptable to the presenter or sender. The *negotiated* reading is the act of contesting the preferred meaning of a sign (its code) such that its meaning is only provisionally accepted and held up to critical evaluation. The *oppositional* reading rejects the preferred meaning as false.

• *representation* is a likeness, picture, copy of something which attempts to be closely analogous to the object represented.

• *stereotype* is a caricature of something which may convey a general or partial truth about the object represented, but in so doing reduces its actual complexity to such a simplistic level that it distorts its truer meaning.

• *culture and ideology* is respectively the signifying and symbolic system (*culture*) within which a particular group generates its own beliefs and meaning (*ideology*).

(terms adapted from Fiske, 1990, pp. 39–114, 164–188)

Before entering this discussion it is helpful to recall the instructional context in which visual images in the K–8 series were meant to be understood. This is important because it speaks to the issue of realism and how visual images, especially photographs, are conventionally considered to mirror reality as naturalized representations. In Chapter 2 there was discussion about the "Talking Ear of Corn" in the *About Your Book* section, where a distinction was made between "real" and "unreal" images (see Fig. 2.3, chap. 2). This true/false criterion is operative throughout the series. This principle could probably have been derived from the guidelines for instructional media in the California Framework (1988) which stress that "visual nonprint materials" should be "accurate, objective, current and appropriate" (p. 120). In general this is basically the standard for visual material used in social studies. To serve this principle the third-grade textbook introduces the concept of *captions* (see Fig. 2.4, chap. 2). It is largely this denotative function for which captions were designed in the K–8 program.

As stated earlier, *denotation* "is the direct meaning of a word, sign, or image." The captions in *A Closer Look* or *A Moment in Time* were meant to function in a denotative fashion. The captions were supposed to "anchor" the image, that is, tie it down to a specific meaning. The function of *anchorage* is basically just this: to hold, if not restrict, the image to a particular meaning (Meggs, 1989). In most instances this was largely nonproblematic because the majority of images were primary source archival images, hence realistic. But the *Moments* were imaginative renderings with only the most tangential connection to historical events. In these more controversial *Moments,* as we shall see, even the captions could not anchor the intended meaning conceived for the image, instead actually serving to connote other meanings. Generally, this is because images tend to be *polysemic.* Simply put they can signify many (poly) meanings. Being polysemic, images with or even without a caption, tend to connote, that is they can suggest meanings counter to the apparent one.

The Power of Naming

In every respect *A Closer Look: The Grand Canyon* (Fig. 6.1) is similar to the standard visual/verbal format specifications followed for other *Closer Looks* in the Series (see Fig. 2.9 in Chap. 2: *History in the Details*). As signs, one can interpret the layered background, central, and detail images as falling broadly into the three types of categories: *iconic, indexical, and symbolic* signs listed above. An *icon* has a one-to-one resemblance with the thing it represents (Meggs, 1989, p. 8). The detail photographs of the pick hammer and pieces of rock are just that: a rock, a hammer. However, at the same time the icon pick hammer would be used by a paleontologist and so it can be seen as *indexical* image having a "factual or causal connection" pointing directly to that field. While the central layered images of the Grand Canyon function iconically they also can be viewed *symbolically.* For instance, the Canyon can be interpreted as a symbol for the immensity of cosmic time (Meggs, 1989, p. 8).

However, the image that became a symbol of some controversy is in the top right center of *Grand Canyon*. In the background above the hammer there is a small black and white oval shaped photograph identified by the caption to its right. Given its small size, it is uncanny how "loaded" this image/text inset is. When Roland Barthes (1977) talks about "the text loading the image with a culture, moral, [and] imagination," he can be said, though in a narrow sense, to be describing the signifying function of the caption to *anchor* the image with a specific meaning. At the same time, when he includes "imagination" he is alluding to the possibility of *connotation.* Yet in a wider sense he is describing how *culture* and *ideology* communicate a meaning *encoded* in the designed visual/verbal object such as the photograph/caption of John Wesley Powell. One might look at the Thumbnail Process as the point in the design process of these textbooks where this image of John Wesley Powell was *encoded* with its *preferred meaning.* As an entry into this discussion of its controversial elements, one might even apply the same questions used by the Thumbnail team. You may recall there were four questions the team would constantly ask: Why is that image there? What is it doing or showing? What kind of explanation is there for it? And, what concept is it trying to get across? (see Chap. 2: The Terms of Apportionment).

What is immediately apparent when these four questions are applied is that the original caption seems to be inadequate on all counts. In fact, critics weighed in against this caption because it names only one person, John Wesley Powell, the explorer, and not the Indian. Until the 1994 revised edition the Indian had no name. A comparison of the 1991 and 1994 captions suggests a great deal about the nature of the historical omission when read in conjunction with viewing the photograph:

> John Wesley Powell, standing on the right, explored the Grand Canyon by boat, in 1869. (1991)
>
> In this 1873 photograph, John Wesley Powell talks with Tau-Gu, Chief of the Paiutes, near the Grand Canyon. (1994)

In the first, the Indian is not even mentioned though he is right there towering above Powell in the photo. In the second, his name and actual status were fortunately discovered. Still, given the suggestive richness of the photograph one might conceive of another possible caption which reads: Tau-Gu, Chief of the Paiutes, shows John Wesley Powell the rock formations of the Grand Canyon. Such a role reversal where a Native American and not the heroic White explorer determines the narrative feeds into a larger ideological issue. According to the original caption: "Few people knew about the canyon's beauty until Powell shared information he learned on his journey." In the revised caption, "Few people . . ." is changed to "Few *White* people knew about the canyon's beauty . . ." Embedded in this visual/verbal trope is the clash of two opposing cultural imaginaries. In the original, the heroic White explorer charts an unknown Western Frontier. Here a Eurocentric motif of discovery and exploration is reinforced. In the other, a multicultural history from below, the explorer seems to become guest and pupil who is on a guided tour of the local chief's backyard. Yet such an interpretation is possible only when we go beyond the caption and really look at the picture. Are visible traces of countermeaning embedded in the body language of Powell and Tau-Gu, or is it just wishful projection? Such a clash of imaginaries is perhaps inevitable with the two track narrative that Nash employed (Gitlin, 1995). In this case, the intended balance did not result.

Consequently, this visual/verbal imbalance compelled adoption critics to question the cultural politics of the designers. Here even the reasonable explanation of the author, Gary Nash, did not suffice. That Ligature's image acquisition researchers simply couldn't identify either the person or his tribal affiliation for the first edition was taken as a subtle unconscious slippage which betrayed a Eurocentric bias. Though unintended, their critical audience *read* it as a textual erasure of an all too visible Other.

Here is a case where the designers should "say only what you can see," but didn't. The opposite of this admonition was recommended for the visual/verbal layering strategy devised for the *Moments* and *Closer Looks* (see Chap. 2: Say

A CLOSER LOOK

The Grand Canyon

The power of a river can change the earth. The Colorado River has formed a huge canyon by working its way through layers of rock. Every year, for millions of years, the canyon has become deeper and wider.

Millions of years ago, sand, gravel, and boulders were swept along by the river. These materials scraped away layers and layers of rock.

What was once a river bed is now the Grand Canyon. The Colorado River started out on flat land. Today it is a mile deep and almost 20 miles wide in some places.

John Wesley Powell... explored the... Few people... until...

Fossils may be found where the Colorado River has cut down through layers of rock. Fossils are the remains or traces of past plants or animals. This fossil shows a fern that once grew in the canyon.

FIGURE 6.1. John Wesley Powell and Tau-Gu in a Closer Look: The Grand Canyon, Grade 3, pp. 20–21.

What You Cannot See). This absence is an excellent example of the importance of captions in altering the content of images. There are any number of classic cases, especially in photojournalism and propaganda, where a mere caption can totally deceive the viewer (see Goldberg, 1991). Here, though, the intention was hardly to deceive or even mislead. Rather from a multicultural perspective a small oversight becomes loaded with significance. In the revision the first man to see the Grand Canyon became the first *White* man, and Tau-Gu's name was discovered and added.

These may seem small added traces of meaning, yet together they serve to wholly re-orient the narrative away from a Eurocentric point of view. Such details are like cracks in a well overlaid structure through which we can peer to discover that we are seeing the Grand Canyon for the first time, through the eyes of Tau-Gu. In expanding the narrative to a multiperspectival dimension such shifts are both revealing and instructive.

Visualizing a Remote Present

In the next example it is not the questionable text of a *caption* but the *con-text* of the lesson in which the *Moment in Time* is set which became controversial. Again, this visual/verbal doubling effect was at work. The evocative opening section of the lesson served to realign the *preferred* meaning of the *Moment*. The juxtaposition was so jarring it produced multiple negative *connotations*.

Lesson 2: *The Development of Culture,* which includes the *Moment in Time: A Cro-Magnon Toolmaker,* found in the sixth grade text *A Message of Ancient Days*, would hardly seem to have enough pages to discuss a development which covers a time span of over two million years in human evolution. In a mere five pages the lesson abruptly jumps from discussing the appearance of Homo habilus in Africa to Homo erectus in Europe. The Lesson Focus is on the development of language and toolmaking. It begins with the text encouraging the student reader to participate in a visualization exercise. To stimulate this imaginative construction the lesson page format provides a beautiful setting photograph of a lush east African plain depicting a lone tree holding center stage in a vast expanse of grass, mountains, and sky. At the top of the page a red and gold timeline marks off the timeframe of the Lesson which runs from 3,500,000 to 40,000 B.C. The year is 2,500,000 B.C. Using the photograph as a visualizing ground, students are asked to imagine an encounter with "two naked, dark-skinned people," who are supposed to represent "our early ancestor Homo habilus." Compelled by hunger, the student's only means of survival is to make friends with his "dark-skinned" peers through sign language.

> You put on a friendly smile and walk toward them. Their first reaction
> is to laugh. . . . You point to your open mouth to show them you are
> hungry. They nod, talk to each other in a strange language, and motion
> for you to wait. One person walks off toward a field. The other person
> picks up two rocks and begins striking one against the other to make a

sharp edge. Soon the first person returns with a bloody bone. The people place it on the ground and pound it with the sharpened stone. They invite you to eat the red marrow oozing from the bone. (*A Message of Ancient Days*, Grade 6, 1991, pp. 97–98)

With this mental image of "dark-skinned" creatures eating a bloody bone now suggestively framed the lesson introduces toolmaking practices by contrasting the primitive tools made by Homo habilus with the more sophisticated toolmaking of Homo erectus. The jump from Homo habilus to Homo erectus is made by turning the page. The mental image is followed by a visual image of a *Cro-Magnon Toolmaker circa 11:17 AM, April 23, 12,011 B.C.* (Fig. 6.2). The lesson ends with a section titled, *Using Language,* which states that "People often communicate with one another without using language."

Ironically, this jarring juxtaposition of images did communicate nonverbally and not just to adoption critics. Gary Nash felt that the Cro-Magnon looked strikingly contemporary. The rendering reminded him more of a California surfer who could have just stepped off the beach at Malibu than an ancient toolmaker. To Joyce King, the only dissenting member of the California Curriculum Commission who later resigned to vigorously oppose adoption of the Houghton Mifflin textbooks, these images together had a much darker connotation. She argued that the "juxtaposition" of these images were deeply "problematic" because they alluded to the worst sort of racial and cultural "stereotypes" (Reinhold, 1991, p. 46). With only the turn of a page the naked "dark-skinned" African is superseded by a clothed white-skinned European. The crude binary logic of stereotypes seemed to be reinforced when the primitive toolmaking of the Homo habilus which produces only a "bloody bone" is matched with the sophisticated tools attributed to the Homo erectus Cro-Magnon man. In this *Moment* the callouts describe a clean shaven man with a variegated diet of grains and meat.

Beverly Armento commented that there was so much trouble with the *Moments in Time* because, since these were imaginative recreations, the artists could only resort to stereotypes. The tendency to unwittingly produce such stereotypes only seemed to increase as the connection to an actual historical event grew more tenuous. For example, consider the acceptability of the stereotypical Knight and the Samurai (see Figs. 2.7 and 2.8, Chap. 2) because they used actual historic events as a background setting for the image. In the *Closer Looks* features, stereotyping seemed to be less a problem in general because the presentation was thematically constructed around archeological and historical artifacts, archival visual material, photographs, and primary source documents.

Nevertheless, the problem of realism and representation remains for both. Although the photograph of John Wesley Powell and Tau-Gu obviously documents a real historic moment, its caption mis-represented what the photo was showing. In the *Development of Culture* lesson the *representation* is based on the best archeological evidence and scientific speculation to date. Yet in trying to picture such a remote past, artist and writer unwittingly fell back on the worst sort of

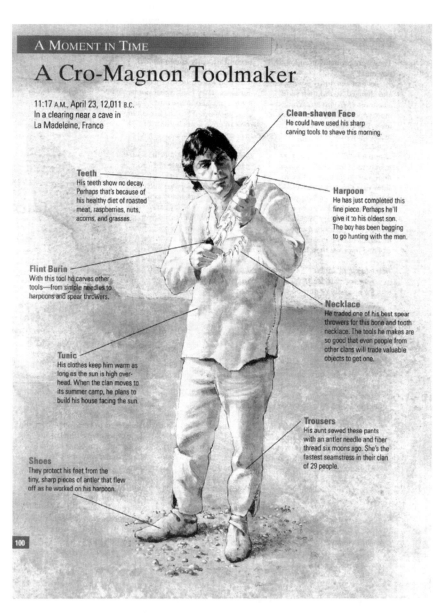

A MOMENT IN TIME

A Cro-Magnon Toolmaker

11:17 A.M., April 23, 12,011 B.C.
In a clearing near a cave in
La Madeleine, France

Clean-shaven Face
He could have used his sharp
carving tools to shave this morning.

Teeth
His teeth show no decay.
Perhaps that's because of
his healthy diet of roasted
meat, raspberries, nuts,
acorns, and grasses.

Harpoon
He has just completed this
fine piece. Perhaps he'll
give it to his oldest son.
The boy has been begging
to go hunting with the men.

Flint Burin
With this tool he carves other
tools—from simple needles to
harpoons and spear throwers.

Necklace
He traded one of his best spear
throwers for this bone and tooth
necklace. The tools he makes are
so good that even people from
other clans will trade valuable
objects to get one.

Tunic
His clothes keep him warm as
long as the sun is high overhead. When the clan moves to
its summer camp, he plans to
build his house facing the sun.

Trousers
His aunt sewed these pants
with an antler needle and fiber
thread six moons ago. She's the
fastest seamstress in their clan
of 29 people.

Shoes
They protect his feet from the
tiny, sharp pieces of antler that flew
off as he worked on his harpoon.

100

FIGURE 6.2. A Moment in Time: A Cro-Magnon Toolmaker, Grade 6, p. 100.

cultural stereotypes: Africans are primitive, naked, and dark-skinned, whereas Europeans are civilized, clothed, and White. And when inadvertently combined, the expressive power of images and words became a negative charge to the critical eye. In the revised edition the words "dark skinned," "bloody," and "oozing" were omitted. But the Cro-Magnon surfer remains.

Empowering the Powerless Image

The problem of stereotypes was even more pronounced in the *Escaping Slave–Moment in Time,* in the fifth-grade text *America Will Be* (Fig. 6.3). Even though the image was easily supported by the historic record—it depicted a slave in his flight North along the Underground Railroad, circa 1848—it nevertheless ran into trouble. The presentation of the *Moment* followed the standard format which built up textual layers of detail through an array of callouts set around the central image of the slave. In every respect these captions scrupulously adhered to historical standards of evidence. Every detail was plausible and could easily be based on accounts of the Underground Railroad. From the standpoint of a historian it was a fair and accurate representation. Gary Nash argued that it not be removed from the revised edition.

With the Cro-Magnon/Homo habilus one could argue that the juxtaposition was chance, or that the Thumbnail team responsible for the design of this lesson spread really missed because what they were attempting to depict was impossibly remote. But with the *Escaping Slave,* even though the image had a basis in historical fact, such explanations were not enough. What then was wrong with it? In a word, the place to start is with the *viewing position* of the respective audience. In general, the audience brings to a visual image a complex set of intellectual and cultural presuppositions which reflect the individual background of the viewer (Williams, 1995). From the perspective of a historian one could examine the image of the barefoot slave and see history. Yet from the perspective of African American academics, the image of the barefoot slave appeared "more akin to an animal than a . . . human being" (Cornbleth & Waugh 1995, p. 67).

To gain a better understanding of how such opposing views can follow from the same image, it is necessary to look again at the unintended dual function of the callouts that complement the image. For it is safe to say that both the image and the callouts can be subjected to a double reading. That is, depending on the *viewing position* of the audience both interpretations are equally valid. Whether you see an animal in flight or a slave soon to be free can be a projection reflecting your own viewing position. Similarly, it could be read in the textual and figurative codes embedded in the image which correspond to cultural stereotypes, or both. If we start with the callouts which surround the images the connotative possibilities inherent in nearly every description tend to build on each other and greatly increase the likelihood that the caption will not so much be plainly read but *read into*. That is, the *preferred reading* can be *negotiated* into an *oppositional* one which contradicts the intended denotative function of the description.

There are seven callouts. Counterclockwise from left to right there are callouts titled: *Eyes, Back, Papers, Feet, Clothes, Straw*, and *Stomach*. Of the seven, four refer directly to various parts of the body image. What is interesting about three of these body descriptions is that each can readily imply stereotypic traits and characteristics associated with both humans and animals. For example, the escaping slave's eyes are described as "accustomed to night travel. He hopes to avoid being captured by traveling at night and sleeping by day." Such a description is analogous to the traits of nocturnal animals who are also active at night and sleep during the day. Similarly, the stereotypical description of the slave's scarred back can also suggest the whipping of animals. This analogy to animals culminates with the exposed and vulnerable bare feet of the slave, which is reinforced by the callout. Although it is historically plausible to assume that slaves, especially "field hands," were more likely to be barefoot than to wear shoes, the common stereotype suggested by bare feet is that slaves were held to be no different than the farm animals who worked the fields with them.

One might ask that while it may be historically accurate to depict a slave poised at the moment of his liberation, why did its African American critics not find it empowering? My close reading found suggestive double messages there. These callouts and the image suggest that the visual/verbal doubling effect which Wittig describes can work both ways. Unfortunately he only saw the positive potential in such devices. But if I could easily see and read countermeanings, why couldn't the other California Curriculum Commission members? Why were the *connotations* so obvious to Joyce King and her teenage children, whom she said responded "without any prompting from her" (Cornbleth & Waugh, 1995, p. 67)?

Given our *viewing position* we bring to the image what Roland Barthes (1977) calls our own "culture, morality and imagination." Less subtly we bring all our baggage with us. At the same time the image by itself is already "burdened," as he says, with the same. It already bears the traces of other similar images and other readings since neither was it made in a vacuum nor is it viewed in one. Rather, it is part of a larger *index* of images within a cultural system, of which the practice of history is a part. But in a multicultural system of representation what kind of imaginative historical reconstructions are acceptable? In the 1994 edition the image of the *Escaping Slave* was replaced with the *Black Abolitionist*. This image depicts a newspaper editor standing before his press holding a notice for an antislavery meeting he has just printed.

When Rob Wittig spoke about multiculturalism being "at the heart of everything we're doing here these days," he was alluding to the fact that they were already responding to the adoption critics' evaluation of the *Escaping Slave*. They were in the midst of trying to *negotiate* with the *oppositional* view, to bring them-

A MOMENT IN TIME

Escaping Slave

3:09 A.M., October 12, 1848
At a safe house near Baltimore

Eyes
The carpenter's eyes are accustomed to night travel. He hopes to avoid being captured by traveling at night and sleeping by day.

Stomach
The scent of coffee and fresh bread makes his hungry stomach growl. The "stationmaster" who prepared breakfast is a freed slave. He often waits up for the "passengers" that come into his "station."

Back
He can still feel the scars from his master's whip after his first escape attempt.

Straw
Hiding for four hours in a "conductor's" hay wagon left bits of straw on his clothes. The conductor, a Maryland farmer, has transported hundreds of escaping slaves along this 20-mile stretch of the Underground Railroad.

Papers
The forged documents that he has just received say he is a free man. These papers might help if slave hunters capture him.

Feet
The journey has made his feet tired. Except for tonight's uncomfortable trip in the wagon, he has traveled on foot for the last four nights.

Clothes
He is a skilled carpenter, but his clothes make him look like a field hand. Many "passengers" on the Underground Railroad wore disguises to fool slave hunters.

454

FIGURE 6.3: A Moment in Time: Escaping Slave, Grade 5, p. 454

selves to that threshold where they could see from the Other side. It's impossible to know if they succeeded with the *Abolitionist*, since the multicultural "common ground" he hoped for was less than utopian. However, Cornbleth and Waugh (1995) note that it "provided a more positive reflection of African American struggles than had the earlier illustration," which "Joyce King and others had found demeaning" (p. 175). Yet the next image illustrates that what we hold in common, those mythologies that burden our imagination and instead hold us, may really be at the heart of what prevents us from reaching that multicultural goal.

Textbook Orientalism

> One aspect of the electronic, postmodern world is that there has been a reinforcement of the stereotypes by which the Orient [Middle East] is viewed. Television, the films, and all media's resources have forced information into more and more standardized molds. So far as the Orient is concerned, standardization and cultural stereotyping have intensified . . .
>
> —Edward Said (1978, p. 26)

With the last "hot spot" there was no disagreement. Both sides saw that it was, in Gary Nash's words, "a mistake" (Gitlin, 1995). This *Moment in Time: A Caravan Camel* (Fig. 6.4), is found in a unit on Islam in the seventh-grade textbook *Across the Centuries*. This unit reveals a fundamental lack of basic knowledge about Islam and Arab culture that may reflect a gap in textbook developer expertise or may be part of a larger cultural deficit which is typically American, or both. Aside from adverse reaction to the camel, three images of Mohammed also appear in the same unit. But these were editorially removed before the adoption of the textbooks was approved by the state. That images of the Prophet are a cultural taboo for Muslims is a fact that perhaps most American people would not generally know. But that such images seem to continually reappear in textbooks may be a more telling sign. During the last adoption cycle of social studies textbooks in California, a report on "Arabs in American Textbooks" (Al-Qazzaz, Afifi, Pelletiere, & Shabbas, 1975) was submitted to the California State Board of Education in June of 1975. The report is a "detailed analysis of twenty-four social studies textbooks" then up for adoption. You don't have to delve deep into the report to find this critical notation on a book submitted for approval by a major publisher. It states, "Pictures of Mohammed are shown with no explanation that Islamic teaching forbids portrayal of Mohammed as a safeguard against idolatry"(p. 4). The introductory comments also offer this summary evaluation on the majority of the books under review.

> Despite the importance of the Arab world in the past and the present, information about the area is distorted both in the mass media and textbooks. . . . Most textbooks for grades 1–4 present the Arabs as a nomad

with camels and tents in the desert, although Arab nomads represent
less than 5% of the Arab people. (p. 2)

Hindsight two decades hence has Gary Nash coincidentally in the strange
position of belated agreement. The camel, he said, "plays on the stereotype of
the Arab as a camel jockey" (Gitlin, 1995, p. 12). That stereotypes of racial and
ethnic minorities continually reappear in textbooks and American popular culture would probably not surprise many, certainly not Native Americans, Africans, and Arabs. Whether American or not, the three groups represented by the
"hot spots" have all been consistently depicted in a stereotypical fashion by film
and television (see Berkhofer, 1978; Bogle 1994; Shaheen 1984, 1996).

Yet even this seventh-grade textbook *Across the Centuries* in which the Caravan Camel appears attempts to deal intelligently with this phenomenon, but within
the context of European wars fought over religion. To make the concept more
accessible to seventh graders the *Understanding Relationships* feature uses a
more contemporary illustration to show how sex roles were stereotyped in American society of the 1950s. In *Identifying Stereotypes* a photograph shows a typical
white American middle class family packing the trunk of their automobile, getting ready to go on vacation (p. 471). The feature defines a stereotype as "an
oversimplified idea about a group of people. . . . Because they are often based on
partial truths stereotypes can be hard to recognize." On the right side of the family photograph we see a father, in red shirt white cardigan, pipe in mouth and
fishing rod, while his son who stands directly in front of him wears a bright red
football helmet with a baseball bat propped on his shoulder. Seated next to him is
his Lassie look alike pet collie. The symmetry of gender position in this photo is
most revealing for directly opposite we see the smiling blonde mother wearing a
blue dress. In front of her is their daughter also in a blue dress and clutching a
doll.

As insightful as this image may be for gender stereotypes it would seem to
be woefully lacking as a mental setting for students when it asks them to deal
with the much darker reality of European history. The text of the feature notes
that "During the 1500's, Europeans made slaves of the peoples of Africa and the
Americas." This was possible because they "accepted the stereotype of Africans
and Indians as less than human." This substitution of a positively banal image to
illustrate a much more brutal and tragic fact is curious to say the least, though it
may inadvertently point to a more fundamental contradiction at work in these
problematic images.

The stereotypes projected in these images do not reflect a multicultural perspective but a culture, at least in its perception of the Arabs and the Middle Eastern cultures, in a state of arrest. That a report on Arabs in textbooks submitted in
1975 to the California State Board of Education is pointing to the same mistakes
being made again in the next cycle of adoption is perhaps a strong indicator of a

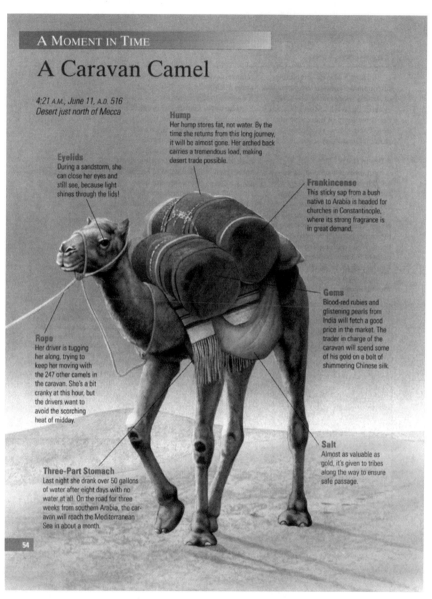

A MOMENT IN TIME

A Caravan Camel

4:21 A.M., June 11, A.D. 516
Desert just north of Mecca

Hump
Her hump stores fat, not water. By the time she returns from this long journey, it will be almost gone. Her arched back carries a tremendous load, making desert trade possible.

Eyelids
During a sandstorm, she can close her eyes and still see, because light shines through the lids!

Frankincense
This sticky sap from a bush native to Arabia is headed for churches in Constantinople, where its strong fragrance is in great demand.

Gems
Blood-red rubies and glistening pearls from India will fetch a good price in the market. The trader in charge of the caravan will spend some of his gold on a bolt of shimmering Chinese silk.

Rope
Her driver is tugging her along, trying to keep her moving with the 247 other camels in the caravan. She's a bit cranky at this hour, but the drivers want to avoid the scorching heat of midday.

Three-Part Stomach
Last night she drank over 50 gallons of water after eight days with no water at all. On the road for three weeks from southern Arabia, the caravan will reach the Mediterranean Sea in about a month.

Salt
Almost as valuable as gold, it's given to tribes along the way to ensure safe passage.

54

FIGURE 6.4. A Moment in Time: A Caravan Camel, Grade 7, p. 54.

public culture whose collective thinking about racial and ethnic minorities has remained, to a substantial degree, at that same stereotypical level.

Our visual culture has so thoroughly colonized our society, our collective mental and physical space, that oftentimes we do not see these images as constructed, but simply as part of the natural order of public perception and common knowledge. Because this mediated social reality is so naturalized we often do not see it as part of a larger network and system which disseminates information as a commodity and not out of any fundamental social obligation to the viewer. Yet institutionally the mass media performs unevenly if not benignly. Taking the good with the bad and ugly, the Media is still our primary electronic window on a multicultural world. On the one hand it can disseminate the worst sort of cultural stereotypes and reduce complex sociopolitical realities to the simplistic black and white terms of a Western. At the same time none of this is so mystifying and impenetrable that it cannot be *seen* for what it is, and used as a bridge to a larger, more nuanced worldview. In a multicultural visual education Rob Wittig observed we would want the students to ask not only, "Who's missing from this picture," but also "invite kids to look at the man behind the curtain."

WHAT YOU SEE IS NOT WHAT YOU GET

The production and arrangement of images in textbooks draw *intertextually* on a media language that saturates the popular culture inside and outside the school. . . . [These images are part] of a larger system . . . that positions minorities . . . in relation to dominant whites. In many cases our students depend on the media, more so than on textbooks. . . . We must therefore find some way dynamically to interrogate the current production of images in popular culture . . . in the classroom.

—Cameron McCarthy (1993, pp. 296–297)

Recasting Harold Rugg's words at the beginning of this chapter, we might ask what is the "task" of the "forward looking" social studies "curriculum-maker" in a multicultural present? Rather than asking how the National Identity was visually rendered in the books, we have looked at how the Nation's collective unconscious, our public Imaginary, refracts our understanding of particular cultural groups into visual stereotypes. This act of visual analysis or decoding, I would suggest, is one critical "task" which should be brought to bear in evaluating the visual content of multicultural curriculum materials, and likewise a necessary visual learning skill in any multicultural curriculum strand.

In this review, we saw a 19th-century photograph of an anonymous Native American standing alongside a famous White American explorer. Next, a vivid mental image of our hominid ancestors was set against an illustration of a Cro-Magnon toolmaker who looked more contemporary than ancient. Another illustration of an escaping slave seemed to evoke markedly different responses depending on the racial composition of the audience. And lastly, we see a rope leading off the page and beyond the frame of the picture where a caravan camel holds center stage. Who is holding that rope? One photograph, one mental image and three illustrations intending to represent from various perspectives elusive historical realities and multicultural identities. In each of these visual artifacts the symbolic dynamics at work destabilized the image such that the denoted or intended meaning became suspect, thus allowing multiple readings on the part of the viewer. In so being the image reveals connotative symbolic layers not apparent to the artist. These countermeanings in some instances reflect ideologies of racial and ethnic stereotyping, and cannot be understood in terms of the real/unreal criteria of accuracy and objectivity held as guidelines for the series.

In each case we might ask, where do these images come from? Is the cultural space of the artist who created the image and of those who were represented the same? Can the National Identity and these other cultures actually share that same space? And lastly, what does it mean *to see in*, or *from*, a multicultural perspective? How do we know when the image captures that intangible order of correspondence between viewing subject and viewed object, such that a racial, ethnic, religious or gender group see themselves reflected in that image? In each of these images, that which was intended by the artist was not seen by the viewer. We do not see "their idea" of how they "see themselves as a people." Had a Native American written the caption for the Tau-Gu and John Wesley Powell photograph, how would it be phrased? How would that moment in the Grand Canyon be described? How would Joyce King's children render their version of an escaping slave? These "hot spots" are like cracks and fissures in the edifice of the National Identity which reveal the gap between American ideals and the way things are.

In the present we can understand neither our National Identity nor multiculturalism without first coming to terms with how our visual culture is a window on both. It is certain that when Rugg made his pronouncement the printed textbook had a status it does not enjoy now. For Social Studies then, textbooks were at the educational nexus of a print culture which shaped the educational discourse of citizenship. In our postmodern world we are cast in the role of spectators. Political discourse has largely become political sound bites and photo-ops. This alone would seem to require that we give a critical visual edge to citizenship education, to begin as it were to articulate how our visual culture underpins the social and political dimensions of American society. Douglas Kellner (1995a) contends that a "postmodern pedagogy" calls for "reading images critically." He believes that such a reading "involves learning how to appreciate, and interpret images concerning both *how* they are constructed and operate in our lives and *what* they communicate in concrete situations" (p. 64). Kellner (1995b) suggests that such a visual learning strategy would also be important to a "critical multicultural approach." Within this perspective the study of images would

> involve analysis of relationships of domination and oppression, the way
> stereotyping works, resistance on the part of stigmatized groups to domi-
> nant representations, and the struggle of these groups to represent them-

selves, to counter dominant and distorting representations, and to produce more positive ones. "Multicultural" here thus functions as a general rubric for all those attempts to resist the stereotyping, distortions,
and stigmatizing of the dominant culture. (1995b, p. 94)

Though their protest was to little or no avail, at least at the state level, Joyce
King and Toni Cook may have understood the inherent "problem," if not outright
contradiction, in trying to satisfactorily represent a multicultural perspective from
the standpoint of the dominant culture. The *real politik* of the adoption battle was
largely orchestrated for media attention in Oakland. On the day the Los Angeles
Unified School District voted to adopt, Joyce King strode up to a bank of micro-
phones and a wall of video cameras outside district headquarters with an enormous box of Aunt Jemima in hand, making a dramatic gesture about cultural stereotypes that perhaps few understood. Like Toni Cook of Oakland, she seemed to
understand that the "National Identity" is largely constructed by and lived through
the mass media.

Publishing is also a mass medium. The California Framework was a document reflecting a consensus of elite educational experts on a definition of
multiculturalism that would appeal to a majority of Californians on both sides of
the political spectrum. Textbooks, always a mass market product, are designed to
meet the requirements of the state and the educational needs of a culturally diverse
yet nevertheless mass audience. What is politically possible is not usually visionary, yet oftentimes quiet revolutions begin with small steps. Although the California Framework and the adopted textbooks which accompanied its implementation
may represent only a "first stage multiculturalism," they nevertheless set the stage
for what will come (Jones & Maloy, 1996). Like the mass media, textbooks represent a broadcast model of communication. The same product with uniform content is disseminated to all. The publisher produces, the state allocates, the teacher
instructs, and the student turns the page. As the adoption process illustrates, it's
very hard to change channels.

As an educational phenomenon, multiculturalism may be more akin to a distributed computer network. In the California Framework you have the force of
two contending symbols: the National Identity and Multiculturalism. Whereas the
latter pushes for an inclusive narrative with equal coverage and representation for
all, the former forces a common identity to center stage and presents a master
narrative in which all these lesser voices are subsumed. In the textbook series, the
narrative structure followed the Framework, producing, in effect, "two contradictory stories" (Gitlin, 1995). In a sense the inherent limitations of the print medium
produce an "additive approach" to multiculturalism, in which these lesser voices
are, in effect, added onto the master narrative (Banks, 1995).Though speaking
about the content issue of adequately representing ethnic minorities, Gary Nash
indirectly alludes to the material constraints of the textbook medium.

You can't produce a book which is all inclusive. You can't emphasize the Chinese in San Francisco *and* the Armenians in Fresno *and* the Portuguese in San Pablo *and* the Italians in the North beach *and* the Koreans in L.A. You can't write the history of every ethnic group in California. You certainly can't do it for the entire country. (Gitlin, 1995, p. 19)

Multiculturalism seems to create a burden of representation that may be impossible to fulfill, at least in a textbook medium. Reduced to such material terms, Nash seemed to agree. On another occasion he remarked that if one attempted such an inclusive history "you'd have to carry the book around in a wheelbarrow."

In addition to the material constraints and narrative contradictions of multicultural inclusion, the introduction of all the features, visual or otherwise, seemed to further expand the field of the narrative, thus adding to the apparent structural fragmentation, and thereby making it look more like a "scrapbook" than a textbook (Gitlin, 1995). Echoing a view that Gilbert Sewall and Arthur Woodward would certainly share, Todd Gitlin comments that

the books' thematic disjointedness is embodied in, and even intensified by, their format, which gives them the look of scrapbooks. . . . The layouts get in the way in an attempt to be hip, multimedia, and all that. The books don't put the fragments together. . . . Indeed, to anyone raised on linear texts, these books bear a disconcerting resemblance to MTV. (p. 21)

However, this type of evaluation may reflect a bias or conservatism of another type. Rather than looking at "scraps" we are actually seeing designed modules, carefully crafted nodes of visual/verbal information, not "fragments." Having introduced some basic semiotic terms to critically evaluate the "hotspots" in the series, we also need to shift to a semiotic perspective in order to grasp the structural conventions of information design, discussed in previous chapters, which do indeed "put the fragments together," though obviously not in the conventional linear terms with which Gitlin is more at ease.

It may be that the source of this basic unease with multiculturalism in the adoption controversy is not so much its message as the inherent limitations of the textbook medium to contain it. The innovative visual features in this series, such as *A Moment in Time* and *A Closer Look,* failed to adequately represent a multicultural viewpoint. But even these shortcomings perhaps only reflect the limitations of the artist, and not of the inspired visual/verbal format, for presenting complex themes and information. The material constraints of breadth and depth of coverage in a textbook were also overwhelmed by the basic demand for inclusion which multiculturalism makes. As an author, Gary Nash is right to fear the demands for inclusion which multiculturalism makes, since it means, at least at one level, the end of linear master narratives and monolithic textbooks, which cannot easily support or integrate multiperspectival viewpoints. It may be that the emerging technologies of multimedia offer multiculturalism a medium appropriate to its inclusive message. A database doesn't need to be "carried around in a wheelbar-row," and a network isn't carried at all. Yet regardless of his disdain for the hipness of the formats and the "scrapbook" feel, Gitlin has a point. Neither book nor network will provide us with the "bridges" necessary to access a cultural space in which differences can be held freely and in common, a truly "public imagery" where all the fragments come together as "stories well told." Because multiculturalism as an educational phenomenon seems to reveal the inherent limitations of the textbook as a representational medium, the next chapter explores a few steps beyond the cultural boundaries of the book. The emerging technologies which brought this visual/verbal textbook series to its realization are also mapping the electronic learning spaces of today and the borderless cultures of tommorow.

A Window in the Text

There is nothing outside the [screen].

Imaginary waves are actually breaking on an imaginary beach . . .
—Richard Mark Friedhoff and William Benzon, *Visualization:
The Second Computer Revolution* (1989)

Close to the end of research on this project I was invited to speak at the annual meeting of the Hawaiian Social Studies Association. Never having been to the Islands, I gratefully accepted. It was October, 1994. The day before the talk I gave a brief presentation of my Visual Turn research findings to a small group of faculty at the College of Education at the University of Hawaii, Manoa. This talk was relatively easy to give because it was a summary of the principal issue arising from the study which concerned reading visual/verbal information in textbook formats. However, the talk I had planned for the Social Studies Association had caused me a great deal of anxiety. At the end of a long research project I had wanted to "envision," like Tufte, beyond the results of my study which connected visual/verbal thinking to speculation about how children might learn from the graphical interface of the computer. There was also the desire to render the "big picture" about how the physical space of the classroom was soon to be virtually co-terminus with cyberspace. This convergence point was traceable, I felt, in the beautiful visuals nested in the white space of the Houghton Mifflin books. All were like windows in the text through which kids, unlike most teachers or parents, could look to see what was on the other side.

Given this anxiety, I pieced together half of the college talk with part of a paper entitled *Virtual Mario*, although I told the Association people I would give something called "Steps Toward the Virtual Classroom." Being in Hawaii, and following Ligature's visual approach to unit openings, I thought it appropriate to begin with a picture of a surfer riding a wave. The wave, I said, symbolized the changes occurring in the computer industry. Awkwardly I suggested that doing my study was like riding that wave. Any speculation about the end of the textbook could be made incredibly shortsighted if not instantly irrelevant by the accelerating pace of change. But as soon as I displayed the image of the surfer while catching a look at my audience I knew that my point, along with my nerve, had already been lost.

Yet there was a much greater change implied by the surfer which my fractured talk entirely omitted. Several months later I had a lunch meeting with a brilliant computer engineer at Sun Microsystems. We walked out to a nature reserve area adjacent to their campus-like research park. We had only just met, brought together by the suggestion of a mutual friend, and I was very interested in sharing some of his insights. But there was barely a moment to talk and get acquainted. He was constantly answering his cell-phone in order to walk his kids through configuring the operating system of their new Power Mac so that it could access the Internet. A few days later I was having dinner with friends at a restaurant on the east shore of Lake Washington. The course of the meal was interrupted several times as we paused to watch groups of Microsoft personnel who, alighting from a company shuttle at a nearby dock, boarded a huge powerboat with the company logo emblazoned on its stern. Apparently they were being taken to the waterfront Xanadu that Bill Gates was building down the lake. A few days later I was in Portland where I met with Frank Loose, the former Ligature art director who designed the Houghton Mifflin textbooks for Grades 1–3. I had only talked with Frank Loose twice by phone and had had no sense of the man. Face to face we instantly connected. It was a fitting closure, meeting the designer of what were considered to be the best books in the series. The string of those coincidental moments strangely illustrated, unlike any image or word could, how important actual human contact still is in a world becoming increasingly mediated by electronic communications.

Of course there is a certain irony in these fractured moments. In a social environment increasingly saturated by electronic technology which, like those cell-phone interruptions, is reordering every lived moment to a new digital time-space, how does one speak about one's vision of the near future when it appears to be here already? Typical millennial anxiety generated by the American mythos of techno-utopias perhaps, yet more fundamentally the question is still posed: How do we make human contact through an electronic interface when oftentimes we barely connect face to face? In a larger sense we might then ask: How is the social (in Social Studies) being shaped by these new electronic communication technologies?

The progress of this book has followed on the heels of that trajectory of change that began when I first opened that Houghton Mifflin textbook, and ends, as Sherry Turkle (1995) would say, with the beginning of our collective "life on the screen." I characterize the cognitive aspect of this "life" as a visual/verbal dialogue now framed by the special kind of interactivity inherent to the digital medium. As educators, we face the challenge to understand the nature and potential of this new medium, and how it may irrevocably alter our social fabric. The cultural dichotomy which relegates text and images to autonomous spheres of cognitive activity has marked every chapter of this book. Yet images have brought that divisive containment into question. The purpose of this work has been a reflective movement to decipher the larger significance of this graphic difference.

In the opening, Ligature's principal of binding visual and verbal elements in book form (one fundamental dichotomy, given the privileged position of *text*) only came to be fully realized by de-materializing that text in the neutral but infinitely plastic electronic space of the computer. On screen, image and text temporarily lose the respective cultural codes which enforce the fundamental dichotomy that separates each off screen. In the reduction to another code, binary digits, text potentially loses its inherent linearity, and the image, because of its virtual malleability (due to digitization), loses its exact correspondence to the world it supposedly mirrors. Despite these transfromations, in the end, the gain (in terms of production), was the "beautiful book" which had been envisioned.

In the second chapter the problem of moving beyond conventional book forms regulated by the dichotomy of editorial and design roles was illustrated by the ingenious in-house rituals of socialization to raise consciousness. In bringing the teams up to the creative level required for the Thumbnail Process, the inherent dichotomy of visual form versus verbal content was transcended. The partnership of the editor/designer team then effectively translated into a "partnership of information." The motto *"content is everything"* became realized on the wall of the Thumbnail room. Outside that room Ligature designers advanced plans to "codify" visual/verbal text structures to maximize the communication potential of both components in special features like *A Moment in Time* and *A Closer Look,* thus breaking the apparent visual/verbal dichotomy and the "flatland of the page."

In the third chapter the turn to aesthetics transformed this "flatland," while raising the question whether a spatialized 3-D *text*book is a contradiction in terms. The fourth chapter showed this hyper-realist space to be in conflict with the readerly imperative of the "considerate" text. In the fifth chapter, the question of how to link the scripting and instructional support in the Teacher Edition effectively to the visual/verbal architecture and Openers posed another visual/verbal dichotomy, albeit in instructional terms. What is the status of Visual Learning in the Social Studies curriculum if its use is not properly assessed? Is its intended purpose overlooked? Or even worse, are the visuals given a quick, casual look so that teacher and student can move on to the real content?

In the last chapter the canonical authority of the textbook representing a multicultural perspective aligned with the California Framework was called into question by adoption critics. Here the division was not so much between text and images as between the perceptions of various groups who were actually being depicted. Instead of "empathy" being "triggered" by the visual/verbal layering of callouts with image in features like *A Moment in Time*, the recursive combination did just the opposite. Instead of seeing what the designers intended, ethnic, religious, and racial minorities saw Eurocentric stereotypes. The designers seemed to overlook the obvious: Images can have more than one meaning, and the meaning depends largely on the audience receiving it. Here, another dichotomy was exposed: The difference of one's own cultural standpoint cannot always be bridged. Images that were supposed to represent multicultural realities in fact mirrored the stereotypical perceptions of our dominant cultural system. And in a multimedia world where the power of images suffuses everyday life, visual learning would seem to require a deeper understanding of images than simply distinguishing the real from the unreal. In a multicultural/multimedia world, the adoption controversy suggests that the social studies curriculum requires critical media savvy skills, visual learning with a critical edge so that students can get beyond the surface of images and events in our spectacle driven culture.

In shifting to a semiotic perspective we can also see the culture and economy of the textbook design and production as an artifact of this system. In the *Visual Turn* this meant looking at the development of an instructional textbook not from an editorial or even educational standpoint, but instead as a project largely inspired and directed by graphic designers. As presented chapter by chapter, such a view overturns a number of categories (or ways of thinking) fundamental to a text-based curriculum. In broader terms it might be said that underlying these dichotomies are two cultures in conjunction: one emergent, the other long established; each with respective symbol systems and epistemologies, which seem to be in opposition. As this conjunction was posed in the fourth chapter, the culture and codes of the printed book seem to be in conflict with the ascendancy of a postlinear visual culture of digitized information, as it took form in the visual/verbal design.

Whether high or low/popular culture or academic discourse, the sense is that a threshold has been crossed into another era. Are we not all at dockside waiting for that boat to shuttle us to some fabulous electronic future? We must recognize that the evolving visual culture, depending on the frame of reference, really has no definitive beginning. As sketched in the second chapter it is possible to trace a continuum which reflects a pedagogy that is not strictly textual. Considered in terms of technical innovation, it can be asserted that society is now rapidly proceeding through a series of technological changes which have introduced new forms of visual representation (photography, film, television, video games, computers) that have successively constructed a cultural space sustaining a "human attention structure" oriented largely to visual thinking (Lanham, 1993). This change in orientation is now profoundly under the sway of computer technology. Our cultural space is a lattice of electronic networks. "Cyberspace," Sherry Turkle (1995) observes, "is now part of the routines of everyday life" (p. 9).

Whatever the larger effects of such a cultural movement may be, they are perhaps less important for our purposes than how one situates this change in terms relevant for education. How have these "routines" encroached upon education, and how is the design of the Social Studies Program reflected in this change? Certainly the design does not reflect dominant instructional models. At the curricular level the serious attempt to advance a program for Visual Learning in the Scope and Sequence reflects in its own way a profound re-orientation that attempts to deal seriously with visual information, instead of just advancing the traditional instructional goal of text comprehension. The "attention structures" Ligature designed were not exclusively "semantic." Regardless of its connection to the wider cultural sphere beyond education, the question remains: "What might the implications of this textbook design be for learning and instruction?"

Perhaps the major influence shaping this program is the most obvious: its connection to the culture of design. What does design as process and product tell us about how our current educational practices are organized by the textbook? The innovative features of the textbook series were largely determined by the responsiveness of Ligature designers to advances within their profession. To understand the nature of innovation as it becomes embodied in a product, we might first return to consider the highlight of that design process. As indicated by the account of the final production processes, the computer served the strategic purpose of realizing Ligature's goal to create a "beautiful book." It provided the means to "finesse" visual/verbal design at the "backend" of the production process. Yet at the same time the computer points beyond the fixed format of a paper textbook medium. Because the computer provides a medium where language, number, and images can merge and complement each other, it raises questions about why the practice of learning and instruction is not organized, much less integrated, in the same way. In this concluding discussion we consider how the textbook is being transformed by these innovative forces which carry a revolutionary potential of no less magnitude than the coming of print.

WYSIWYG: WHAT YOU SEE IS WHAT YOU GET

> I do not think that we have begun to scratch the surface of training in visualization—whether related to the arts, to science, or simply to the pleasures of viewing our environments more richly.
>
> —Jerome Bruner (1966)

In the mythology of Macintosh computer culture the acronym WYSIWYG is a standard, now universal in the industry, which evolved over the design concern for how text typed in a word processor application would appear the same on screen and printed out. What we see as input is what comes out. Mac interface design people extended this innovative principle taken from the earlier research done by Alan Kay (1990) at the now legendary Xerox PARC (Palo Alto Research Center) to their concept of how all the functional aspects of any application should look and feel.

> Don't hide features in your application by using abstract commands.
> People should be able to see what they need when they need it. [They]

> should be able to find all the available features. . . . If you find a need to
> initially "hide" features, do it in a way that gives people information
> about where they can find more choices. A stepped interface, by re-
> vealing relevant information to users in steps, shows the choice most
> users want . . . while providing a way . . . to get more choices.
> —Apple Computer Inc., *Macintosh Human*
> *Interface Guidelines (1992, p. 8)*

In the same fashion, the key to the textbook program was the "self-revealing presentation" of their pages. The goals of the art director, like the approach of the
Macintosh guidelines, lie in their shared insight as to the relevance of *seeing*.
WYSIWYG is central to understanding the transformation of the textbook. The
sensibility of graphic design does not so much privilege seeing as it acknowledges
the necessity of its cultivation. The *Visual Learning* strand, which reflected the
larger aesthetic intentions of the Ligature designers, also recognized such necessity, by providing a basic framework for its cultivation.

What We See then also implies how we see it. The key to understanding how
the textbook will be transformed by computer technology begins with considering
the fundamental philosophical shift it introduces to the curriculum. In the opening
discussion we consider how such a step involves the cultivation of visual and
spatial thinking, and in turn how such thinking relates to the electronic transformation of the textbook.

This leads us to exploration of the wider implications for the Social Studies of
What We Get as we pose it as a question about the future. As the adoption controversy revealed what we see is not always what we actually get. The meaning we
may take from a representation, whether text or image, is not necessarily transpar-
ent or understood by everyone. But what will we get from the new communication
technology? Are computers really going to transform learning in any profound
way? What we may envision for education is not what we may actually get.

Sherry Turkle (1995) very wisely suggests that what we should be asking
about the emerging digital culture is not "what computers do *for* us," but "what
they do *to* us—to our relationships and our ways of thinking about ourselves."
Because Social Studies is primarily about "us," about how we assist young people
in developing their sense of self and identity in relation to society and the world,
asking finally what we get from computers may mean seeing not only how they
will transform textbooks, but us.

Post-Piaget and the Return of the Concrete

> "What is the use of a book," thought Alice, "without pictures . . ."
> —Lewis Carroll (1982)

Is it at all strange that the same dichotomy which marks the divide between visualists
and verbalists reaches into the brain itself and the nature of cognition? In a more

global sense the visual/verbal dialogue described in Chapter 2 is more fundamentally about the nature of cognition, both individual and distributed, about how we perceive the world as image and then construct representations of that world, making sense of it through language, or image and number. The mind, then, is the final ground on which this opposition plays itself out. Rival camps in the field of cognitive science have been arguing for the past decade about the function of images and propositions in cognitive processing, with the latter even denying that mental images exist in and of themselves.

Relative to this ongoing "debate," Preece and Keller (1994) noted that "imagists believe that images are [a] distinct . . . form of mental representation . . . and play an important role in thinking and reasoning." On the other hand, "propositionalists believe that images are a by-product, . . . are of no purpose to cognitive functioning, [and that only] propositional representations underlie all mental processing" (p. 127). Although the complexity of this "debate" is beyond the scope of this discussion it is nevertheless important to note, because it mirrors at a deeper level the same intractable dichotomy of image and text underlying this study (see Pylyshyn, 1973, 1981). And because the way taken here is to embrace images in all their potential and not to dismiss them, we shall briefly consider the work of the chief "imagist" in this "debate" as it may bear on this shift to the visual in postprint learning environments.

Stephen Kosslyn's (1994a) extensive work in visual cognition has successfully articulated the theoretical basis for accepting "visual mental imagery" as fundamental to cognitive processing. Key to his argument is the linking of visual perception to cognition and his recognition that the underlying neural mechanisms of visual object identification and visual mental imagery have "solid implications for visual display design" (p. vii).

In *Elements of Graph Design* (1994b) Kosslyn explores this topic of "visual display design" as it may apply to the communication of quantitative data in graphs. Interestingly enough, he introduces most of the same principles of gestalt outlined in Chapter 4. Under the "maxim" that "the mind is not a camera," he explains how the mind organizes visually perceived elements into groups or units of meaning. The importance of this maxim is in its suggestion that the eyes are not passive "receiving systems." Instead of being "like a TV camera [which] register[s] the world as it is," he emphasizes that the eyes with the brain "actively organize and make sense of the world" (p. 3). This stress on the active dimension of vision is important in understanding the perceptual basis underlying any shift to screen-based learning environments.

Kosslyn's point on the constructive aspect of visual cognition should be aligned with Piaget's earlier theory of concrete operations in children's cognitive development. We should look at Piaget's work as an important precedent. Like the later work of Kosslyn, Piaget points to the importance of visual and spatial thinking in cognition. In the context of the previous chapter, what is particularly interesting about Piaget is his characterization of these operations as the "semiotic" or "repre-sentational" function (Ginsburg & Opper, 1988). Although the "semiotic func-tion" which Piaget describes should be seen in the narrow sense of a child's for-mative ability to devise and create symbolic representations (which he calls "signifiers") of their emerging world, its connection to the larger field of culture as a "signifying system" which was the critical focus of the last chapter should be fairly evident (Williams, 1981). For Piaget "concrete operations" are dominated by "figurative cognition," that is, mental imagery (Ginsburg & Opper, 1988). Such cognitive activity was studied by Piaget in three ways. Subjects could verbally describe their images, draw an object previously observed, or select out of a col-lection of pictures one that most closely resembled the object under scrutiny (p. 164). In all cases Piaget, like Kosslyn, describes these visually based cognitive processes in constructive terms. Our perceptions do not mirror reality but are built up and refined through expression. Children are naturally disposed to "active look-ing," not "passive watching" (Stafford, 1996). Such "active looking" combines visual and spatial thinking. According to Thomas West (1991), visual thinking as described by Kosslyn and Piaget involves "that form of thought in which images are generated or recalled in the mind and manipulated. . . . Spatial [thinking] is closely related to visual thinking but emphasizes those elements of three-dimen-sional space [which can be manipulated for instance through the technique of draw-ing, like] mass, volume, proportion as well as distance, momentum, leverage, bal-ance, and the like" (pp. 21–22).

However, I believe, with Seymour Papert, that Piaget's work in particular falls short in this area. Papert (1993) suggests that this kind of cognitive *"activity"* calls for a return "to more concrete ways of knowing." In making this point, he draws into question a fundamental tenet of Piaget's stage theory of cognitive de-velopment (p. 137). The peculiar weakness of this theory is the status to which it relegates the second stage of "concrete operations," which Papert notes is "coex-tensive with the elementary school years," years covered by the Social Studies Program (p. 153). In working from a theory of knowledge acquisition which pre-sumes that logic and abstract thought represent the pinnacle of mental develop-ment, Papert argues that Piaget "failed to recognize that concrete thinking . . . was not confined to . . . underdeveloped children" (p. 151). In fact, visual and spatial thinking typical to "concrete operations" are traits characteristic of the most cre-ative artists, writers, and scientists (see West, 1991). Papert advocates an "alterna-tive epistemology" that would "strengthen and perpetuate" concrete thinking. Papert believes the "new media," especially the new computer communication technolo-gies, presage a return to the concrete (pp. 155–156).

From White Space to Viewing Space

> We should talk less and draw more. I personally would like to renounce
> speech altogether and, like organic nature, communicate everything I
> have to say in sketches.
> —Johann Wolfgang von Goethe (see West, 1996)

Up to now the dialogue of text and image has been the principal focus. Images can illustrate, or complement, add information or provide context, reveal, explain, or elaborate relationships which the text alone cannot make apparent. In the last chapter we saw what images and text can do to the viewer in provoking a negative reaction. Because the ideal of visual/verbal integration is only revealed through its visibility, that is of actually seeing the two elements juxtaposed, only the act of viewing can make the distinct parts a whole. On the page or screen we see the separate elements. The mind alone creates a gestalt. But what do images do to us by themselves, how do they communicate? How can we encourage "active looking" and cultivate visual–spatial thinking? In other words, what do we do with the window in the text?

If we wish to follow seriously David Perkins' (1994) appeal for cultivation of "wide spectrum cognition" (noted in Chap. 3), we must begin with facing the broader implications of Piaget and Kosslyn's work on visual–mental imagery. We must recognize along with Stuart Murphy, the creator of this Social Studies Program, that school is not arranged for the visual learner. Rudolf Arnheim (1979), one of the more erudite advocates for visual thinking, has argued compellingly that our culture's basic mistrust of images manifests itself by regarding "perception and reason" as distinct and unequal "mental functions." Howard Gardner (1993) to the same effect observed that of the three universal symbol systems, "language, picturing, and mathematics," only alpha-numerical literacy is considered necessary for serious study. The curriculum is blind to *sight* and its aesthetic cultivation. How then are we to make a place for this excluded-middle in the curriculum? It is not so much the "new media," which herald, as Papert claims, a return of the concrete. The return reflects a much older sensibility, as the work of Comenius, noted in Chapter 3, demonstrates. "Picture this, . . ." is an ancient evocation stimulated by an even more primal impulse. The difference in the power of the image is in the medium. But the computer screen, unlike the printed page, cannot be as easily dismissed. The electronic window stares back at us. Its luminescent frame frames the issue: Visualization takes command of the curriculum; a return of the repressed. The white space of the printed page now is in transit to an unknown digital destination.

At CHI96, the annual meeting of the special interest group on Computer-Human Interaction, which is one of many professional organizations under the international Association for Computing Machinery (ACM), Betty Edwards gave the keynote address. This renowned art educator has gained international recognition for her espousal of basic drawing techniques in books such as *Drawing on the*

Right-Side of the Brain (1979) and *Drawing on the Artist Within* (1986). What may have been prescient about the moment was that here was an artist with admittedly little knowledge of computers speaking to an assembled audience of the world's digital elite. "This," she said, "is a new audience" which normally she wouldn't have imagined speaking to. Nevertheless she felt the occasion held great importance, a view with which Arnheim would almost certainly concur. And she brought a disarmingly simple message to this high-tech audience: "That drawing is a valuable thinking skill." Drawing, she said consists of "five basic perceptual skills." These are:

- The perception of edges (e.g., the contour of shapes)
- The perception of spaces (e.g., the negative space between objects)
- The perceiving of relationships (e.g., proportion and perspective)
- The perception of light and shadow
- And, the perception of the thing itself
  (Copyright © 1996, ACM)

In completing her comments about the second skill, which concerns the perception of space, she mentioned that prior to her talk she had been speaking with one of the editors of *Interaction*, CHI's quarterly publication. She "was fascinated" to hear "that the arrangement of data and the spaces between is becoming an important part of computer interface" design. She was quite "thrilled to hear that," because it reinforced her intuition that such aesthetic sensitivity has importance not only for articulating pictorial space, but also for the presentation of data on screen in a visual display.

She concluded her talk by citing Edward Tufte (1983). "What is sought for designs for display of information is the clear portrayal of complexity. . . . The task of the designer is to give visual access to the subtle and the different; that is the revelation of the complex." That "revelation," she thought, is part of a nonverbal aesthetic response. Such a response, she stated, "is not translatable into words." This is something, she said, "which is very hard for people involved in the manufacture of words to swallow." However, she believed that "as time goes on, our word dependent culture [would come] to value it." Like Papert, she seemed to be suggesting that the "new media" would play a part in bringing about this acceptance.

In fact, LOGO, the programming language developed by Seymour Papert which initiated the Constructionist movement of computer-based learning environments for children, has provided a number of interesting and provocative spinoffs which form something of a precedent for visual and spatial thinking (see Harel, 1990). First is a course called *Problems in Visual Thinking*. James Clayson (1988), the creator, talks about his initial experiments in trying to devise a course that could "teach visual thinking to those students who had problems doing it naturally." Papert's LOGO computer language, he believed, was "an appropriate medium of instruction" for both art students and quantitative types. However, this is not drawing in the sense Edwards is advocating. Rather, Clayson's is "a structured approach to seeing." The structure he refers to is provided by the LOGO programming code. Students in his course learn to model shapes in a largely two-dimensional information space.

Judy Sachter (1990), a colleague of Seymour Papert, assembled a number of students who were proficient in the LOGO language and introduced them to a 3-D computer language she developed called J3D. This software allows children to "manipulate one or more basic geometric polyhedral objects by changing their size, proportions, position, and/or orientation in space." The intention of her study was to provide "a cogent learning environment for children to explore spatial concepts." The geometric constructions possible in J3D encouraged students to represent their designs in "visual, verbal, and formal modes." The underlying rationale for the study was largely shaped by Piaget's work in mapping children's developing spatial abilities in the concrete operational stage (Piaget & Inhelder, 1967).

Both these projects indicate the graphical potential of the LOGO language. Yet at the same time they predate the introduction of visual interfaces, since LOGO and J3D represent command line interfaces which are functional only by entering precisely coded commands in their proper order and sequence. It is noteworthy that Papert's call for a reconsideration of "concrete thinking" in his book, *The Children's Machine* (1993), is important because it reinforces the principle of WYSIWYG. The widespread use of graphical user interfaces (GUI's) which was first popularized by the Macintosh has in the 1990s become almost a universal standard. At the high end of computer innovation this "object-oriented" trend in interface design (GUI by another name) has only accelerated with the advent of visual computing.

Basically, visual computing involves the integration of 3-D computer graphics and digital image processing in a computer application in which complex data and physical phenomena can be visually represented and manipulated on screen (see Cruickshank, 1996; Gross, 1994). A good example of how the potential of visual computing is currently being used in primary and secondary education is the IPT Project, *Image Processing for Teaching*, which was initiated by Richard Greenberg, Director of the Science and Mathematics Education center at the University of Arizona in 1989. The objective of the IPT project is to train K–12 teachers in basic digital image processing which they could then introduce in their classroom (Greenberg, 1996a, 1996b; Raphael & Greenberg, 1995). Greenberg (1996a) "thought that visual learners might find image processing a more attractive entree into science and mathematics than traditional language-based methods." His belief was based on basic human physiology. "People," he states, "are physiologically structured to learn visually. From the standpoint of information theory, images are by far the fastest and most efficient way to deliver information to the human brain" (p. 224).

Richard Friedhoff (Friedhoff & Benzon, 1989) foresaw that such "visually oriented computers, computers with a window, open up a whole new kind of communication between man and machine" (p. 113). As Jakob Nielsen (1993) noted, "the next generation of user interfaces" will have "full dimensionality" and operate in "three or more dimensions" (p. 62). Such an interface will include "real-time animation, sound, or voice, as well as a true third spatial dimension in the form of virtual reality systems." But such interfaces are now in fact available, although at the high end still quite expensive. Yet it is the high end of development in visual computing that inevitably will make availability at the middle and low end widespread, and soon will make the window in the text a door to all worlds.

ON PAPER OR SCREEN: THE SEMIOTICS OF BOOK FORM

> I believe that the motion picture is destined to revolutionize our education system and that in a few years it will supplant largely, if not entirely, the use of textbooks.
> —Thomas Edison, 1922 (see Soloway & Pryor, 1996)

During the second visit to Ligature's Chicago Office in 1993 I saw for the first time a page from the Social Studies Program up on the screen of a large color monitor. In hindsight this moment of seeing at the electronic threshold seemed like a brief glimpse of the future of the book. Or was it? Seventy years after Edison's remark textbooks are still with us. If the medium, as McLuhan said, *is* the message, that is to say, form and content are one, it seems that Edison, as brilliant as he was, did not understand the necessary formative dialogue between the new technology and its emergent cinematic form which had to occur before the medium could evolve. Words and pictures tell stories differently than text. Today we are immersed in images and are rapidly introducing networked computers into the classroom, but do we understand the medium of print any better than we comprehend the global Network localized on each computer screen? Film is quintessentially a visual/verbal medium. But its medium and the kind of messages it could convey took decades to evolve. Cinematic culture is now universally appreciated, its grammar and technique widely disseminated. Much less understood perhaps is film's dependence on and transformation of literary conventions like narrative, plot, character development, and storyline. But these visual equivalents of the novel could only have evolved through much experiment over time.

Had Edison not been so blinded by the revolutionary potential of a new medium, he might perhaps have been better able to step back and ask much simpler questions like, "What is it that film does with content that textbooks cannot?" Or to paraphrase Wilbur Schramm (1977), the renowned communication theorist, Is it the delivery system (the medium) or what is delivered (the content) which makes for the learning experience (p. 14)? In the same sense we should perhaps ask what it is about the medium of print, as it has evolved in the form of the textbook, which has provided a durable, if not revolutionary, model of pedagogy and instruction. Seeing images and text up on the computer screen seemed to confirm Tufte's (1983) basic insight that "pictures and words belong together," but as with Edison, I wonder whether we are not being blinded by another new medium of extraordinary potential, without understanding the broader implications of how its message is shaped and in turn will shape us?

Rob Wittig, the designer responsible for the visual feature *A Moment in Time,* expressed reservations about computers replacing books. He referred to a "chart," (Fig. 7.1) which "appeared in the premiere issue of *Wired* magazine" (February 1993). In his comments on it, he stressed that the "interactive computer people tend to paint" an inaccurate picture of the versatility of books. The "chart" which he noted was called the "Interactivity Matrix." The Matrix, Wittig said,

> purports to show the future of virtual reality techniques by opposing a horizontal scale of interactivity and a vertical scale of vividness (how close it looks to real life). Books are put at the lower left hand corner of the whole chart [which means no interactivity. . . . The problem is . . . that for ninety percent of interactive media I have seen, especially if you do a structural analysis of how a person interacts with it, everything that you can do there, you can do with a book. And the thing is, books are faster. . . . There is no CD-ROM that can do that.

The question of interactivity figures large in this discussion, and the Matrix can serve as a frame to focus the forthcoming discussion. On the Matrix cyberspace is located at the extreme diagonal point *opposite* books. Obviously, the Matrix privileges a kind of interactivity found in virtual environments (VE).

In his comprehensive review, Jonathan Steuer (1995), creator of the "Matrix," distinguished between traditional notions of interactivity in communication studies, and interactivity "based on a telepresence view of mediated communication." "Telepresence," a term coined by the artificial intelligence (AI) expert Marvin Minsky, can generally be understood as "the sense of being physically present at a remote operator site." More generally it can mean the subjective reaction of a user immersed in a virtual environment (Rheingold, 1991; Stuart, 1996). In medicine, telepresence, or remote operator robotic techniques, has allowed surgeons to perform delicate operations without actually being on site with the patient (Heim, 1993). From this perspective Steuer (1995) defined interactivity as "the extent to which users can participate in modifying the form and content of a mediated environment in real time" (p. 46). Coincidentally, Steuer, like Wittig, noted that the principal "limitation" of defining it in these terms is that it "does not include control over how the medium can be experienced." Echoing what would seem to be Wittig's more traditional sense of interactivity he remarked that

> a book, which cannot be changed easily in real time without cutting it apart, is not considered interactive, though one can certainly read a

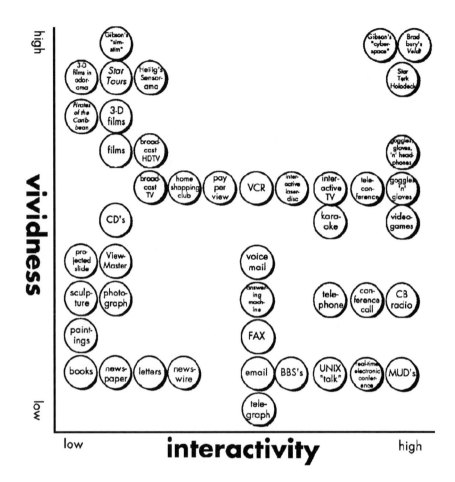

FIGURE 7.1. The "Chart."

book interactively, jumping at will from page to page and from chapter
to chapter. (p. 46)

Strangely though, this doesn't quite suffice. If the mark of difference is as Steuer
says the immaterial "malleability" of one and not the other, it still reduces book
interactivity to physical interactions with the page, ignoring how the user acts
upon the book cognitively and discursively to cut it up through close reading and
annotation. Although an electronic medium certainly enhances such textual interventions and in the process re-invents the form of the book, telepresence, like
interactivity, begins with the viewing subject. Mediation is conscious perception.
Interactivity involves aesthetic contact with the object, even if only through sight.

Bran Ferren of Disney Imagineering puts the notion of interactivity in a more elemental perspective.

> We need to realize that interactivity is not an emerging technology. There's been interactivity since the first creature crawled around on the surface of the earth. Human beings are born interactive. . . . We live in a richly interactive world, except that electronic media forgot this for a few years. The notion that interactivity is a new concept is ridiculous. (Greenberger, 1994, p. 181)

Nevertheless, rather than saying that books are more or less interactive, a more fruitful frame of comparison is to ask what kind of interactivity the form of each inspires. Rightfully, we should not expect a CD-ROM to *do* what a book can, and vice versa. What is more important is understanding what each does best as a medium, or does differently, such that respective characteristics and qualities of each can be seen to suit different kinds of learning and objectives.

For the purposes of discussion here, interactivity in a print medium and on screen can be distinguished in two ways. The first is made in formal terms as a set of material conventions which have their own "hard" and "soft" structures (Bolter, 1991). A "hard" structure would be the pages, binding and book cover. "Soft" structures would be, for example, the unit, chapter, lesson titles or heads, blocks of chunked text or paragraphs, the table of contents. Here we are primarily concerned with the "soft" visual structures that were designed to present visual/verbal information. The second kind of interactivity will deal with the viewing and/or reading that each form facilitates.

Interactivity as it is plotted along the horizontal scale of the Matrix runs from books to MUDs. A MUD or *Multiple User Domain* is basically an online site in which people can interact through coded commands and typed messages. Although the Low to High progression is from printed text on paper to electronic text (as in newspapers, letters, and email which appears midway), the mode of interactvity is strictly text-based, that is, communicating through language, though in the former text is fixed in print, whereas in the latter it can be modified and changed.

The vertical scale of *Vividness* on the Matrix is from the 2-D printed page to 3-D simulations. This movement from painting to sculpture and dioramas calls to mind the kind of concrete interactivity that visual and spatial thinking promote. Although it may be reductive, the Matrix might also be viewed in visual/verbal terms, with *Vividness* analogous to the visual mode and *Interactivity* the verbal. We can look at both scales metaphorically as vectors of transformation pulling the form of the textbook away from print. Between these two scales of change, the unmarked path which can be traced from books to cyberspace should be imagined not so much as a linear trajectory with cyberspace the ultimate destination, but as a bridge linking the printed page of the book to the electronic window of the screen.

Formally, what should be kept in mind is that both are information spaces in their own right, which are designed as, shall we say, semiotic systems for the transmission and acquisition of knowledge. What is overlooked by the visionary intent of the "Matrix" is how the accumulated precedent of typographic conventions bound up in the book can serve as a transitional structure for the electronic medium. Given this, the principal limitation of the Matrix, as Wittig and Ferren indicate, is that it defines interactivity only in terms of the computer, and not for the rich and complex phenomenon it actually is. Nevertheless, the transformation of the textbook begins with an understanding that a "powerful link" exists, as the art director said, between the page and screen. And that "link" (or bridge) in part is this sharing of the same formal conventions of typographic organization which contribute to the visual appearance of the book.

The art director of the K–8 series spoke about interactivity in the structured sense when he described this "link" as "an interesting tension." He said, "You can use the semiotics of book form" in a hypertext format, because "the book convention is a very powerful one." This "tension" alone is a form of interactivity, albeit a cultural one between a traditional form and an emerging one. Electronic and printed text share the same typographic conventions. In Chapter 3 it was shown how the textbook is transformed into a "self-revealing" structure. Ordinary book conventions like chapter titles and lesson headings are given a highly visible color coded structure. The thematic exposition of the unit, chapter, and lesson is made visible by the textual diagrams of the graphic organizers in the Teacher's Edition. The text itself is visibly chunked into definite segments, and significant terms and meanings are highlighted by bold typeface which is visually linked in the Scholars Margin and the text of each lesson. This interactivity of the eye, the art director felt, was "an indicator of the changing sensibility of how we look at information."

Like the art director, Stephen Kerr (1986a), a noted authority on educational technology who has been mapping this cultural transition, agrees that "page and screen share certain similarities," but at the same time "are separated by certain unique characteristics" (p. 207). The most obvious, Kerr noted, is the materiality of each presentational "surface": paper page versus pixel refreshed screen. The surface of a screen, which is coated with phosphorous and hit with a beam of electrons, is a light source, and a pixel, short for picture element, is the smallest unit appearing on a screen as a color or intensity, represented by a number of bits (Sun Microsystems, 1991). Irrespective of this "surface," Kerr (1986b) holds that "the same rules" commonly used by graphic designers "are worth adhering to in [either medium]. These include, he said

> use of distinctive typefaces, carefully determined (and generous) allocation of white space and headings in text, intelligent application of graphics and color (making full use of the capabilities of the technology), and design with the user's need to have the text interesting to read. (p. 377)

This same sensitivity to visual design is obviously found in the visual/verbal page. However, Kerr (1986a) noted that, in moving from page to screen, another set of priorities also assumes importance. In addition to this general adherence to graphic design principles, "preparation" of the graphical user interface involves attention to:

1. The *immediate* structure (the directions and finding aids that are provided on page or screen);
2. the *internal* structure (the helps for using the materials that are part of it, but not always present on any given page or screen);
3. the *external* structure (aids that are external to the material itself; p. 377).

Concerning these three electronic "wayfinding" structures Kerr noted that in "print materials there is typically not much [wayfinding] provided . . ." (p. 378). Yet in the Social Studies Program the elements of "self-revealing architecture" crucial to the visual/verbal presentation including the Scholar's Margin and section heads for "immediate" and "internal" structures, and the Teacher Edition Margins for the "external," were designed as "wayfinding structures." Though static, these structures are remarkably similar in principle to the nature of graphical interaction facilitated by a well designed GUI (graphical user interface).

Nevertheless, the interactivity the printed textbook affords is for interaction with a stable material object. The fixity of type on a page, its logical sequence and hierarchy of content exposition, and ease of linear access ("books are faster") allow for an "intensive" reading experience in which working memory has a stable object of comprehension, and content can be gone over and reflected on in depth (Bazin, 1996, p. 160). The linear conventions of printed text reflect a similar set of cognitive categories. One, for example, is "textual coherence," which was discussed in Chapter 4, and is crucial to certain learning styles.

But in a hypertext environment the stable printed surface is foregone, and its defining attributes just the opposite. Text is neither linear or fixed and can be combined with nontextual elements. The screen interface is a window opening upon "a never-ending book" without boundaries or limits (Bazin, 1996, p. 161). Hypertext implies another kind of cognitive structure in which the learner has to construct a system (or mental map) of knowledge from bits of information (Lansdale & Ormerod, 1994). This cognitive process follows a logic and order determined by the learner, neither of which is linear or has any necessary sequence, beginning or end. In hypertext, each bit of information, text or otherwise, is regarded as a *node*. Hypertext systems allow the learner to link these nodes in associative networks (Jonassen, 1989). Perhaps the most common example of a hypertext is Macintosh's *Hypercard*, in which the cards are considered as nodes and can be linked to other cards. Further, because the cards can contain not just text but images, video, animation, and audio clips it is more properly understood as a hypermedia software, that is, multimedia and hypertext combined.

Bazin (1996) compared the "intensive" model of reading the printed book offers to the "extensive reading" possible on screen (p. 161). In the emerging global network any text can potentially be linked to any other. "Extension" can be conceived in terms of connection across digital networks, archives, databases, libraries, and sites. Linkages appear limitless. The expansive relationality of hypertext systems affords an interactivity in which context overshadows the content of the nodes. Typically, large hypertextual information spaces are composed of hundreds if not thousands of nodes and links. On screen, the user may not be able to see more than a few layered and windowed nodes at a time, much less conceptualize the whole. Although hypertext environments offer a dynamic interactivity connecting multiple texts and even users, "navigation" of the links in the system and knowing "when and how to access" information are two of the most common problems (Jonassen, 1996).

This shift from an "intensive" to an "extensive" model of reading, and correspondingly from content to context reflects this "changing sensibility" which the art director describes. But this change is not only about *how* we look, but also *what* we can look at and interact with. The stable world of information constructed by the conventions of linear text is not the world we look upon today. In the present mediascape the most prevalent characteristic of "information" is its overwhelming quantity, multiplicity and multimodality. As Tufte (1990) would say all the "more interesting worlds" are "multidimensional" in character. The paradox of a multimedia world is that text alone cannot represent its overwhelming complexity, yet at the same time it is fundamental to making sense of that world and is still an integral component in its representation.

Given this change, it is still something of a paradox to see a textbook that combines the traditional conventions of text—"linearity," a "fixed" sequence, and clearly "demarcated" content with a precise beginning and end—with the highly graphical conventions of a computer interface (Landow & Delany, 1991, p. 3). When Wittig exclaimed, "No CD-ROM can do that," he is alluding to those "soft" and "hard" structures which shape interactivity with the book (Bolter, 1991). We expect to see a preface at the beginning and an index in the back pages. All these conventions shape a cognitive space for the reader and organize the material space seen on the page. In creating a "self-revealing" structure which makes these conventions *more* visible, the designers demonstrated how these typically background structures can serve as a visualizing frame interacting with an expanded field of information.

These highly structured conventions are very different from the data spaces seen on the screen interface which are generally only as visually stable as the "consistency" of the graphical representations designed to mediate with them (Tognazzini, 1990).

The mediating functions modeled by interactive system design generally recognize eight interaction styles:

- Menu-based interaction

- Question-and-answer
- Function-key interaction
- Voiced-based interaction
- Graphical direct manipulation
- Forms fill-in
- Command-line interaction
- Text-based natural language
  (Newman & Lamming, 1995)

The GUI (graphical user interface) is also referred to as a WIMP and NERD system. WIMP is the acronym for windows, icons, menus, and pointing device (mouse), and NERD is for navigation, evaluation, refinement, and demonstration (Chignell & Waterworth, 1991). Generally this interface combines several of these interaction or "dialogue" styles with the interface: direct manipulation, menu selection, question-and-answer, and form-filling interactions (Lansdale & Ormerod, 1994). Of these, the "primary" interaction style is direct manipulation, or "point and click" (Shneiderman, 1992). Again there is this interaction of the eye since users can "see" and manipulate "symbolic objects" on the screen (Vacherand-Revel & Bessiere, 1992).

Of course, the underlying principle of graphical interaction is WYSIWYG. This principle is derived from the work of Alan Kay (1984) who is generally credited with creating Windows as well as providing the theoretical impetus for "object-oriented" interface design. He spoke about this kind of human-computer interaction in the most visual of terms. "Any direct interventions *on* the image corresponds for the user to a change in a predictable state of the machine," or as he said more succinctly elsewhere, "Doing with Images makes Symbols" (Kay, 1990). Here Kay is following Jerome Bruner's (1966) reinterpretation of Piaget's stage theory, which decomposed his developmental sequence into "cognitive potentials" which can remain latent or become developed. Kay (1990) adapted Bruner's "enactive, iconic, and symbolic mentalities," eventually using these as a model for the first graphical interface developed at Xerox PARC. Though we are now far from the printed page, the more powerful "link" Kay et al. reveal is the importance of the "iconic" dimension of interaction which connects active seeing to symbolic knowing at the visual interface. Vision is the link connecting the structuring of information in both media.

THE LAST WORD: READING UNDER RE-VISION

I think that reading texts like that is not easy, because you have to *bounce* around. And I think if it's not easy for skilled readers it may even be more difficult for novices. All the data we have suggests that kids' ability to read and comprehend textbooks is pretty dismal. I do think it's an empirical question. The jury is out on whether it's a good idea.

—Karen Wixson (1993)

Reading the complex electronic page demands an attention to text, image, and their relationships. Readers must move back and forth from

> the linear presentation of verbal text to the two-dimensional field of electronic picture writing. They can read the alphabetic signs in the conventional way, but they also must parse diagrams, illustrations, windows, and icons. Electronic readers therefore *shuttle* between two modes of reading, or rather they learn to read in a way that combines verbal and picture reading.
>
> —Jay David Bolter, Writing Space (1991)

Of course, the *"bounce"* Wixson, the reading specialist, alludes to is that *window* in the text, that is, visual images. "Shuttle" is a term suggesting control and volition; whereas "bounce" not only implies a lack of reader control, but suggestively infers what happens when kids encounter visual information like photographs and illustrations. Their eyes "bounce" over it to the next section of text. They have no innate ability to intelligently view visual information in a way similar to a model of reading, but which is in no way discursive. But is this an accurate description, or does it simply reflect a linguistic mind set, in which images are considered inferior to and reducible inevitably to words? Does "bounce" mask a deeper suspicion of images, like the graphic designer noted in the Introduction of this study, which views these textbooks as marking the end of narrative and the book.

The window is, in effect, a black hole in which the coherence of text is disrupted if not lost. No doubt if we rank the visuals from the series on the scale of *Vividness* in the "Matrix" we would have to admit that the intention to design a virtual 3-D space on the page was quite successful. Images that the eye was invited to step into and objects that you could almost pick up cannot be read, they must be aesthetically viewed and inspected. But why is this kind of intelligent viewing any different in quality of focus and attention than the act of reading itself? At this visual threshold the linguistic model of reading ends, but only in part. As J. Hillis Miller (1992) recognized,

> both text and image are something seen with the eyes and made sense of as a sign. What, in fact, is the difference between reading a word and making sense of a picture? This is just the question. (p. 73)

If the first kind of interactivity concerns the kind of information spaces and visual structuring each medium supports for content (image and text), this next kind of interactivity is about how such spatially structured information is viewed/read and comprehended in its temporal and concrete totality.

How do children learn to "shuttle" rather than be "bounced?" The second level of interactivity considered here concerns how children learn *to read* "in a way that combines," as Bolter (1991) suggested, "verbal and picture reading" (p. 71). The key to such a "combination," as Hillis Miller suggested, resides "with the eyes." The ordinary act of reading Estrock (1994) notes, "is a complex process involving many elements, including visual scanning of the page, recognizing of graphemes [literally, the material letter as typographic form], and semantic comprehension" (p. 178).

The act of visual scanning is the axis point of this visual/verbal combination. The process of scanning involves a series of rapid automatic eye movements known as "saccades," in which the eye moves over the surface of an object in a series of fixations and fluctuations (Bloomer, 1990, p. 39). These movements proceed until the object has been wholly grasped by the eye. A diagram of this movement would show a series of lines and fixation points mapping the entire surface of the object. Gandelman (1991) noted that the prominent art historian, Alois Riegl, posited that there are two types of visual scanning: the optic and the haptic. "The optical eye," Gandelman said, "scans objects according to their outlines, . . . it focuses on surfaces," [and] "the haptic, or tactile, eye penetrates in depth . . ." (p. 5). "Optical scanning," Gandelman continued, is like that saccadic mapping of the object, whereas "haptic vision . . . is concentrated in the points of fixation between the saccades" (p. 8).

But Gandelman carries this analogy further. Underlying this optic/haptic dichotomy he suggests is another: metaphor and metonym. Metaphors are generally understood as figures of speech in which something symbolically serves as a substitute for another idea. For example, the eagle can serve as a metaphor for the United States or American patriotism. By contrast, a metonym is a figure of speech in which a part serves to symbolically represent a larger whole. For example, a policeman can serve to symbolize the Law and our system of justice. Asserting that "the eye does not read only pictures; it also reads texts," Gandelman (1991) argued that

> one should speak of two fundamental axes of visual scanning. . . . One axis is that of *metaphoric, optic* scanning, which proceeds through semantic jumps from one corner of the picture or text to another. The other axis is that of *haptic* or *contact* vision, which bores through texture and color and fixes on nonsemantic elements in pictures or text. (p. 12)

It is interesting to note that Gandelman discusses this optic/haptic axis in the context of children's psychological development. One of Alois Riegl's most famous students was the psychologist Viktor Lowenfeld. In his seminal work, *Creative and Mental Growth*, Lowenfeld (1952) took Riegl's optic/haptic "dichotomy" and applied it to his own theory of creativity and psychological development in children. In Lowenfeld's theory children could be of either of two types: visual or haptic (Gandelman, p. 9). Though Lowenfeld's psychological categories and theory of apperception have not stood the test of time, the dichotomy nevertheless stands as a powerful symbol of recognition for widening the scope of reading to include, as Wittig also argued, a "cinematic" mode which scans the visual/verbal information of the page to make associative and semantic connections.

If a "tension" exists between text and hypertext, part of this tension rests in defining the scope of reading as related to text alone, because a hyperlinked environment is a multimedia information space where linked text is just one possible element. As posed in Chapter 4, this dichotomy was between texts that are "semantically structured," a linear hierarchical structure common to most textbooks, and those that are "format structured" (Reinking, 1992, p. 18). Given the problems raised concerning "considerate" text structures in that chapter, it seems apparent that the visual/verbal design was being evaluated in the basic linguistic terms which reflect a "semantically structured" text, though it can only be properly understood as a "format" structure. Here, the term "format," as in *form* and *formal*, is emphasized because it suggests the visual or graphic aspect.

Yet does not Gandelman's synthetic move beyond the visual/verbal dichotomy call for collapsing even this distinction between a "format" and "semantic structure"? In a graphical interface not only are semantic structures (chunks of text) embedded within larger format structures, but on screen the "semantic comprehension" which Estrock (1994) referred to has an expanded meaning. Semantics in the narrow linguistic sense is occupied solely with the signification and meaning of words. But in a wider sense it also includes semiotics, the study of signs (iconic, symbolic, indexical), and what they refer to. The standard GUI employs the use of all three kinds of signs as representational devices, most notably, the correspondence between the iconic, which generally concerns pictures, but with the interface has also come to mean icon buttons. Because a GUI involves, in Shneiderman's (1992) terms, "direct manipulation," it requires that a "semantic directness [or] adequacy" exist between what the user sees on screen and the interactions with those symbolic objects and representations (Hutchins, Hollan & Norman, 1986 p. 345). Thus meaning at the interface also has a "concrete" or visual mode, and from the standpoint of the interface, the term *semantic* includes nonlinguistic information.

Therefore, this combined act of viewing/reading will be dominated by "the process of visual search [which] is based upon the ability to find reliable and discriminable indicators of structure in the screen display" (Lansdale & Ormerod, 1994). Yet learning to scan complex information sets that are multi-windowed and extend beyond the frame of the screen no doubt will place a large burden on the young learner. Although scanning may be learned informally ("Kids can handle it"), the larger question of importance is to what extent the informal can be formalized. Here, research done on "focal attention" or the ability of learners to actively scan a field of information and focus on elements making up this field (whether visual, verbal, or both) would be useful in constructing a conceptual framework for further study (Jonassen & Grabowski, 1987, p. 127).

Such research is important because the "architecture" of the Social Studies Program was meant to be scanned as the designers suggested. Nevertheless, the means *to read* in this fashion were not articulated except in the most general of terms in the Visual Learning strand. This is an important gap. Research has shown that, when children are not properly trained to scan pictures, they tend to focus on the "dominant feature" in the composition, without moving to the total configuration of the object depicted. In gestalt terms they get lost in the parts and do not easily grasp the whole. Consequently, unless children are given cues and directions to make the "broad eye movements [necessary to] sample all the most informative aspects of the display," they will not easily be able to identify and understand the depiction (Gardner, 1978, p. 338). Here semantic coherence might be said to be secondary to the overall coherence and context of the "format." In Bower's (1972) terms, the visual structuring of information must support the gestalt patterns which stimulate "strong associations" in working memory, such that the "semantic fixations," or haptic pauses that occur between saccadic movements across a field of information, conform to the actual pattern of meaning intended by the information as displayed (p. 86).

To the extent that the "structuring of information" follows "the perceptual laws of grouping," for example, proximity, similarity, consistency, and so forth, these kinds of visual "associations" linking form to the content of information can occur (Preece & Keller, 1994, pp. 101–102). Ultimately, the "tension" between page and screen (text and hypertext) is between the kinds of interactivity possible in each medium. This "tension" plays itself out in the three areas we have reviewed here:

- perception of the "self-revealing" information structure,
- direct manipulation of the graphical representations on the interface,
- learning how to read visually/verbally which involves the ability to "navigate" through layered and linked series of windowed information spaces. (Alesandrini,1987; Kerr, 1986b)

Each information space and structure supports certain kinds of interactivity and in turn cognitive styles and actions corresponding to the nature of the medium. In fact, the center of the conventional curriculum is not so much the printed textbook as the *spoken word*. Text privileges voice. In general terms, Teacher/text/student is the primary communication model of instruction. Language, whether spoken or in printed form, orients learning to verbal literacy. However, in the shift to an on-screen learning environment, voice is undercut by vision. This is the basic distinction between the two media. One privileges voice, the other foregrounds sight. If this "changing sensibility of how we *look* at information," which the art director of the series spoke about, begins with being "comfortable with the idea of things being windowed and layered," how in terms of learning will this transformation end? Are the conventions which he regarded as "so accepted" merely a superficial accommodation to computer culture or do they reflect an incremental step in a profound cultural transition?

In 1966 Jerome Bruner observed that we have barely "scratched the surface of training in visualization." With visual computing and the ongoing revolution in chip technology, which will continue well into the next century, we seem now to be just below the "surface." How deep can we and must we go? Barbara Maria Stafford (1996) believes that "being digital requires designing a post-Gutenbergian *constructive* model of education through vision" (p. 3). This does not mean an "obliteration of the past" (Negroponte, 1995). This is not the end of textbook, but only a changing sense of what a textbook is or can be. Stafford (1996) advocates a transformative praxis which engages both past and present while looking to the future. Central to this praxis, she invokes John Dewey's most "evocative phrase . . . the in-viewness of ends" (p. 15). True to Dewey's pragmatic sensibility this means ending the "unproductive conflict between ideas and experience." This conflict has resonated at many points throughout this study. Certainly, the dichotomy of images (and) text participates, as we have seen in this chapter, in this polarizing battle which separates cognition (ideas) from perception (experience). "Developing an integrated, nonpolarized view of the varieties of visual experience" can begin, Stafford believes, by acknowledging "that perception is a significant form of knowing." It is, she says, to be considered an episteme in its own right; one that is fundamentally "constitutive." Experience as vision constructs the world. Stafford (1993) calls this "constitutive form" of visualization, "Educated Seeing" (p. 473). In a digital world "visual proficiency" means a form of praxis that would be able to "assimilate, integrate, and understand a holographic multi-disciplinary reality through three-dimensional imaging" (p. 462).

Such a radical agenda which runs counter to the linguistic orthodoxy of present curriulum theory and pedagogy may seem far beyond the design agenda of a visual/verbal textbook. Nevertheless, in an embryonic sense such an agenda can be traced in every aspect of its design and development. Speaking to the larger significance of the visual/verbal ratios calling for "*more and better* visuals," Frank Loose, like Stafford, has the same end *In*-View. Of the three designers, Loose was easily the most outspoken about the trajectory of visual/verbal design thinking. To him, the ratios introduced in the textbook series represented an elemental step in a logical transition progressing to a distributed multimedia classroom not dependent on textbooks. Implicit in the design was the end of the textbook as we presently know it. If the larger goal of the Social Studies Program was to advance Visual Learning, the computer in his mind was the instructional tool to ultimately realize this goal. Whereas the agenda of the original "Social Studies for the 21st Century" was for the design of a printed textbook, its innovative curricular goals for Visual Learning are in the same spirit as Stafford's "educated seeing." We may hope that this form of visual praxis will be the norm, not the exception, in the electronic learning spaces of the near future.

In the next, and last, chapter, the effect this form of visual *praxis* may have on our present understanding of the Social Studies curriculum is discussed. Because our electronic windows reveal a transnational–multicultural world, in which everyday reality is merging with the virtual space of the Internet, this vision may be something of a paradox for the Social Studies. In a profound sense, the present hyperreality may undercut our basic beliefs about the nature of democracy and citizenship. On the other hand, to actively engage the virtual may be the only means we have to transform our present understanding of the Social Studies in terms suitable for the future.

CHAPTER

8

Face-to-Face or Interface: Social Studies in Cyberspace

The electronic environment makes an information level outside the schoolroom that is far higher than the information level inside the schoolroom. In the nineteenth century the knowledge inside the schoolroom was higher than knowledge outside the schoolroom. Today it is reversed. The child knows that in going to school he is in a sense interrupting his education.

—H. Marshall McLuhan, March 19, 1967 (see Cremin, 1990)

What we have made, makes us.
—Myron W. Krueger (1993)

Although McLuhan's observation was made when broadcast television (then an analog medium) was reaching its zenith, the notion of the school as a space set apart from the world just for learning is still with us today. Yet in the present, McLuhan's "reversal" is itself reversed. The online information level in the classroom now far exceeds any "level" McLuhan could ever have imagined, just as it easily surpasses what can be found in any printed textbook. Inside is outside; potentially there is nothing outside the classroom. If the television was once thought of as a window on the world of physical time and space, today the computer has become a window on a virtual world seemingly unconstrained by either. All reversals aside, McLuhan's larger point about "information levels" reflecting electronic media's potential for extension is well taken.

The "extension" of electronic technology that McLuhan (1994) envisioned brings with it a paradox of enormous "social consequence," as he rightly saw. The lost point of the Virtual Mario talk in Hawaii, opening Chapter 7, was not so much that we would all be surfing the Web, to which the opening overhead of the Wave alluded only by sheer coincidence, but that the connectivity McLuhan foresaw would not only "abolish time and space," but would also create the possibility of a parallel virtual space of "simulation." Consciousness could likewise be "collectively and corporately extended" in both planetary space and cyberspace. In the summer of 1992 I watched the progress of Bill Clinton's first campaign for president in Auckland, New Zealand via Sky TV. Usually, as we watched, my friend's kids would be playing Mario on their Nintendo Gameboys. In the summer of 1994 we watched Jupiter rendezvous with a comet big enough to destroy our planet. At that time the Internet created an "instant global community" of comet watchers through email. "The net result of all this interaction," Robert Cowen (1994) reported, "was [the] emergence of a dense observing network covering the globe." At the time, the scale of interactivity which this coming together represented was truly phenomenal and perhaps without precedent. Cowen noted:

> At its peak, the information flow was almost overwhelming. The ESO in Garching, a major data gatherer, reported: "A true barrage of e-mail messages about new results [sic] arrived from all corners of the globe and sometimes the pace of events is simply breathtaking." It was almost as though a new kind of organism called "global observatory" had arisen, complete with telescopic senses and an electronic nervous system. (p. 13)

In Hawaii, November of 1994, this prescient report, which I omitted from my *Virtual Mario* talk, was the connecting link threading the concepts together. The Wave of technology's advance would soon link Gameboy, television set, and computer anywhere on the planet. A few years hence, NASA's July 4, 1997 Mars Pathfinder landing of the Sojourner rover demonstrates how this "global observatory" has moved off planet and on-site, transforming content into real-time event. With the power of the Web extended from NASA's JPL scientists to citizens, "looking down" has become the digital capability to look upon, and take a "closer look." But how will Social Studies embrace this transformative power? In the Hawaii talk I stressed that the *social* dimension of Social Studies which orients children to the notion of their *place* in the community and world now includes this virtual dimension. If the Gameboys of the near future will be linked, like our cellphones, to a global complex of networks, how is the instructional *space* of the classroom altered, and what may be the place of a typical textbook in such an expanded setting for learning?

Further, how might such electronic connectivity affect the nature and goals of the Social Studies as articulated by, for example, the traditional "Expanding Horizons" curriculum? Does being able to extend ourselves electronically in actual and virtual space draw us any closer socially? We need only think about television as McLuhan conceived of it, to wonder how this new medium will re-shape our society, since we are a "global village" only in the sense of being ever-present spectators. We are online and turned on. How easy it has become to think of society and social relationships in these terms. Electronically we can disengage with a click and a switch.

Connectivity may enhance the possibility of communication, but it does not necessarily dispose us to make actual contact. In the end, the human element of sociability may be irreducible. The desire to reach out and extend oneself, to share and form groups, is not advanced by becoming cyborgs, but by the simple power and presence of conscious volition.

But, does the computer and the virtual interactivity it brings advance the democratic aims of citizenship? Will it bring an electronic agora, a new public space for political discourse, or instead provide a medium for social, political, and economic balkanization? This is ultimately perhaps the core issue, the heart of the Social Studies, though it is one having no easy answer, if in fact it is answerable at all.

Nevertheless, we will attempt to grapple with these issues in the concluding discussion, beginning first with the fate of the textbook in the classroom without walls. Such questions are perhaps the easiest to answer, because, as we shall see, scenarios already exist linking the textbook to the electronic textuality of the Web. Text is *still* text whether printed or electronic.

However, in this transitional moment, a curriculum that can create and sustain linkages between our identity as U.S. citizens and our beliefs about the nature of democracy is not so easily mapped onto the labyrinthine spaces of the Internet, where there are no borders and only flow. What we may be able to say with any certainty about how this technology will impact the traditional Social Studies curriculum is extremely limited.

Yet at the same time our electronic window on the future is now open. We can see things taking shape, even though we may not know their ultimate impact. Consequently, we are free to envision, to imagine what shape the Social Studies may take. Hopefully then, my own scenarios will serve as a provisional base for further reflection on how we might engage this virtual dimension opening up on the screen before us.

A DIFFERENT ENGINE

> The print component is not ultimately or necessarily at the center of an educational system, but just a piece. . . . I've never felt that a book alone works. When you really think about how a teacher [actually] teaches, a program has to be a multisensory, multicomponent one to work for a learner empowered environment. We do find that students using multimedia programs get tired of them. They do like to turn them off. So again it's a combination. [Our own] program architecture is getting more diagraphic, almost a kind of guidebook approach than a read-about book.
>
> —Joe Godlewski (1993)

Different media do certain things better than others. One is not necessarily superior to another. Nor can one medium work alone. Don Norman's (1993) observations about the present state of education leads him to similar conclusions. "Multimedia education captures the experiential nature of the optimal experience, but at the neglect of all the rest" (p. 37). Learning, however, requires the optimal "combination of experiential and reflective modes of cognition." One kind of "reflective" activity encompassed by this latter mode, he suggests, is the use of textbooks (pp. 37–39). This "combination" is nearly identical to the distinction Bazin (1996) makes between the "intensive" and "extensive" kinds of reading determined by print and hypertext environments.

That Norman, like Godlewski, recognizes that optimal learning environments provide experiences that support different cognitive modes, different kinds of constructive interaction with information, a point that Papert would no doubt share, again is indicative of this dynamic "tension" that the art director senses between the book and hypertext. The visual/verbal textbook design combining the visual information structures typical of screen display with the conventional text structures of a book does not resolve this "tension," but instead only heightens it.

Instead of stable text structure the design foregrounds a visually stable graphic structure for information. It captures the essential point about this digital transition. With or without books we still need some kind of stable structure to support learning. And yet this attempt at stability is very much at odds with a medium that heightens disequilibrium, disorientation, and cognitive overload. So, it should not be automatically assumed that a more technologically sophisticated medium supplants one less so. That really does not capture the nature or complexity of technological change. If it were otherwise, textbooks would have disappeared as Edison expected.

Learning, similarly, is not an either/or situation, it is both/and. The computer can enhance a curriculum of different learning styles and cognitive modalities, but so too can paper and pencils. All options are really just "springboards," the art director said. He did not "see teachers pinning their hopes on media or classbound activities." Ideally, he believed teachers "want kids out of the classroom." Whatever the "materials" might be were simply a means to a learning "experience."

After the completion of the K–8 Social Studies Program, the art director eventually moved on to Houghton Mifflin where he took part in implementing this same "multicomponent" strategy merging textbooks with hypertext. Houghton Mifflin's web site *Education Place* has a home page interface with several icons referring to core curriculum subject areas like math and reading/language arts, called "Centers." When you click on the *Social Studies Center* icon you reach a screen with several more icons, one of which is for their new K–6 Social Studies Program, *We the People*. When you click on this icon you see the introduction screen which states:

> On these pages, We the People is supported by Internet resources directly tied to the print materials. We hope that these free materials will make it easier for you to make the wealth of the Internet available in your classroom. (Copyright © 1996 Houghton Mifflin Company)

Below this is a field of information titled, *Curriculum Resources*, which has "materials being developed for each unit of the K-6 series." When you click on a Level 1/Grade 1 you see a list of the six themes covered in the textbook, *Grow and Change*. For example, Theme 1, *We Are a Family,* has "materials which are arranged as a set of theme related resources and links." Some of these links are quite interesting. The first links the student to the Buchanan Family Web, which is the web site for an actual family, the Buchanans. It consists of a home page for each of the children, their father, and also their own list of "recommended Internet links." With other "theme related links" you tour the White House and look at an "annotated photo scrapbook" of previous "presidential families." You can also go to *Edu Web* connecting you to a "Learning site in Great Britain," which in turn can connect you to other web pages of schools "around the world."

Aside from the excellent electronic page design—simple, elegant, good use of white space, color used sparingly, and in hue intensities that correspond to children's perceptual and cognitive level—the only thing that is perhaps noteworthy about this site recalls the art director's words about how quickly we have embraced a screen "sensibility." Social Studies sites like this are now commonplace. The National Council of Social Studies (NCSS) web site has pages which are remarkably similar in design and intent. For example, at the *Kids Connected* link, a button in the *NCSS Online* Main Menu, students can "find cool stuff from around the world." Four buttons organize the information so you can "Look, Listen, Learn, and Laugh." When you click on the *Look* button you go to a list of clickables in which you can see "live pictures" of cities and places from around the world, which in some cases are television cameras connected to computers, though even these do not appear to be in real time. The list starts with Washington, D.C. and ends with New York City. In between and in any order you can link to pictures of Antarctica or Mt. Fuji, New Zealand or Dublin, Ireland, Rhodes, Greece or Main St., Walt Disney World, among many others. Unfortunately, these pictures are single shots with no related links describing the place further or its global geographic context. But the potential is there.

As information spaces re-mapping the field of Social Studies in a virtual n-dimension (n as in infinite), both sites are still under construction. Because the idea of mapping is a core concept of the field, we might consider how these linked spaces recreate the notions of both social and geographic space. In one we can move from a family's home to the White House, and then, if we like, to schools around the world. In the other we can visually jump from place to place, moving to various geographic points on the planet. In the former we could assume that a traditional Social Studies curriculum as defined by the K–6 scope and sequence is just being filled out by an as-it-were electronic ancillary. In the latter the basic core concept of *place* is conceived as an electronic list of unlinked pictures, which if one can hold a mental image of the earth in mind, could be looked upon as a series of visual frames connected to points mapped over its surface. In both, digital space is imperceptibly re-constructing physical time and space, adding a new kind of representation; not just text and/or image, but both/and. In the process this digital conversion compels a new look at the Social Studies curriculum.

The key then to understanding where the *text*book fits in the networked classroom lies in separating the overarching principle of *textuality* from the printed form of the material book. No doubt, the conventions of text are being transformed by the medium of the computer, and new hypertextual conventions are emerging as the word is reconceived electronically. Athough "Content is Everything," is potentially realized on screen, the appropriate linkages between instructional materials must still be intelligently made. This expanded field of information places the book *in* a system of relationships defined by its potential interaction with like or unlike media. Meaning is constructed by the process of interaction, not by viewing a fixed authoritative source. As such, the textbook is neither at the center or periphery of instruction, but an integral component in an array of instructional tools. The "tension" between the textbook and the screen (text and hypertext) is really about the kind of creative linkages between materials that can be envisioned. Although the curriculum may now have at its disposal a multimedia array of information, the engine driving instruction is still the reflective practitioner. That is the real difference.

VR/RL: VIRTUAL REALITY OR REAL LIFE

In his excellent overview, *Digital Technology and Social Studies*, Ronald Pahl (1996) stated that social studies instruction "must be driven by the curriculum." There are, he said, "three basic traditions of instruction" which concern the traditional curriculum:

- transmission of basic citizenship values and beliefs
- acquisition of social science and history knowledge
- [and], analysis and making decisions about major social problems

Assuming that "digital-based instructional activities" be looked upon as just a new classroom resource, he holds to the proposition that "curriculum drives instruction." Digital technology can "augment" the knowledge base of the second, and "assist" with the third, but the first tradition is of central importance. "How," he says, "does . . . digital technology affect the transmission of societal values and attitudes?"

Rather than contesting the validity of a firmly established educational proposition, let us instead simply suspend its logic and reverse the terms. Ask instead, how digital technology may now be driving the Social Studies curriculum? As Sherry Turkle (1995) suggested the present cultural moment calls for asking not what this technology can do *for* us, as just a new and powerful resource, but what is it doing *to* us, and the established traditions on which the Social Studies curriculum is based. Pahl sees this because he asks how it may "affect the transmission of societal values." He has a very good survey of the major social and cultural issues that digital technology introduces into the classroom. However, in a less cautious and more exploratory manner, I would suggest that he doesn't go far enough. What lies beyond this instrumental view of instruction, where technology is *introduced* just as another input to produce an instructional effect?

Turkle (1984) sees computer technology not just as another tool, but as a power shaping our sense of identity and perception of the world. To assert, as she does, that the Internet introduces a "culture of simulation" where our on-screen lives can become as important, if not synonymous with, real life requires serious consideration (1995, p. 10). To redirect our attention to the psychological dimension of technology, away from our typical, all too American, fascination with the newest and the latest high-tech gizmo, is to address what an instrumental view of technology, quite frankly, tends to avoid.

Rather, we should ask how this "culture of simulation" is fundamentally altering our "life world" (Idhe, 1990; Sobchack, 1994). This can be regarded as the lived space we create socially in our day to day lives. This space has both interior and exterior dimensions. First of all, it consists of our psychological well-being. And secondly, it consists of civil society that provides the setting for "transmission" of American identity and values to occur. At present, the most striking characteristic of our lived experience is, as Turkle notes, its simulated nature. If there is an irony to technological "extension" it is that it creates new boundaries and insurmountable distances just as easily as it seems to dispel them. But now, in addition, comes the final "extension." Standing in the shadow of our already overmediated "life world" is a new simulated one, cyberspace.

Because the discussion so far has been primarily concerned with vision and interface (what we *see*), it is directly related to how our mediated existence is largely taken up with how we participate in this "moving-image culture" (Sobchack, 1994). Like Edison, Vivian Sobchack (1994) a noted American film historian and cultural critic, has recognized the power of cinematic technology to shape our perceptions and define our lives. But all our screen technologies, film, television, and now computers, she says, do not just create media effects but "transform us as *subjects*." Each medium in its own way "demand[s] and shape[s] our presence to the world and our representation in it," that is, each defines our range of perceptual possibility and to a great extent shapes our conceptual horizons.

Whereas film and television, being photographic media, reference the "lived" and embodied space of the "concrete *world*," the virtual spaces being opened up by the new digital technology reflect, to use Turkle's term, a "nascent culture of simulation" (1995, p. 10). In recent Social Studies publications dealing with digital/interactive technology there is a distinct unease with the terminology of digital culture. For example, in a chapter looking at citizenship education and online learning communities, Lynn Fontana (1997) states that she will "avoid the use of the term *virtual* . . . since the term implies that the interactions and the learning are unreal." Pahl (1996), citing a series of articles by Doris Ray (1991a, 1991b) in the journal *Computing Teacher*, argues that the "image of a cyberspace education [is] unrealistic."

Like images that are either "real" or "unreal" these safely erected dichotomies prevent us from seeing the present. By viewing technology solely in instrumental terms, that is, what technology can *do* for us, they avoid facing what it is doing *to* us. We are not going to be able to grasp, much less understand, how, for instance, the *transmission* of citizenship will change in a digital world, unless we come to terms with the power these technologies have as dynamic engines of representation which will recreate the personal and public spaces of American society and culture.

A WINDOW THROUGH . . .

> What if you walk along and everything that you see is more than what you see—the person in the T-shirt and slacks is a warrior, the space that appears empty is a secret door to an alternate world? . . . Perhaps it is a doorway to another place. If you choose to go inside you might find many unexpected things.
>
> —Sigeru Miyamoto (1993, p. 37)

Just as this project began in the dark, gazing at a videogame interface, so too without quite realizing it, did I have my initial encounter with cyberspace. What made Sigeru Miyamoto's evocation so compelling when I first saw it was that he was the creator of Nintendo's *Super Mario* game. If the children that I watched in that dark hall had already crossed over, when would I make my choice to go inside? Outside/Inside? Real/Virtual? These are spatial terms implying movement from one place or point to another. Rather than seeing the Social Studies curriculum as now being *driven* by digital technology, let us instead see it as being reconfigured (that is redrawn, remapped, or envisioned).

Like Betty Edwards hearing that "the arrangement (configuration) of data and the spaces between" is now essential to interface design, we might perhaps consider how the three traditional strands in the curriculum could be visualized as data objects that are part of a larger Social Studies information structure which will, like the *NCSS Online* site, exist virtually in cyberspace. Perhaps the key to seeing things virtually is to understand the space in terms of a microworld built of bits, digits of zeroes, and ones. No doubt because we can't actually see these infinitely small worlds composed of 0/1s, we might try to imagine them like Miyamoto, in more conventional terms as places with streets you might walk along. That is, we might begin to think of them spatially.

Michael Heim (1993) explained "the *virtual* in virtual reality" in the most fundamental hardware terms. He said that "computer scientists use *virtual* memory to mean computer RAM (Random Access Memory) set aside in such a way that the computer operates as though memory exists beyond the actual hardware limits" of the computer. The distinction he makes between the "formal" (RAM set aside) and the virtual" can only be described metaphorically. Virtual space being an "informational equivalent" of physical space can "make us feel as if" it were real, he says.

This "as if . . ." should be seen not as unreal, but as an actual microspace inside the computer. This is, perhaps, the first elemental step in coming to terms with the *virtual*. We should see that it is, in fact, directly related to its silicon base, even though being microscopic it is no doubt extremely difficult to conceptualize. It is this sheer invisibility that is, more than likely, one significant factor contributing to our unease with such terms as "virtual" and "cyberspace." Nevertheless, it is ironic that this microworld provides, as it were, the silicon ground for the infinitely complex and multidimensional information space of the Internet. At the same time, and this may be a another factor contributing to our *virtual* anxiety, it allows us, if we so desire, to imaginatively project a "life on the screen," which need not have any direct connection to the identity we assume in real life (Turkle, 1995).

A less magical definition of cyberspace than Miyamoto's, and one closer now to our everyday experience, is Michael Benedikt's (1991). He says that

> Cyberspace is a globally networked, computer sustained, computer accessed and computer generated, multi-dimensional, artificial, or virtual, reality. In this reality every computer is a window, seen or heard objects are neither physical nor, necessarily, representations of physical objects, but are rather, in form, character and action, made up of data, of pure information. (pp. 122–123)

Of course in emphasizing this purely virtual space we might tend to miss how much it depends on the everyday conventions of the natural world to be comprehensible. What makes the virtual real and the real also real is that they both are constructed symbolically. Both are representations we sustain and actively create, and both are now in a process of merging. There need not be anything mysterious about this emergent reality. For instance, Heim (1993) talks about the experience of cyberspace being as simple as the space we open up during a telephone call. Our voice signals are reduced to "pure information" sent back and forth and instantaneously reassembled such that we hear what seems to be the recognizable voice of another "as if" we were talking face to face. There's nothing "unreal" about that. As all forms of communication become more digitized, social interaction has this invisible "as if" quality added on, meshing with the real. To the extent that we participate in any online activity, we are moving in both dimensions. In time, however, this "as if" dimension will become more visible.

Traditionally, Meredith Bricken (1991) noted, "an interface is a surface forming a boundary between . . . the information environment and the person accessing the information." Presently, most interface "*surfaces*" are just that: two-dimensional pages of text and pictures with links to other sites of similar page-like quality. Web sites are by and large text-based information environments that are proliferating by the millions. Communication in path breaking online communities such as the WELL (Whole Earth 'Lectronic Link) is also text based (see Rheingold, 1993). Groups interact by keyboard. The WELL home page describes itself as a "place made of words . . . a word palace" (WELL, 1997). However, in *City of Bits: Space, Place, and the Infobahn*, William Mitchell (1995) noted that as the Network infrastructure develops "higher bandwidths" and "ever-greater processing power" it will erode that "traditional boundary." Virtual cities, which will not necessarily have any geographic location since they are entirely "software constructions," will begin to take shape on the Web, Mitchell (1995) said. Every traditional urban space will have its "soft" counterpart, including the school. Interactivity in these information spaces will be "multimodal" and will not be restricted to exchanges of text (p. 19). Like the Unit and Chapter openers which a student could "step into," the classroom will have electronic learning spaces which students will be able to step into (Von Schweber & Von Schweber, 1996).

One place Mitchell's cyber-city has been taking shape for "the K-12 Global Schoolhouse" is the on-going *Cityspace project* (Spence, 1994, p. 145). *Cityspace* is a collaborative project for students sponsored by SIG Kids. Kids is a group affiliated with ACM—SIGGRAPH (Association for Computer Machinery—Special Interest Group for Computer Graphics). SIGGRAPH is the professional group within the computer industry devoted to research and development of high-end computer graphic and visualization applications. With *Cityspace* "students collaborate" from various real world city sites all over the planet "by submitting digital images and objects for inclusion in a 3-D virtual world kept alive by a Silicon Graphics Onyx system" (Spence, 1994, p. 145). Students can observe this digital urban counterpart being constructed on screen. Like IPT, this project should be of interest to educators because it demonstrates the possibility of students freely interacting across global networks to achieve a creative goal: the creation of a virtual world of their own design and making. In generational terms, such a project reflects the possibility that as children become more acculturated in a world shaped by computers the distinction between the virtual and the real will become less problematic than it is presently to some adults, who have grown up in the more naturalized cultural environments of film and television.

However, the question remains and our unease lingers. Even if we embrace cyberspace and engage this new virtual dimension invisibly emerging in our midst, will it provide a new social space for interaction, in which human connectivity and community are realized? Even the optimistic, more utopian inclined commentators on the emerging digital culture have questioned whether computer-mediated-communication (CMC) has the potential to create "genuine community" (Rheingold, 1996, p. 417). Howard Rheingold wonders openly whether "virtual communities" have merely appropriated the "aura" of real communities. Since "online relationships," he noted, generally "lack the genuine personal commitments to one another that form the bedrock of genuine community," how can they be considered actual communities? Later in the same article he introduces an important historical footnote on the origins of the Internet, which adds a strange gloss to the issue he raises, though one which he appears to entirely overlook. He notes that "computer-linked communities [were] predicted twenty years ago by J.C.R. Licklider and Robert Taylor," who also set in motion in the late 1960s the creation of the ARPAnet by the Defense Department, which is the electronic backbone for the present day Internet (p. 421). The "online interactive communities" of the ARPAnet (Advanced Projects Research Agency), described by Licklider and Taylor in 1968, "will consist of geographically separated members, sometimes grouped in small clusters and sometimes working individually. They will be communities not of common location, but of common interest" (Rheingold, 1996, p. 421). What Rheingold fails to elaborate on is why these communities have *no* "common location," and what this "common interest" might be. ARPANet was devised by the Pentagon as a communication network that could survive a nuclear war. This "closed world" of connected underground command and control bunkers, and as we know now, entire artificial communities for select scientists, military personnel, and politicians, was designed to survive the lethal radioactive fallout following a first strike of Russian intercontinental missiles (Edwards, 1996). It is difficult to dismiss the darker absurdity upon which the present Internet has its origins. One might ask, what kind of "genuine community" might have been realized, had such sinister scenarios, no doubt in the defense of freedom, tragically occurred?

No doubt, the Cold War is gratefully past, yet we still should ask just how Licklider and Taylor's prediction about online communities has been realized in the present. One area at which we might look, which is also important for the Social Studies, is the post-Cold War transnational economy. Here, the relationship between "community and the technology marketplace," which is overwhelmingly reliant on the Internet, is strikingly ambivalent (Miller, 1996, p. 321). In discussing how "the requirements of a vibrant market economy" are at odds with "stable communities," Steven Miller (1996) observes that "some commentators are now predicting the elimination of traditional, geographic-based communities" which will be replaced by "work communities," or in Licklider's terms communities of "common interest" (p. 322).

Like the dehumanized "closed world" of the Pentagon's ARPAnet, which had only one apocalyptic purpose, the electronic flow of information and transnational capital can selectively destroy communities in its relentless pursuit of profits, without any regard for the basic human needs and interests which are generally characteristic of "geographic-based communities."

Though it is difficult enough to judge even the local effects of the information economy on a case by case basis, much less determine how it may affect social and economic conditions on a global scale, it is nevertheless appropriate to look beyond the more optimistic rhetoric on where the "information superhighway" is taking us. The present practices of big business are hardly anything new, but if current predictions regarding the break-up of "stable geographic communities" fully materialize in our society, then the basic democratic principles underlying the Social Studies are indeed threatened, if not made entirely meaningless. If "technology is," as Miller (1996) asserted, "a social construction," so too is cyberspace. Our metaphors make us. If we conceive of the computer as an instrument of control and domination, rather than as a tool to facilitate communication and disseminate information, the darker potential of cyberspace will no doubt materialize (Edwards, 1996). The cutting edge of high technology may also be a razor's edge on which our present "life world" is poised. If, electronically speaking, there is really nothing outside the classroom, we nevertheless still need to filter the enormity and complexity of that world, so that what gets inside the school serves our ideals, and does not add to the darkness. Such responsibility requires only that we try to see things whole, and struggle with drawing out all aspects of a phenomenon, to represent it from all sides, in shadow and light. Regardless of its origin, the network computer is in search of a metaphor which will make the future appear hopeful. Cyberspace need not be populated by Terminators.

Even if we creatively configure cyberspace, this merging of virtual space with social reality seems to prefigure a number of profound shifts in the curriculum largely involving moving beyond the "transmission" model of knowledge acquisition, which tends to dominate the curriculum. The textbook is, of course, key to this traditional model, which is fundamentally about how we communicate with each other, and pass on what the curriculum has deemed to be important. This is usually a master narrative of cultural reproduction, which ensures society's status quo. Around this "story well told," the transformative point of this concluding discussion is reached.

TRANSMISSION IN TRANSITION

A book changes because it does *not* change while the whole world changes around it.
—Roger Chartier and Pierre Bourdieu (see Bazin, 1996)

Through even the smallest window the eye can reach the most distant horizon.
—A. Bergman (see Shneiderman, 1992)

The dominant metaphor of the Social Studies curriculum, like the Curriculum in general, is defined by the notion of transmission. Considering this from the vantage point of communication studies, one might say there are two competing models of the curriculum. In the first, the curriculum is looked upon as the "transmission of messages" or selected knowledge (Fiske, 1990, p. 2). In the second the curriculum is viewed as the "production and exchange of meanings" (1990, p. 2). In the first, curriculum is a linear process in which the teacher (the sender) transmits a message (text) to students, who receive the intended meaning. In the latter, "exchange" can be conceived as a complex interaction in which students construct (or produce) the meaning of the text within the context in which it is received. In the first model, the sender and the message are considered to be of primary importance. Reception or the effect of the message on the receiver depends entirely on the sender's ability to control the transmission of the intended message. In the second model, the meaning taken from the message assumes critical importance. Its recipients, in effect, construct the meaning, which may or may not coincide with the intended message.

The transmission model roughly corresponds to the making of a textbook. The first chapter described a process in which Ligature and the publisher consulted with California state social studies officials to produce a series of textbooks conforming to the new state Framework. This product, once adopted, would be transmitted by teachers in conformity with the Framework to students in the classroom. However, Chapter 6, on the California textbook adoption controversy, reflects the second model, in which the transmitted curriculum is contested and its meaning is negotiated. The conflict revealed that the textbook is not as stable and fixed as it normally appears. Author and audience (sender and receiver) roles were momentarily reversed. The adoption critics contested the author's privilege to present a multicultural message which reflected their understanding and actual position in the dominant culture. They wanted control of the message and the medium. Here, I likened textbook production to a broadcast medium which didn't best suit the reality of a multicultural world.

No doubt the question of transmission framed here may be conceived too abstractly. The best contemporary example of a transmission curriculum model is E.D. Hirsch's highly prescriptive *Cultural Literacy* program. This approach, which is reminiscent of Mortimer Adler's *Great Books of the Western World* curriculum, puts forward a model of what properly constitutes the cultural dimension of American civil society. Culture, like civilization, is to be understood largely as a matrix of facts, dates, and ideas transmitted to students for memorization, with the teacher functioning as sort of a stand-in oracle who authoritatively disseminates the best of the West. Citizenship transmission has its ideological counterpart in notions like the *National Identity*, the central symbol of controversy in the California adoption struggle, which prescribes a view of citizenship, that is, what it means to be an American, in largely Eurocentric terms which are incontrovertible and beyond question (the "American creed"). Such social reproduction models, which incidentally regard book literacy as key to culture's continuity and conservation, tend to view citizenship education in terms of compliance with authority and observance of the letter of the law and the status quo. This conservative view of civil society leaves little room for seeing citizenship in broader critical terms, least of all virtual ones (Parker & Jarolimek, 1997, p. 63).

Yet in moving from a traditional curriculum model which assumes textbook-based instruction to a multimedia network model in which the textbook is no longer dominant, the idea of *transmission* fundamentally changes. Most obviously, the medium of transmission changes. Paper bound text is not a screen display. We are no longer in a classroom where teachers talk and students listen. On screen the word can be viewed, heard, and rewritten. Transmission shifts from the spoken word to the electronic address of a network. The privileging of text shifts to a wider field of electronic context. This expansion transcends both cultural and national boundaries. All cultures and nations are potentially linked. The "intensive" information space of the book is framed by an "extensive" electronic window. Civil society is repositioned both globally and virtually. This is the digital horizon.

By contrast, the California History–Social Science Framework, as well as the series of textbooks Ligature designed, both conform to a traditional scope and sequence curriculum pattern known as "expanding horizons" (Allen, 1996). Marker and Mehlinger (1992) commented that this been the most frequently employed scope and sequence pattern used this century. It is conceived as a series of "concentric circles" oriented to a student's growing awareness of their place in world. In kindergarten this relational movement begins with a sense of self, the innermost circle, progressively expanding to understand home and family, school and their local community, then state, country, and the wider world. This spatial movement of geographic breadth is expanded further in the temporal dimension by consideration of ancient and contemporary world history and cultures, though the global perspective gives way to a national one in the later grades with the usual focus being on U.S. government and civic education. Except for its institutional and historic precedent Marker and Mehlinger (1992) admit with a tinge of irony that there is nothing about the "expanding horizon" (they refer to it as "expanding environments") curriculum which makes it "necessary." As long as "the classroom presentation is pitched to a cognitive level appropriate to the age of the student, practically any content can be justified and taught legitimately at any grade level," they said (p. 833).

Actually the naturalness of the "expanding horizons" curriculum seems to work well with a series of graded textbooks, because it is basically linear and progressive. Contrast this kind of contained expansion with the behavior of an inquisitive child who has access to a Netscape browser. Given the right search engine and search queries a child could just as easily be investigating the coincidence of geography and cosmology in the design of ancient Chinese cities, or be studying the water tributaries and wetland ecosystems of the Mississippi river. Digitally, a child can leapfrog across time and space, histories and cultures. Who or what provides the appropriate frame and sets a context for closure? Such topics could perhaps be just as easily engaged in the "expanding horizons" format, but a networked computer problematizes the nature of scope and sequence in a way that fundamentally challenges our present understanding of how a curriculum can or should be organized. Further, not only does it offer limitless expansion of transdisciplinary subject matter (a boon for Social Studies), it also draws into question the basic articulation of self and society which the "expanding horizons" pattern successfully contains.

In his seminal book, *No Sense of Place: The Impact of Electronic Media on Social Behavior*, Joshua Meyrowitz (1985) articulated the deeper and more lasting significance of Marshall McLuhan's oracular pronouncements on American popular culture. His basic contention is that television creates a new kind of social space (a "life world") which blurs the "perceived differences among people of different social groups" by dissolving their distinctive "experiential worlds." Instead television creates an electronic "stage for socialization," collapsing the natural distinction one could formerly make between face-to-face interactions and their mediated counterpart. "Electronic media affect us," he says, "not primarily through their content, but by changing the situational geography of social life" (p. 9). Computers, which interestingly enough he regards as a sort of hybrid medium combining television and books, can only serve to accelerate this social phenomenon which levels group identity and experience.

One of the more interesting chapters of Meyrowitz's book deals with how television has profoundly altered the way presidential campaigns are conducted and the mediated fashion in which public office is held. Over time, the substance of political discourse has been diminished to personal style and the articulation of political issues reduced to photo-ops and sound bites. None of this of course raises an eyebrow, because it's just the way things are. Yet, just imagine how far the present mediated spectacle is from the terms on which American civil society and citizenship are actually based. The concept of a "public sphere" is historically derived from the Enlightenment political philosophy which is also foundational for American democracy. This "sphere" is conceived of as a social stage for political activity and self-expression, which is separate from the government and the economy (Habermas, 1989). Similarly, the Enlightenment conceived of a citizen acting in this sphere as an autonomous subject who through reason and consensus participates in the democratic polity which in turn influences the exercise of government. However, in present day America the social, political, and economic spheres have merged. The Market largely defines the normative terms of social and political discourse. Freedom becomes synonymous with consumption. Democracy is less something in which one participates in than a phenomenon that one simply watches.

Paradoxically, the institutional pattern of the Social Studies curriculum and the central tenets of citizenship education are reproduced within the field of Social Studies as if the Enlightenment categories on which both are predicated are perennial truths untouched by the force of history or the engine of a transnational economy. No doubt the new digital technologies can "augment" and support the basic curricular "elements of democratic citizenship education" (Parker & Jarolimek 1997, p. 63). All these elements on which civil society and participatory democracy are based:

- Knowledge
- Discussion
- Decision Making
- Values
- Character Dispositions
- Community Service/Action

might easily be envisioned in virtual terms. Howard Rheingold (1993) has argued as much, though his optimism that the "public sphere" can be reinvented in digital terms is tempered by his critical awareness that formidable market forces are coalescing against it. Just as the Internet is presently regarded, like television was at its inception, as a revolutionary medium that will fulfill the ideals of participatory democracy, it is also well on its way to becoming a more sophisticated broadcast medium explicitly designed for tailored consumption (see Miller, 1996, chap. 11; and *Wired*, March 1997). In a culture of simulation where education and entertainment appear to be merging, will our children know how to make such a critical distinction? Unless the curriculum conversation in Social Studies moves beyond an instrumental view which looks upon computers as just another means of improving instructional delivery, we, like our students, will imagine that our horizons are expanding when in fact they are shrinking.

If the "heart" of the Social Studies is about decision making, as Shirley Engle (1978) believed, then might we not have to come to terms with how both we and the discipline are being transformed by the computer? It has been said that "the purpose of computers is insight, not numbers"(Hamming, 1962). When the heart flows with the deliberations of the mind, we have insight. Part of that insight might involve the recognition that the Social Studies curriculum has up to now largely been a product of "traditional" and "progressive" forms of pedagogy, both of which assume a mode of instruction centered on the textbook (Cummins & Sayer, 1995). Just as the authors of the textbook series examined here did not quite comprehend the way in which a phenomenon like multiculturalism radically alters conventional standards of narrative and representation, so too might the Net computer be viewed simply as an electronic ancillary. Authorial privilege did not, at least at first, recognize that their multicultural audience was the real voice in the text. In a multicultural world a story is not well told unless the author speaks in the same voice as the audience represented. Given the exclusive limitations of the textbook, such a multitextured voice was not possible, at least in printed form. Even if the author fully identified with the role of "architect," which Ligature's art director felt was more appropriate to the task, at some point the arrived at whole might still exclude a necessary but omitted part. But in a multicultural sense it might turn out to be the foundation stone of an inclusive textual edifice.

Yet, because the role of an author more closely corresponds to a communication model of transmission, the metaphor of architect might be more suitable as a role for the Social Studies teacher in the emerging multicultural/multimedia society. In practice, architects, like graphic designers, may at the outset envision a grand design or have an initial ideal conception. But from process to product that vision is constantly refined. This nearly always involves intense collaboration and consultation. Great buildings or complex systems are rarely the result of a mythic visionary individual, but the synergy of a collective highly organized vision. In the exercise of design all practitioners visualize. Architects with their design teams draw up countless plans and diagrams. Space is mapped and allocated down to the most minute structural detail. Good design requires the expert guidance of a well articulated layout and plan in which *clarity* and *complexity*, as Tufte maintains, are not mutually exclusive.

In an electronic learning space the social studies teacher can well be seen as something like a architect and a guide and most definitely a facilitator of collaboration and inquiry, reflecting the best of the progressive tradition. Textbooks will no doubt remain, though in both print and electronic form, but will perhaps be more like a "guidebook" showing all the possible ways into a subject area, rather than a definitive text. Though it may be that, the change to an electronic format will be more abrupt than gradual. Recently, the Texas Board of Education, the nation's other trend setting market, announced that it was seriously considering purchasing laptop computers for students, instead of replacing obsolete social studies textbooks with the newly printed edition. Just as we have followed how this digital medium transformed the printed textbook, so too is it paradoxically ushering in the end of that print pedagogy by opening a window of possibility extending far beyond the classroom centered on textbook instruction.

Jim Cummins and Dennis Sayer (1995) maintain that U.S. society of the 21st century will be characterized mainly by an electronic multiculturalism in which local and "global networks" will cross all national, cultural, and geographic boundaries. They believe that a "transformative pedagogy" would provide students "with a broad range of experience in using such networks for intercultural collaboration and critical thinking." The key to understanding the "instructional landscape" that "global networks" offer is in viewing instruction as a constructive dialogue, and not as "top-down" transmission. Education as broadcast needs to be "reframed" by the metaphor of a network. Students are not made knowledgeable, they make their own knowledge. Information, like cognition, is distributed through a web of interrelationships. And soon, these intercultural collaborations will have a visual as well as virtual dimension. Difference will be mediated by electronic presence. Interface will give way to face-to-face encounter. Text, voice, and image will be immediate, but distant, constructed and even possibly delayed, as each viewer is so inclined.

The extraordinary potential this connective presence will offer might well be regarded as the visual/verbal mark of a "transformative pedagogy." And over time it will likely shift the entire process of education as we know it to an active cultivation of this emerging visual dimension. Cummins and Sayer assert that the "transformative" approach is more in keeping with the ideals of participatory democracy necessary for a multicultural world. Such pedagogical models are certainly not foreign to Social Studies, although they are perhaps undervalued because they diminish more traditional forms of instructional control.

Ultimately then, the transformation of the textbook is less about expanding the power of representation by extending the range of media in which knowledge can be represented, than it is about moving beyond the social constraint invested in a pedagogy centered on textbook instruction. Yet we really do not have to imagine its coming technologically because it is already here. The boundaries of belief maintained by our institutional patterns of seeing and knowing ritually transmitted to our children, largely through the medium of the traditional textbook, can only temporarily prevent us from being led by them across that transformative threshold.

The coming of such "pedagogy" then is perhaps less by design and more by the random activation of electronic presence taking place collectively across the interface, and across the planet. Likewise, the horizon of the social, like Social Studies, shifts from the nation to the network. Potentially, identity becomes multiple and transnational in makeup. In such a digital transition, we move from representation to real-time, from content to event, as the local becomes synonymous with the global. In this fundamental repositioning, the textual does not so much give way to the visual, as it is re-integrated with it. Yet, there are many unforeseen steps in this transition. This book marks only an embryonic point where it has begun.

References

Al-Qazzaz, A., Afifi, R., Pelletiere, J., & Shabbas, A. (1975). *The Arab in American textbooks: A detailed analysis of treatment of the Arabs in elementary and junior high school textbooks for the California State Board of Education, June 1975* (p. 4). Albany, CA: NAJDA (Women Concerned About the Middle East).

Alesandrini, K. (1987). Computer graphics in learning and instruction. In H. A. Harvey & W. M. Willows (Eds.), *The psychology of illustration, Volume 2: Instructional issues* (pp. 157–187). New York: Springer-Verlag.

Allen, R. (1996). What should we teach in social studies? And why? In B. G. Massialas & R. F. Allen (Eds.), *Crucial issues in teaching social studies, K–12* (pp. 1–26). Belmont, CA: Wadsworth.

Allington, R., & Weber, R. M. (1993). Questioning questions in teaching and learning from texts. In B. K. Britton, A. Woodward, & M. Binkley (Eds.), *Learning from textbooks: Theory and practice* (pp. 47–68). Hillsdale, NJ: Lawrence Erlbaum Associates.

Anderson, T. H., & Armbruster, B. (1984). Structures of explanation in history books. *Journal of Curriculum Studies, 16*(2), 181–194.

Anderson, T. H., & Armbruster, B. B. (1985). Study strategies and their implications for text design. In T. M. Duffy & R. Waller (Eds.), *Designing usable texts* (pp. 159–177). Orlando, FL: Academic Press.

Apple Computer, Inc. (1992). *Macintosh human interface guidelines* (p. 8). Reading, MA: Addison Wesley.

Armbruster, B. B. (1981). The problem of "inconsiderate text." In G. G. Duffy, L. R. Roehler, & J. Mason (Eds.), *Comprehension instruction* (pp. 203–217). New York: Longman.

Armbruster, B. B. (1986). Schema theory and the design of content area textbooks. *Educational Psychologist, 21*(4), 253–267.

Armbruster, B. B., & Ostertag, G. (1993). Questions in elementary science and social studies textbooks. In B. K. Britton, A. Woodward, & M. Binkley (Eds.), *Learning from textbooks: Theory and practice* (pp. 69–94). Hillsdale, NJ: Lawrence Erlbaum Associates.

Armento, B. J. (1986). Research on teaching social studies. In M. C. Wittrock (Ed.), *Handbook of research on teaching* (pp. 942–951). New York: Macmillan.

Arnheim, R. (1979). Visual thinking in education. In A. Sheikh & J. T. Shaffer (Eds.), *The potential of fantasy and imagination* (pp. 215–223). New York: Brandon House.

Banks, J. A. (1990). *Teaching strategies for the social studies* (4th ed.). New York: Longman.

Banks, J. A. (1995). Multicultural education: Historical development, dimensions, and perspectives. In J. A. Banks (Ed.), *Handbook of research on multicultural education* (pp. 3–22). New York: Macmillan.

Barthes, R. (1977). Rhetoric of the image. In *Image, music, text* (pp. 32–51). New York: Hill and Wang.

Bazin, P. (1996). Toward metareading. In G. Nunberg (Ed.), *The future of the book* (pp. 153–168). Berkeley, CA: University of California Press.

Benedikt, M. (1991). Cyberspace: Some proposals. In M. Benedikt (Ed.), *Cyberspace: First steps* (pp. 122–123). Cambridge, MA: The MIT Press.

Berger, J. (1972). *Ways of seeing.* London: The BBC and Penguin Books.

Bergman, A. (1992). Visual realities. In B. Shneiderman. *Designing the user interface* (2nd ed.), (p. 335). Reading, MA: Addison Wesley.

Berkhofer, R. F. (1978). *The white man's Indian: Images of the American Indian from Columbus to the present.* New York: Alfred A. Knopf.

Bliss, T. (1990). Visuals in perspective: An analysis of U.S. history textbooks. *The Social Studies, 81*(1), 10–14.

Bloomer, C. M. (1990). *Principles of visual perception.* New York: Design Press.

Bogle, D. (1994). *Toms, coons, mulattoes, mammies, and bucks: An interpretive history of blacks in American films* (3rd ed.). New York: Continuum.

Bolter, J. (1991). *Writing space: The computer, hypertext, and the history of writing.* Hillsdale, NJ: Lawrence Erlbaum Associates.

Boring, E. G. (1957). *A history of experimental psychology.* New York: Appleton-Century-Crofts.

Bower, G. H. (1972). Mental imagery and associative learning. In L. W. Gregg (Ed.), *Cognition in memory and learning* (pp. 51–58). New York: John Wiley.

Brammer, M. (1967). Textbook publishing. In C. B. Grannis (Ed.), *What happens in book publishing* (2nd ed.), (pp. 320–349). New York: Columbia University Press.

Bricken, M. (1991). Virtual worlds: No interface to design. In M. Benedikt (Ed.), *Cyberspace: First steps* (pp. 363–382). Cambridge, MA: The MIT Press.

Bruer, J. T. (1993). *Schools for thought.* Cambridge, MA: The MIT Press.

Bruner, J. S. (1966). *Toward a theory of instruction.* Cambridge, MA: The Belknap Press.

Calfee, R. C., & Chambliss, M. J. (1987). The structural design features of large texts. *Educational Psychologist, 22*(3 & 4), 357–375.

Calhoun, C. (Ed). (1992). *Habermas and the public sphere.* Cambridge, MA: The MIT Press.

California State Department of Education. (1988). *History social-science framework.* Sacramento, CA.

Carroll, L. (1982). *Alice's adventures in wonderland* (p. 37). Berkeley, CA: University of California Press.

Cazden, C. B. (1986). Classroom discourse. In M. C. Wittrock (Ed.), *Handbook of research on teaching* (pp. 432–463). New York: Macmillan.

Chall, J. S. (1977). *An analysis of textbooks in relation to declining scores.* Princeton, NJ: College Entrance Exam Board.

Chall, J. S., & Conrad, S. S. (1991). *Should textbooks challenge students?* New York: Teachers College Press.

Chall, J. S., & Squire, J. R. (1991). The publishing industry and textbooks. In P. D. Pearson, R. Barr, M. L. Kamil, & P. Mosenthal (Eds.), *The handbook of reading research, Vol. II* (pp. 120–146). White Plains, NY: Longman.

Chartier, R., & Bourdieu, P. (1996). Toward metareading. In G. Nunberg (Ed.), *The future of the book* (p. 160). Berkeley, CA: University of California Press.

Chatman, S. (1978). *Story and discourse.* Ithaca, NY: Cornell University Press.

Chignell, M. H., & Waterworth, J. A. (1991). WIMPS and NERDS: An extended view of the user interface. *ACM SIGGCHI Bulletin, 23*(2), 15–21.

Clayson, J. (1988). *Visual modeling with Logo*. Cambridge, MA: The MIT Press.

Cornbleth, C., & Waugh D. (1995). *The great speckled bird: Multicultural politics and education policymaking*. New York: St. Martin's Press.

Cowen, R. C. (1994). On-line astronomy links Jupiter watchers. *The Christian Science Monitor*, August 3, p. 13.

Cremin, L. A. (1990). *Popular education and its discontents* (p. 51). New York: Harper & Row.

Cruickshank, D. (1996). The inevitable engine: The evolution of visual computing. *IRIS Universe*, No. 34, 17–22.

Cummins, J., & Sayer, D. (1995). *Brave new schools: Challenging cultural illiteracy through global learning networks*. New York: St. Martin's Press.

de Beaugrande, R. (1984). *Text production: Toward a science of composition*. Norwood, NJ: Ablex.

Debes, J. L. (1970). *The loom of visual literacy: An overview* (pp. 1–16). New York: Pitman.

Dondis, D. A. (1973). *A primer of visual literacy*. Cambridge, MA: The MIT Press.

Duchastel, P. C. (1978). Illustrating instructional texts. *Educational Technology*, November, pp. 36–39.

Duchastel, P. C. (1986). Computer text access. *Computer Education,* 10, 403–409.

Edwards, B. (1979). *Drawing on the right side of the brain* (pp. 36–37). Los Angeles, CA: Tarcher.

Edwards, B. (1986). *Drawing on the artist within*. New York: Simon & Schuster.

Edwards, B. (1996, April). A new look at the art of seeing. Plenary Session, *CHI 96: Conference on Human Factors in Computing Systems*, Vancouver, BC: Association for Computing Machinery, New York.

Edwards, P. N. (1996) *The closed world: Computers and the politics of discourse in Cold War America*. Cambridge, MA: The MIT Press.

Elkins, J. (1996). *The object stares back: On the nature of seeing*. New York: Simon and Schuster.

Engle, S. H. (1978). *Decision making: The heart of the social studies instruction-Revisited*. Bloomington, IN: Social Studies Development Center, Indiana University, Occasional Paper Number 1.

Estrock, E. J. (1994). *The reader's eye: Visual imaging as reader response*. Baltimore, MD: The John Hopkins University Press.

Febvre, L., & Martin, H. J. (1958). *The coming of the book: The impact of printing, 1450–1800*. London: New Left Books, Verso, 1990 edition.

Finocchiaro, M. (1989). *English as a second/foreign language,* (4th ed.). Englewood Cliffs, NJ: Prentice-Hall.

Fiske, J. (1990). *Introduction to communication studies* (2nd ed.). London: Routledge.

Fitzgerald, F. (1979). *America revised: History schoolbooks in the twentieth century*. Boston: Atlantic-Little Brown.

Fontana, L. A. (1997). Online learning communities: Implications for the social studies. In P. H. Martorella (Ed.), *Interactive technologies and the social studies: Emerging issues and applications* (pp. 1–26). Albany, NY: The State University of New York Press.

Fredette, B. W. (1994). Use of visuals in schools. In D. M. Moore & F. M. Dwyer (Eds.), *Visual literacy* (pp. 235–236). Englewood Cliffs, NJ: Educational Technology Publications.

Friedhoff, R. M., & Benzon, W. (1989). *Visualization: The second computer revolution* (p. 113). New York: Harry N. Abrams.

Fullinwider, R. K. (1996). Patriotic history. In R. K. Fullinwider (Ed.), *Public education in a multicultural society: Policy, theory, critique* (p. 204). New York: Cambridge University Press.

Gagnon, P. (Ed.). (1989). *Historical literacy: The case for history in American education*. Boston, MA: Houghton Mifflin.

Gandelman, C. (1991). *Reading pictures, viewing texts*. Bloomington, IN: Indiana University Press.

Gardner, H. (1978). *Developmental psychology: An introduction*. Boston, MA: Little, Brown.

Gardner, H. (1982). *Art, mind and brain*. New York: Basic Books.

Gardner, H. (1993). *Multiple intelligences: The theory in practice*. New York: Basic Books.

Gates, B. (1995). *The road ahead* (1st ed.). New York: Viking Penguin.

Gates, B. (1996). *The road ahead* (2nd ed.). New York: Viking Penguin.

Ginsburg, H. P., & Opper, S. (1988). *Piaget's theory of intellectual development*. Englewood Cliffs, NJ: Prentice-Hall.

Gitlin, T. (1995). *The twilight of common dreams: Why America is wracked by culture wars*. New York: Metropolitan Books, Henry Holt.

Goldberg, V. (1991). *The power of photography: How photographs changed our lives* (p. 96). New York: Abbeville Press.

Gombrich, E. (1979). *The sense of order* (p. 4). Ithaca, NY: Cornell University Press.

Grabowski, B., & Schroeder E. E. (1994, April). *Learned activities matched with individual differences: An examination of interrelated styles*. Paper presented annual meeting of the American Educational Research Association, New Orleans, LA.

Greenberg, R. (1996a). The image processing for teaching project. In C. Fisher, D. C. Dwyer, & K. Yocam (Eds.), *Education and technology: Reflections on computing in classrooms* (pp. 221–222). San Francisco: Jossey-Bass.

Greenberg, R. (1996b). The ITP project: Image processing for teaching. *T.H.E. Journal, 24*(5), 61–65.

Greenberger, M. (Ed.). (1994). *Content and communication: Technologies for the 21st century* (p. 181). Santa Monica, CA: Council for Technology and the Individual.

Greenfield, P. M. (1990). Video screens: Are they changing the way children learn. *Education Letter, 6*(2), 1–4. Cambridge, MA: Harvard Graduate School of Education in association with Harvard University Press.

Gross, M. (1994). *Visual computing: The integration of computer graphics, visual perception and imaging*. Berlin: Springer-Verlag.

Habermas, J. (1989). *The structural transformation of the public sphere: An inquiry into the category of bourgeois society*. Cambridge, MA: The MIT Press.

Hamblen, K. (1987). An examination of discipline-based art education issues. *Studies in Art Education, 28*(2), 68–78.

Hamming, R.W. (1962). *Numerical methods for scientists and engineers*. New York: McGraw Hill.

Harel, I. (Ed.). (1990). *Constructionist learning*. Cambridge MA: The MIT Media Laboratory.

Heim, M. (1993). *The metaphysics of virtual reality*. New York: Oxford University Press.

Honig, B. (1989). California's experience with textbook improvement. *Educational Policy, 3*(2), 125–135.

Houghton Mifflin Publishing Company. (1996). *Education Place: Free Internet Resources for K-8*. http://www.eduplace.com/ (All Rights Reserved).

Hutchins, E. L., Hollan, J. D., & Norman, D. A. (1986). Direct manipulation interfaces. In D. A. Norman & S. W. Draper (Eds.), *User centered system design: New perspectives on human-computer interaction* (pp. 87–124). Hillsdale, NJ: Lawrence Erlbaum Associates.

Idhe, D. (1990). *Technology and the lifeworld: From garden to earth*. Bloomington, IN: Indiana University Press.

Jarolimek, J. (1990). *Social studies in elementary education* (8th ed.). New York: Macmillan.

John P. Getty Trust. (1993). *Improving visual arts education: Final report on the Los Angeles Getty Institute for Educators on the Visual Arts (1982–1989)*. Santa Monica, CA: The John P. Getty Trust Publications.

Jonassen, D. H., & Grabowski, B. L. (1987). Assessing cognitive structure: Verifying a method using pattern notes. *Journal of Research and Development in Education, 20*(3), 1–14.

Jonassen, D. H. (1989). *Hypertext/hypermedia*. Englewood Cliffs, NJ: Educational Technology Publications.

Jonassen, D. H. (1993). *Handbook of individual differences, learning, and instruction*. Hillsdale, NJ: Lawrence Erlbaum Associates.

Jonassen, D. H. (1996). *Computers in the classroom: Mindtools for critical thinking*. Englewood Cliffs, NJ: Prentice-Hall.

Jones, B. L., & Maloy, R. W. (1996). *Schools for an information age: Reconstructing foundations for learning and teaching* (p. 244). Westport, CT: Praeger.

Kammen, M. (1989). History is our heritage: The past in contemporary American culture (p. 149). In P. Gagnon (Ed.), *Historical Literacy*. Boston, MA: Houghton Mifflin.

Kay, A. (1984). Les logiciels. In *Pour La Science*, November, pp. 14–22.

Kay, A. (1990). User interface: A personal view. In B. Laurel (Ed.), *The art of human-computer interface design* (pp. 191–208). Reading, MA: Addison Wesley.

Kellner, D. (1995a). Reading images critically: Toward a post-modern pedagogy. In H. Giroux (Ed.), *Postmodernism, feminism, and cultural politics: Redrawing educational boundaries* (pp. 60–82). Albany, NY: State University of New York Press.

Kellner, D. (1995b). *Media culture: Cultural studies, identity and politics between the modern and the postmodern*. London: Routledge.

Kerr, S. (1986a). Instructional text: The transition from page to screen. *Visible Language, 20*(4), 368–392.

Kerr, S. (1986b). Learning to use electronic text. *Information Design Journal, 4*(3), 206–211.

King, J. E. (1995). Culture-centered knowledge: Black studies, curriculum transformation, and social action. In J. A. Banks (Ed.), *Handbook of research on multicultural education* (pp. 265–290). New York: Macmillan.

Kirby, J. R., Moore, P. J., & Schofield, N. J. (1988). Visual and verbal learning styles. *Contemporary Educational Psychology, 13*, 169–184.

Kosslyn, S. M. (1994a). *Image and brain: The resolution of the imagery debate*. Cambridge, MA: The MIT Press.

Kosslyn, S. M. (1994b). *Elements of graph design*. New York: W. H. Freeman.

Krueger, M. W. (1993). Forward in: M. Heim. *The metaphysics of virtual reality* (p. x.). New York: Oxford University Press.

Landow, G. (1992). *Hypertext: The convergence of contemporary critical theory and technology.* Baltimore, MD: The Johns Hopkins University Press.

Landow, G., & Delany, P. (1991). Hypertext, hypermedia, and literary studies: The state of the art. In P. Delaney & G. P. Landow (Eds.), *Hypermedia and literary studies.* Cambridge, MA: The MIT Press.

Langer, S. K. (1957). *Philosophy in a new key* (3rd ed.). Cambridge, MA: Harvard University Press.

Lanham, R. (1993). *The electronic word: Democracy, technology, and the arts.* Chicago, IL: University of Chicago Press.

Lansdale, M. W., & Ormerod, T. C. (1994). *Understanding interfaces: A handbook of human-computer dialogue.* London: Academic Press.

Levin, J. R., & Mayer, R. E. (1993). Understanding illustrations in text. In B. K. Britton, A. Woodward, & M. Binkley (Eds.), *Learning from textbooks: Theory and practice* (pp. 95–114). Hillsdale, NJ: Lawrence Erlbaum Associates.

Ligature, Inc. (1989, May 8). *Social studies for the 21st century: SS21: Social studies plan document,* Chicago, IL.

Lowenfeld, V. (1952). *Creative and mental growth.* New York: Macmillan.

Marker, G., & Mehlinger, H. (1992). Social studies. In P. W. Jackson (Ed.), *Handbook of research on curriculum* (pp. 830–851). New York: Macmillan.

Martorella, P. H. (1985). *Elementary social studies.* Boston, MA: Little, Brown.

McCarthy, C. (1993). After the canon: Knowledge and ideological representation in the multicultural discourse on curriculum reform. In C. McCarthy & W. Crichlow (Eds.), *Race, identity, and representation in education* (pp. 289–305). New York: Routledge.

McLuhan, M. (1994). *Understanding media: The extensions of man.* Cambridge, MA: The MIT Press edition, Lewis H. Lapham, Introduction.

Meggs, P. (1989). *Type & image: The language of graphic design.* New York: Van Nostrand Reinhold.

Meyer, B. J. F. (1985). Signaling the structures of text. In D. Jonassen (Ed.), *The technology of text, Volume II* (pp. 64–89). Englewood Cliffs, NJ: Educational Technology Publications.

Meyrowitz, J. (1985). *No sense of place: The impact of electronic media on social behavior.* New York: Oxford University Press.

Miller, S. E. (1996). *Civilizing cyberspace: Policy, power, and the information superhighway.* New York: The ACM Press.

Miller, J. H. (1992). *Illustration* (p. 73). Cambridge, MA: Harvard University Press.

Mitchell, W. J. T. (1986). *Iconology: Image, text, ideology.* Chicago, IL: University of Chicago Press.

Mitchell, W. J. (1995). *City of bits: Space, place, and the infobahn.* Cambridge, MA: The MIT Press.

Miyamoto, S. (1993). In D. Sheff. *Game over* (p. 37). New York: Vintage Books/Random House.

Monaco, J. (1981). *How to read a film* (rev. ed.). New York: Oxford University Press.

Mulcahy, P., & Samuels, S. J. (1987). Three hundred years of illustration in American Textbooks. In H. A. Houghton & D. M. Willows (Eds.), *The psychology of illustration* (Vol. 2, pp. 2–48). New York: Springer-Verlag.

Naylor, D. T., & Diem, R. A. (1987). *Elementary and middle school social studies.* New York: Random House.

Negroponte, N. (1995). *Being digital.* New York: Alfred A. Knopf.

Newman, W. M., & Lamming, M. G. (1995). *Interactive system design.* Reading, MA: Addison Wesley.

Nielsen, J. (1993). *Usability engineering.* Boston, MA: Academic Press.

Norman, D. A. (1993). *Things that make us smart: Defending human attributes in the age of the machine.* Reading, MA: Addison Wesley.

Nöth, W. (1990). *Handbook of semiotics.* Bloomington, IN: Indiana University Press.

Pahl, R. H. (1996). Digital technology and social studies. In B. G. Massialas & R. F. Allen (Eds.), *Crucial issues in teaching social studies, K–12* (pp. 341–386). Belmont, CA: Wadsworth.

Palmer, S. E. (1992). Modern theories of gestalt perception. In G. W. Humphreys (Ed.), *Understanding vision* (pp. 39–70). Cambridge, MA: Basil Blackwell.

Papert, S. (1993). *The children's machine: Rethinking school in the age of the computer.* New York: Basic Books.

Parker, W. C., & Jarolimek, J. (1997). *Social studies in elementary education* (10th ed.). Upper Saddle River, NJ: Prentice-Hall.

Peeck, J. (1987). The role of illustrations in processing and remembering illustrated text. In D. M. Willows & H. A. Houghton (Eds.), *The psychology of illustration* (Vol. 1, pp. 115–151). New York: Springer-Verlag.

Perkins, D. N. (1988). Thinking frames: An integrating perspective on teaching cognitive skills. In J. Baron & R. Sternberg (Eds.), *Teaching thinking skills: Theory and research* (pp. 41–61). New York: W. H. Freeman.

Perkins, D. N. (1994). *The intelligent eye: Learning to think by looking at art.* Santa Monica, CA: The J. Paul Getty Trust Publications.

Piaget, J., & Inhelder, B. (1967). *The child's conception of space.* New York: W. W. Norton.

Preece, J., & Keller, L. (1994). *Human-computer interaction.* Reading, MA: Addison Wesley.

Print (1993, September/October). Introduction: Computer art and design annual 2.47 (5). pp. 114–124.

Pylyshyn, Z. W. (1973). What the mind's eye tells the mind's brain: A critique of mental imagery. *Psychological Bulletin, 80*, 1–24.

Pylyshyn, Z. W. (1981). The imagery debate: Analogue media versus tacit knowledge. *Psychological Review, 87*, 16–45.

Rand, P. (1985). *A designer's art.* New Haven, CT: Yale University Press.

Raphael, J., & Greenberg, R. (1995). Image processing: A state-of-the-art way to learn science. *Educational Leadership, 53*(2), 34–37.

Ravitch, D. (1995). *National standards in education: A citizen's guide.* Washington, DC: Brookings.

Ravitch, D., & Finn, C. (1987). *What do our 17-year-olds know?: A report on the first national assessment of history and literature.* New York: Harper & Row.

Ravitch, D., & Vinovskis, M. A. (Eds.). (1995). *Learning from the past: What history teaches us about school reform.* Baltimore, MD: The Johns Hopkins University Press.

Ray, D. (1991a). Technology and restructuring—Part I: New educational directions. *The Computing Teacher, 18*(6), 9–20.

Ray. D. (1991b). Technology and restructuring—Part II: New organizational directions. *The Computing Teacher, 18*(7), 8–12.

Reinhold, R. (1991). Class struggle: California's textbook debate. *The New York Times Magazine*, September 29.

Reinking, D. (1992). The differences between electronic and printed texts: An agenda for research. *Journal of Educational Multimedia and Hypermedia, 1*(1), 11–24.

Reiser, R. A. (1987). Instructional technology: A history. In R. M. Gagne (Ed.), *Instructional technology: foundations* (pp. 11–47). Hillsdale, NJ: Lawrence Erlbaum Associates.

Rheingold, H. (1991). *Virtual reality*. New York: Simon & Schuster.

Rheingold, H. (1993). *The virtual community: Homesteading on the electronic frontier*. Reading MA: Addison Wesley.

Rheingold, H. (1996). A slice of my life in my virtual community. In P. Ludlow (Ed.), *High noon on the frontier: Conceptual issues in cyberspace* (pp. 413–436). Cambridge, MA: The MIT Press.

Rice, S. (1978). *Book design: Systematic aspects*. New York: R. R. Bowker.

Robbins, B. (Ed.). (1993). *The phantom public sphere*. Minneapolis, MN: University of Minnesota Press.

Rock, M. (1992, March/April). Since when did USA Today become the national design ideal? *I.D. Magazine, 39*(2), 34–35.

Rugg, H. O. (Ed.). (1926). *The Twenty-Sixth Yearbook of the National Society for the Study of Education*, Chicago, IL: University of Chicago Press.

Rugg, H, O. (1941). *That men may understand: An American in the long armistice*. New York: Doubleday, Doran.

Sachter, J. E. (1990). Explorations into the spatial cognition of children using 3-D computer graphics. In I. Harel (Ed.), *Constructionist learning* (pp. 217–247). Cambridge, MA: The MIT Media Laboratory.

Said, E. W. (1978). *Orientalism*. New York: Vintage Books/Random House.

Said, E. W. (1993). *Culture and imperialism*. New York: Vintage Books/Random House.

Schipper, M. C. (1983). Landmarks in the literature: Textbook controversy: Past and present. *New York University Education Quarterly, 14*(3–4), 31–36.

Schramm, W. (1977). *Big media–little media: Tools and technologies for instruction*. Beverly Hills, CA: Sage.

Sewall, G. T. (1992). Textbook organization and writing: Today and tomorrow. In J. G. Herlihy (Ed.), *The textbook controversy: Issues, aspects and perspectives* (pp. 27–32). Norwood, NJ: Ablex.

Shaheen, J. G. (1984). *The TV Arab*. Bowling Green, OH: Bowling Green State University Popular Press.

Shaheen, J. G. (1996). Disney: The purveyor of racist images. *Islamic Horizons, 25*(6), 26–27.

Shavelson, R. J. (1985, April). *The measurement of cognitive structure*. Paper presented at the annual meeting of the American Educational Research Association, Chicago, IL.

Shneiderman, B. (1992). *Designing the user interface: Strategies for effective human-computer interaction*. Reading, MA: Addison Wesley.

Shohat E., & Stam, R. (1994). *Unthinking eurocentrism: Multiculturalism and the media.* New York: Routledge.

Sinatra, R. (1981). Using visuals to help the second language learner. *Reading Teacher, 34*(5), 539–546.

Singer, H., & Donlan, D. (1989). *Reading and learning from text* (2nd ed.). Hillsdale, NJ: Lawrence Erlbaum Associates.

Smith, K. A. (1992). *Structure of the visual book, Book 95, the revised and expanded edition.* Fairport, NY: The Sigma Foundation, Inc.

Sobchack, V. (1994). The scene of the screen: Envisioning cinematic and electronic presence. In H. U. Gumbrecht & K. L. Pfeiffer (Eds.), *Materialities of communication* (pp. 83–106). Stanford, CA: Stanford University Press.

Soloway, E., & Pryor, A. (1996, April). The next generation in human computer interaction. *Communications of the ACM, 39*(4), 16–18.

Solso, R. L. (1994). *Cognition and the visual arts.* Cambridge, MA: The MIT Press.

Spence, K. (1994, September). Netsurf: See me, hear me. *Wired, 2*(9) p. 145.

Stafford, B. M. (1993). Presuming images and consuming words: Visualization of knowledge from the enlightenment to post-modernism. In J. Brewer & R. Porter (Eds.), *Consumption and the world of goods* (pp. 462–477). London: Routledge.

Stafford, B. M. (1996). *Good looking: Essays on the virtue of images.* Cambridge, MA: The MIT Press.

Squire, J. R., & Morgan, R. T. (1990). The elementary and high school market today. In D. L. Elliot & A. Woodward (Eds.), *Textbooks and schooling in the United States, The Eighty-Ninth Yearbook of the National Society for the Study of Education, Part 1* (pp. 107–166). Chicago, IL: University of Chicago Press.

Sternberg, R. J. (1988). *The triarchic mind.* New York: Viking Penguin.

Sternberg, R. J. (1990). *Metaphors of mind.* Cambridge, England: Cambridge University Press.

Sterns, R. C., & Robinson, R. S. (1994). Perception and its role in communication and learning. In D. M. Moore & F. M. Dwyer (Eds.), *Visual literacy* (pp. 31–52). Englewood Cliffs, NJ: Educational Technology Publications.

Steuer, J. (1995). Defining virtual reality: Dimensions determining telepresence. In F. Biocca & M. R. Levy (Eds.), *Communication in the age of virtual reality.* Hillsdale, NJ: Lawrence Erlbaum Associates.

Stuart, R. (1996). *The design of virtual environments.* New York: McGraw Hill.

Sun Microsystems, Inc. (1991). *An introduction to computer graphics concepts.* Reading, MA: Addison Wesley.

Tharp, R. G., & Gallimore, R. (1988). *Rousing minds to life.* Cambridge, England: Cambridge University Press.

Tognazzini, B. (1991). Consistency. In B. Laurel (Ed.), *The art of human-computer interface design* (pp. 75–78). Reading, MA: Addison Wesley.

Trachtenberg, A. (1989). *Reading American photographs: Images as history from Matthew Brady to Walker Evans.* New York: Noonday, Farrar, Straus & Giroux.

Tufte, E. (1983). *The visual display of quantitative information,* Cheshire, CT: Graphics Press.

Tufte, E. (1990). *Envisioning information,* Cheshire, CT: Graphics Press.

Turkle, S. (1984). *The second self: Computers and the human spirit.* New York: Simon & Schuster.

Turkle, S. (1995). *Life on the screen: Identity in the age of the internet.* New York: Simon & Schuster.

Tyson-Bernstein, H., & Woodward, A. (1989). Nineteenth century policies for 21st century practice: The textbook reform dilemma. *Educational Policy, 2,* 95–106.

Vacherand-Revel, J., & Bessiere, C. (1992). Playing graphics in the design and use of multimedia courseware. In A. D. N. Edwards & S. Holland (Eds.), *Multimedia interface design in education.* NATO ASI Series, No. 76. Berlin: Springer-Verlag.

Venezky, R., & Osin, L. (1991). *The intelligent design of computer-assisted instruction.* New York: Longman.

Venezky, R. L. (1992). Textbooks in school and society. In P. W. Jackson (Ed.), *Handbook of research on curriculum* (pp. 436–459). New York: Macmillan.

Von Schweber, L., & Von Schweber E. (1996, November 5). The web goes 3-D. *PC Magazine, 15*(9), 229–263.

Waller, R. H. (1982). Text as diagram: Using typography to improve access and understanding. In D. Jonassen (Ed.), *The technology of text, Vol. I* (pp. 137–166). Englewood Cliffs, NJ: Educational Technology Publications.

Waller, R. H. (1991). Typography and discourse. In P. D. Pearson, R. Barr, M. L. Kamil, & P. Mosenthal (Eds.), *The Handbook of reading research, Vol. II* (pp. 341–380). White Plains, NY: Longman.

WELL (1997). *About the well.* http://well.com/dip_well.html.

West, T. G. (1991). *In the mind's eye: Visual thinkers, gifted people with learning disabilities, computer images, and the ironies of creativity.* Buffalo, NY: Prometheus Books.

West, T. G. (1996, August). Images and reversals: Talking less, drawing more. *ACM SIGGRAPH Computer Graphics, 30*(3), 81–82.

Westbury, I. (1990). Textbooks, publishers, and the quality of schooling. In D. L. Elliot & A. Woodward (Eds.), *Textbooks and schooling in the United States, The Eighty-Ninth Yearbook of the National Society for the Study of Education, Part 1*(pp. 1–22). Chicago, IL: University of Chicago Press.

Wilen, W. W., & White, J. J. (1991). Interaction and discourse in social studies classrooms. In J. P. Shaver (Ed.) *Handbook of research on social studies teaching and learning* (pp. 483–495). New York: Macmillan.

Williams, L. (Ed.). (1995). *Viewing positions: Ways of seeing film.* New Brunswick, NJ: Rutgers University Press.

Williams, R. (1981). *The sociology of culture*, Chicago, IL: University of Chicago Press.

Wired (1993, February). *Premiere issue, 1*(1), San Francisco, CA.

Wired (1997, March). *Push!: The radical future of media beyond the web, 5*(3), San Francisco, CA.

Wixson, K. K., & Peters, C. W. (1987). Comprehension assessment implementing and interactive view of reading. *Educational Psychologist, 22*(3 & 4), 333–356.

Woodward, A. (1993). Do illustrations serve instructional purpose in U.S. textbooks? In B. K. Britton, A. Woodward, & M. Binkley (Eds.), *Learning from textbooks: Theory and practice* (pp. 115-134). Hillsdale, NJ: Lawrence Erlbaum Associates.

Wynter, S. (1990). *A cultural model of critique of the textbook, America will be.* Letter to California State Board of Education Members, enclosure 2.

Young, M. J. (1990). Writing and editing of textbooks. In D. L. Elliot & A. Woodward (Eds.), *Textbooks and schooling in the United States, The Eighty-Ninth Yearbook of the National Society for the Study of Education, Part 1*(pp. 71–85). Chicago, IL: University of Chicago Press.

Appendix 1

The Houghton Mifflin Social Studies Program, K–8, 1991

Grade

K: *The World I See*
1:    *I Know a Place*
2:    *Some People I Know*
3:    *From Sea to Shining Sea*
4:    *This Is My Country* (California Version titled: *Oh, California*)
5:    *America Will Be*
6:    *A Message from Ancient Days*
7:    *Across the Centuries*
8:    *A More Perfect Union*

Interview Subjects

Carolyn Adams	Marketing Research Director, Chicago office
Beverly Armento	Social Studies subject specialist, Georgia State University, Atlanta
Helen Chandra	Editor of the Program Scope and Sequence, Chicago office
Sara Chavkin	Project Administrator, Chicago office
Joseph Godlewski	Project Art Director, Chicago office
Frank Loose	Project Design Manager, St. Louis office (this office closed after the completion of the project)
Stuart Murphy	Ligature Co-Founder and Project Executive Director, Evanston, Illinois
Gary Nash	History subject specialist, University of California, Los Angeles
John Ridley	Houghton Mifflin Project Editor, Boston office
Dan Rogers	Project Editor, Chicago office
Christopher Salter	Geography subject specialist, University of Missouri, Columbia
Ann Sievert	Production Manager, Chicago office
Rob Wittig	Project Team Coordinator, Chicago office
Karen Wixson	Reading specialist, University of Michigan, Ann Arbor

Visual Turn Chronology

1987   California State Board of Education approves History-Social Science Framework

1988   Ligature begins *Social Studies for the 21ˢᵗ Century* (SS21) Pre-Planning Program Development.

1989   SS21 Planning and Thumbnail Process.

1990   SS21 Production.
April 1:   State of California adoption submission deadline.

1991   Houghton Mifflin Social Studies Program (K–8) First
                                            Edition is adopted by the state of California with revi-
                                            sions.

1992   February 27:   First interview with Ligature designers in Chicago.
                                            Dan Rogers, Joe Godlewski, Rob Wittig
            April 23:   Beverly Armento
            October 10:   Gary Nash
            December 31:   John Ridley

1993   February 26:   Second interview with Ligature designers in Chicago.
                                            Dan Rogers, Helen Chandra, Joe Godlewski, Rob
                                            Wittig
            March 15:   Stuart Murphy
            March 31:   Karen Wixson
            April 16:   Beverly Armento
            July 12:   Carolyn Adams
            August 26:   Sara Chavkin, Ann Sievert, Rob Wittig
            September 9:   Frank Loose
            November 16:   Christopher Salter (declined formal interview)

1994

            February 17:   Frank Loose

Houghton Mifflin Social Studies Program Second Revised Edition is published.

Appendix 2

These tallies are deceptively simple. In a larger sense they point to the need for a pedagogical language that understands and is comfortable with visual information. However, a visualizing grammar that reveals the integral place of seeing in the act of cognition, and the necessity of cultivating the concrete for higher order thinking is at present the underdeveloped symbolic mode in the Curriculum, still largely centered on alpha-numeric literacy. However, as the potential of the computer for visualization is realized this new grammar will be articulated.

Teacher Talk/Student Task Summary

Grade 1

Teacher Talk Script

Have students...	
Identify	8
Describe	6
Find	6
Compare	4
Look at	2
Point to	2
	28

Help students...	**8**
Ask students...	**7**
Point Out	5
Call/Direct Attention to	4
Discuss	3
Explain	3
Brainstorm with	1
Work With	1

Student Task

Answer Question	8	Look at	2	Comment	1
Identify	8	Make	2	Count	1
Describe	6	Point to	2	List	1
Find	6	Read	2	Name	1
Discuss	5	Tell	2	Respond	1
Compare	4	Use	2	See	1
				Study	1
				Summarize	1

Grade 5

Teacher Talk Script

Ask students to...

Question	19
Look at	12
Draw Visual	6
Study	5
Discuss	3
Compare	3
Misc.	13
	62

Have students	**61**
Look at	18
Make Visuals	16
Describe	7
Explain	7
Study	4
Examine	2
Misc.	14
	61

Discuss	17
What (do, were, type of)	8
Call/Direct Attention to	5
Remind	4
Refer to	4
List	3
Point to	3
Work with	3
Help	2
Tell	2

Use	2
Allow for	1
Brainstorm with	1
Compare	1
Do Research	1
Encourage	1
Explain	1
How Does	1
Imagine	1
Instruct	1
Look at	1
Note What Types of	1
Study the	1
Suppose	1
Talk with	1

Student Task

Answer Question	37	Analyze	2	Research	1
Look at	24	Interpret	2	Sketch	1
Discuss	21	Locate	2	Understand	1
Make	10	Organize Display			
Study	8	Study	2		
Draw	7	Work in Groups			
Compare	6	Write	2		
Describe	6				
Imagine	5	Bring to Class	1		
List	5	Design	1		
Examine	4	Evaluate	1		
Identify	4	Explain	1		
Create	3	Find	1		
Determine	3	Measure	1		
Use	3	Read	1		

Grade 8

Teacher Talk Script

Have students...	**62**
Look at	12
Compare	6
Identify	5
Study	11
Examine	4
Describe	3
Misc.	16
	62

Ask students...

Question	20
Identify	5
Compare	4
Explain	4
Describe	3
Study	3
Misc.	22
	61

What	31
How	27
Why	19
Refer to	25
Point out	21
Tell	5
Discuss	3
Explain	3
Call Attention to	2
Compare/Contrast	2
Divide in Groups	1
Encourage	1
Guide through	1
Instruct	1
Request that	1
Review	1
Study	1

Student Task

Answer Question	78	Bring in newspapers	1
Interpret	18	Determine relationships	1
Compare	18	Make inferences	1
Look at	16	Point out evidence in	1
Analyze	11	Find symbols	1
Identify	11	Recall	1
Read	10	Review	1
Study	8	Speculate	1
Use	6	*Scan* text	1
Describe	4	Summarize	1
Discuss	3	Think About	1
Make, Build, Create	3	Understand	1
Imagine (Self in Picture)	2		

Author Index

Subject Index